New Ethnicities, Old Racisms?

New Ethnicities, Old Racisms?

Edited by Phil Cohen

Zed Books
LONDON • NEW YORK

New Ethnicities, Old Racisms? was first published by Zed Books
Ltd, 7 Cynthia Street, London N1 9JF, UK, and Room 400,
175 Fifth Avenue, New York, NY 10010, USA, in 1999.

Editorial copyright © Phil A. Cohen, 1999.
Individual chapters copyright © individual authors, 1999.

Distributed exclusively in the USA by St Martin's Press, Inc.,
175 Fifth Avenue, New York, NY 10010, USA.

Cover designed by Andrew Corbett.
Typeset in Monotype Ehrhardt and Franklin Gothic by
Ewan Smith, London.
Printed and bound in the United Kingdom by Biddles Ltd,
Guildford and King's Lynn.

A catalogue record for this book is available from the British
Library

US CIP data is available from the Library of Congress

ISBN 1 85649 651 1 cased
ISBN 1 85649 652 X limp

Contents

Cultures of Racism

Rethinking Multiculturalism

Postscript

Tables and Figures

Acknowledgements

My first debt is to all the contributors to this book, for their commitment to the project and their forbearance in dealing with editorial questions. I would also like to thank other colleagues whose work it was not possible to include here but who have nevertheless made a notable contribution to the intellectual and cultural life of the Centre for New Ethnicities Research. In particular I would like to thank Linda Rozmovits, Gucharan Virdee, Ashwani Sharma and Judith Hargreaves for their help over the years, and Bill Schwarz and Catherine Hall for their early championing of our cause. More recently the Centre's project manager, Richard McKeever, and Linda John have ensured that the Centre has remained viable as its work has expanded.

I owe a special debt to Alan O'Shea, who made it possible for me to have a sabbatical, during which this book was put together. Mike Rustin helped to set up the Centre and has continued to be a staunch friend. Finally, of course, this book, like the Centre itself, owes an enormous debt to Stuart Hall, whose work not only helped to create the field of study in which we have worked, but whose personal example has served as a source of inspiration for those of us who still believe that the best intellectual work is that which is most engaged, socially and politically, with its subject matter.

Phil Cohen

Contributors

LES BACK is Senior Lecturer in Sociology at Goldsmiths College, University of London. He is the author of *New Ethnicities and Urban Culture* (UCL Press, 1996) and co-author with John Solomos of *Race Politics and Social Change* (Routledge, 1995) and *Racism and Society* (Macmillan, 1996). He collaborated with Phil Cohen and CNER in the ESRC-funded research reported here.

ALICE BLOCH lectures in the Department of Social Policy and Politics, Goldsmiths College, University of London. Her research interests include immigration policies and welfare legislation, refugee communities in East London, ethnic minority rights, and issues of race equality in social provision. Her most recent publication is *Beating the Barriers: the employment and training needs of refugees in Newham* (European Union, 1998).

PHIL COHEN is the director of CNER and Reader in Cultural Studies at UEL. His research interests include the history of multiracist Britain, the cultural geography of contemporary racism (especially in East London), youth arts and urban multiculture, and psychoanalytic approaches to popular racism and nationalism. His most recent books are *Rethinking the Youth Question* (Macmillan, 1997) and two forthcoming collections: *Race and the Other Scene* (Sage) and *The Migrations of Identity* (Macmillan).

BARNOR HESSE is a Lecturer in Sociology at UEL. His current research interests include: Black cultural politics and the African diaspora, Eurocentrism, the politics of race and instutionalised racism in higher education, racial violence and the local state. He is the author of *Beneath the Surface – studies in racial harassment* (Avery, 1996).

JAYNE IFEKWUNIGWE lectures in Anthropology and Sociology at UEL. Her current research projects are on the transformation of 'coloured' identities in post-apartheid South Africa and the multiple genealogies of 'race-mixing'. She is the author of *Scattered Belongings: Cultural Paradoxes of Race, Nation and Gender* (Routledge, 1998).

MICHAEL KEITH is the Director of the Centre of Urban and Community

Research, Goldsmiths College, and the author of *Race, Riots and Policing* (UCL Press, 1993) and co-author with Steve Pile of *Geographies of Resistance* (Routledge, 1997) and *Place and the Politics of Identity* (Routledge, 1993).

REINA LEWIS lectures in Women's Studies at UEL. Her current research interests are focused on the relation between orientalism and feminism, and on the gendered writing of 'race'. She is the author of *Gendering Orientalism – race, femininity and representation* (Routledge, 1996).

IAN MACDONALD is Co-Director of the Centre for Sport Development Research at Roehampton Institute, London. His areas of research include racism in British sport, the politics of UK sport policy, and the role of physical culture in contemporary Hindu nationalist discourse. Ian is currently writing a book, 'Sport and the Making of Modern India', with Sharda Ugra.

PHIL MARFLEET lectures in Third World Studies and is Co-ordinator of the new MA in Refugee Studies at UEL. His research interests include globalisation and the political economy of international migration, trade, aid and unequal exchange, issues in development education, Eurocentrism and 'third worldism'.

JOHN MARRIOTT lectures in History in the Department of Cultural Studies at UEL. His current research is on the metropolis and empire in relation to popular culture and politics. His publications include *The Culture of Labourism* (Edinburgh UP, 1991) and the forthcoming *Imagining the Metropolitan Poor 1775–1910* (Chatto).

PATRICIA TUITT lectures in Law at Birkbeck College and was previously in the Law Department at UEL, where she taught on the MA in Refugee Studies. Her research interests include the legal construction of refugee identities, the discourse and practice of immigration law, and discourse of the Law. She is the author of *The Death of the Refugee* (1998).

SHARDA UGRA is a history graduate from the University of Bombay. She is currently senior sports reporter for *The Hindu*, a national daily newspaper in India, and a sports correspondent for the *Sportstar*, India's largest-selling weekly sports magazine. In 1997, she spent six months in England conducting research on racism in cricket, upon which the chapter in this book has been based. She is collaborating with Ian McDonald on a book, 'Sport and the Making of Modern India', investigating the link between the two.

COUZE VENN lectures in Cultural Studies at UEL. His main research interests are in postcolonial studies, race and postmodernity, and theories of identity and subjectivity.

IN MEMORY OF
STEPHEN LAWRENCE

1

Through a Glass Darkly: Intellectuals on Race

Phil Cohen

Language Games

Race, ethnicity and nation are ever contested terms. What they have been made to mean over recent decades tells its own story about the changing politics of knowledge in postcolonial Britain. The sheer variety of uses to which these three terms have been put in public debate and in strategies of governance not only requires mapping but raises the issue as to what their changing articulation tells us about the deeper and more unconscious dimensions of our social imaginary.[1]

In a recent study of children's intellectual development, Lawrence Hirschfield has argued that in societies where these terms are strongly and visibly indexed to positions of power and powerlessness, they also serve as important conceptual tools which help the growing mind to engage actively – and hence creatively – with the grammars and lexicons of difference that constitute the parameters of the adult world. His conclusion is that race, ethnicity and nation are good to think with but bad to act upon (Hirschfield 1996).

The validity of this distinction and the conditions under which it can be made has been of special concern to intellectuals in their role as arbiters of public debate. For the post-war Western intelligentsia, liberal and modernist in outlook and largely formed by the war against fascism, all three terms were equally bad. Racist theories of intelligence and eugenic philosophies were effectively marginalised, at least within official discourse. Only out-and-out racists considered that race was a valid social descriptor; ethnicity was considered a throwback to forms of culture and consciousness that modernity had long since relegated to the margins of history; as for nationalism, the European experience over the previous two centuries proved how effectively it empowered the imperialisms of the state. The task for intellectuals was thus to purge the public mind and body politic of these archaic residues of irrational sentiment and belief, and help build a world in which such divisions no longer held sway (Lévi-Strauss 1977).

It could be argued that this is still the prevalent view; certainly amongst those intellectuals who have held on to an optimistic view of the mission of modernism, liberalism and the enlightenment project despite, or because of, their profoundly Eurocentric roots (Rorty 1991; Taylor 1994), it is still the main plank of those who argue for an internationalist perspective that eschews any kind of local patriotism. This position has recently been powerfully restated as a means of asserting the priority of equality over difference as part of a universal quest for social justice (Malik 1996).

The 'all bad' position was quickly challenged by a more complex and ambivalent response as intellectuals grappled with the complex allegiances forged by the Cold War and the process of decolonisation; for traditional liberal thinkers race was still a bad item because it constituted a fixed quasi-biological essence operative only within scientific or popular racism; race meant defining people by the colour of their skin, or the shape of their nose; ethnicity, however, was good (or at least better) in so far as it offered a more permeable and open-ended account of identities in which language, culture and religion all played their part in making or marking forms of historical individuality. As for nation, in so far as its meanings became racialised it remained definitely on the side of the baddies; by means of its 'good' ethnic side, however, it was made part of a quite different story, linked to the emergence of newly independent countries in the so-called 'Third World' (Kellas 1988).

More recently we have seen a move towards an even more complicated set of perceptions as a new kind of organic intelligentsia has asserted its presence in the postcolonial world; in the hands of roots radicals, vocabularies of race, ethnicity and nation have been effectively transvalued into powerful tools of ideological resistance, a means of minorities talking back at their oppressors, turning negative stereotypes into badges of pride. Ethnicity is soul food, race is given a new rationality, nation speaks a new, non-territorial language unto nation. By the same token, the reiteration of these same terms discomfits majority populations since it continues to implicate them discursively in forms of exclusion and domination which are integral to the colonial legacy (Gabriel 1994).

This redistribution of values has in some cases been accompanied by a blurring of categorial boundaries. Race becomes ethnicised and ethnicity racialised so that both terms can be used interchangeably in a way that allows their respective elements of fixity and permeability to be conjugated into more subtle idioms of attribution than either on their own could achieve. This both corresponds to a complication of migration histories and provides for a more tactical, context-sensitive kind of identity work. The contemporary performance of Irishness, Africanness and Jewishness, for example, increasingly depends on the ability to deploy a large repertoire

of heterogeneous linguistic, social and cultural signs, even if only in order
to re-establish, often somewhat covertly, the fixed racial, ethnic and national
essences that are otherwise being undermined by this proliferating poly-
semy (Brah 1996).

One way to stabilise meanings in a world of shifting signifiers is to
insist on the observance of set linguistic forms. 'Politically correct' ortho-
doxy in the field of 'race and ethnic relations' is nowadays very much a
matter of orthography. This is how the rule is stated in one recently
influential text: 'When the word black is spelled in the lower case, it will
be a reference to colour or race; when the word black is spelled in the
higher case it will be a reference to ethnic group, ethnic status, ethnicity,
or community' (Wright 1997).

While such concatenations of race and ethnicity have become pervasive
in some institutional protocols of 'community relations', the customary
distinction between the two terms has resurfaced to dramatic effect in
academic debates around different forms of nationhood. Here a new binary
has been introduced between civic nationalism, whose polity is held to be
liberal, rational, forward-looking and inclusive, and ethnic nationalism,
which is seen as illiberal, irrational, backward-looking and exclusive
(Ignatieff 1994; Smith 1991). There are various ways in which this di-
chotomy can be mapped back on to race/ethnicity. For example, in some
of the currents of identity politics that emerged from within the anti-racist
movement in the 1980s, to be black, Caribbean and British was to claim to
be a standard-bearer for an inclusive multi-ethnic form of civic nationalism;
while to be white, English and British was to have a monolithically impacted
identity that confirmed all the narrowest prejudices associated with legacies
of race, nation and empire (Rutherford 1998).

This double standard of representation has had a long gestation and
has only recently fully entered into the currency of public debate. But
from the outset its terms seemed problematic to many academic commentators. It was not that such distinctions did not correspond to how
certain identities were made, but that such a binary model did not allow
for the complexity and fluidity of identifications that actually constituted
the field of so-called 'race and ethnic relations'. It was to address this
problem that a new theoretical paradigm emerged in the 1980s.

New Racisms, New Ethnicities?

The uprisings of 1981 marked a crucial turning point in post-war race
relations in Britain. They signalled through the flames that black and
Asian communities were no longer immigrants: they were here to stay. A
younger and more militant leadership emerged to challenge the power

both of their own elders and of the established, white-dominated race relations industry (Solomos 1993). This produced a diversity of response from the erstwhile 'host' community. Commentators noted the emergence of what they called a new racism: crude biologistic doctrines and stereotypes of innate superiority/inferiority were giving way to a more subtle and indirect discourse that spoke about cultural differences as an 'organic' principle of discrimination (Barker 1981; Gordon 1989). According to this new story-line, it wasn't that the English were innately superior to the Irish, the Jews or the Blacks, they just did things differently and had a thousand years of history to prove it!

The new racism thesis provided an important intellectual resource for the anti-racist movement, enabling it to shift its attention beyond the violent, aversive forms of popular racism towards the more subtle and invisible aspects of cultural stereotyping and discrimination, especially as these operated within institutions of civil governance (Cambridge and Feuchtwang 1991). Municipal anti-racism had by the early 1980s provided a toe-hold for an organic black intelligentsia within the local state. In education authorities, and in social service, law and housing departments, a new generation of evangelical bureaucrats prosecuted race equality policies with a zeal that sometimes made them easy targets for a hostile Thatcherite press (IRR 1989). The media attack cynically exploited potential tensions between their roles as representatives of their own communities and as public servants and state employees. Only black activist intellectuals, it seemed, experienced the dilemmas of dual consciousness, and for them, unlike their 'disinterested' white counterparts, it was an issue of divided loyalties and incompatible choices.

The anti-racist movement did, however, give some hostages to fortune. The complication of the delineation of institutional racism, to encompass its more hidden cultural as well as its structural aspects, was not accompanied by an equally sophisticated strategy of practical engagement (Donald and Rattansi 1991). The application of moralistic and prescriptive agendas, often based on crude reductive theories of who or what was racist, brought some initiatives into public disrepute (MacDonald 1989). This was used by ideologues of the New Right to orchestrate a backlash in which they portrayed themselves as heroic freedom-fighters defending all that was best in the British way of life against the monstrous foreign tyranny of 'political correctness' (Fieldstein 1990).

The sophisticated cultural theory that was largely missing from the politics of municipal anti-racism was, however, being developed elsewhere. The Salman Rushdie affair, the growth of black and Asian youth multi-cultures and the public debate over transracial adoption combined to create a major arena in which the issue of race and representation was being rethought (Rushdie 1991; Back 1997; Gaber and Aldridge 1994). The discursive strategies brought to bear on these various issues split apart the prevailing articulations of race/ethnicity/nation, made each into a relatively autonomous trajectory of identifications, and then, in a final moment, reconnected them in forms of real and imagined community that broke the binary black/white code into a much more complex configuration of positions (Cohen and Bains 1988; Werbner and Modood 1997).

Central to this development was the notion of new ethnicities, first developed by Stuart Hall in the 1980s (Hall 1996). At a time when the New Right was at the height of its ideological power, and the left and anti-racist movement in profound disarray, this seminal text mapped out a way forward that took account of the complex social and cultural changes occurring in Britain's black and Asian communities. To the insistence that ethnicities were invented not given, modern not 'traditional' (Sollors 1989), was added a conjunctural analysis that spoke presciently to the material circumstances and strategies of a new generation of young black and Asian artists and intellectuals in postcolonial Britain.

The new problematic signalled the fact that identities had broken free of their anchorage in singular histories of race and nation and were busy elaborating a play of difference in a way that put in question organic models of culture and unitary definitions of self. Historicist narratives of 'roots' and images of the homeland based on essentialist definitions of community or identity were in any case being challenged at the grass-roots level of popular cultural practice (Hebdige 1989; Gilroy 1993b). The notion of new ethnicities referred to myriad forms of cultural traffic generated by the process of globalisation, and the convergence of transnational and transracial geographies of identification via the opening up of new diasporic networks of communication (Featherstone 1990; Beiner 1999; Brah 1996).

All this made race, nation and ethnicity freshly exciting to think and work with. In the 1980s we were, after all, dealing with a major qualitative transformation in Western capitalism, associated with the expanded role of design and communications technologies in every sphere of production (Sassen 1997). The growth of media and cultural industries threw up what Régis Debray has called, somewhat disparagingly, a mediocracy (Debray 1981). This was a hybrid intelligentsia that straddled – and hence disrupted – established divisions between 'highbrow' and 'lowbrow' culture, while at the same time launching a swingeing attack on the 'middlebrow' as the repository of a residual, but still imperial, parochialism. A new kind of intellectual culture emerged in which the invention of tradition, the pro-fession of modernity, the cultivation of roots and the embrace of liminality were no longer specialised intellectual strategies but could be combined in various permutations to compose a vibrant 'postmodern' mix.

Black and Asian intellectuals and artists were in the vanguard of this movement. Many of them had graduated from the polyversities to join this new 'cultural mass', and found themselves living and working through the digital revolution in information media and mass communications (Sharma *et al.* 1997). Cultural racism was an apt description of the obstacles they faced in their struggle to assert autonomous spaces of creative activity in the art world, the academy and the mass media in a way that secured an adequate space of representation for the issues they wanted to address (Gupta 1993).

It was not surprising (though not inevitable) that many of them saw issues of race and racism primarily through a cultural lens. Although its aesthetic expression took many forms, the cultural fluidity associated with 'new ethnicities' also served to map out a space, both real and imagined, of social mobility. Those who were on the move and 'going places' now had a lexicon to describe their trajectory in terms other than those of the old class geographies, which were in any case shifting (Cannadine 1997).

This was facilitated by the promotion of two other terms that gave the notion of 'new ethnicities ' a spatial rather than a temporal or conjunctural dimension: diaspora and hybridity. Diaspora became 'good to think with', as James Clifford put it, because it could be used to describe the global trajectory of travelling theory, a meeting place of postcolonial minds that was fully compatible with the digital age (Clifford 1998). *En route*, and through a process of projective identification that had little to do with their position in the real world, the refugee and the asylum-seeker were 're-invented' as nomadic 'postmodern' subjects (Cohen 1994).

The notion of cultural hybridity, wrested away from its racial problematic of miscegenation, served as a further resource for representing positively the processes of internal differentiation that were going on in second- and third-generation black and Asian communities. In place of the pathologising notion of young people caught 'between cultures', there was the altogether more constructive vision of an inmixture of influence, where East met West on grounds of neither's making, and forged a dynamic 'semiosphere' that put into question the cultural politics of both separatism and assimilationism (Werbner and Modood 1997).

Taken together, these three terms thus worked to articulate the experience of those who were climbing out of the ethnic ghetto of 'traditionalism' or communalism into the new multicultural middle class. They could now feel that their sense of progress 'onwards and upwards' was part of a wider horizontal movement of ideas and populations across heterogeneous cultural space. *En route*, however, the more dialectical, critical and reflexive elements in Stuart Hall's original formulation tended to be lost. His intervention was expresssly designed to offer a third way between the retreat into essentialist race and/or class politics, on the one hand, and the febrile vacuity of the 'polymorphously perverse' forms of identity politics offered by the postmodern turn, on the other. Yet in much, though not all, of the popular take-up of his ideas, there has been a tendency to rewrite the project in a way that undermines the possibilities of a third way. How did this come about?

Once fluidity and floating signifiers became the aesthetic trademark of a new and youthful multicultural intelligentsia, then, by contrast, fixity and the failure to tolerate ambiguous or multiple identities were all too easily associated with an older generation stuck in their ways, or with a white and black 'underclass' immobilised at the bottom of the social ladder. The temptation to institute a new moral binarism between a 'good, new' ethnicity, which celebrated healthy, happy hybridity, and 'bad, old' ethnicity mired in pathological purity was often difficult to resist.

At the same time, the links between structural and cultural racisms that Hall was concerned to articulate in his conjunctural analysis tended to be lost the more spatialised (and hence postmodernised) the imagery of diaspora and hybridity became (Young 1995). In place of Hall's complex map of social dislocation and disjuncture being worked through (and against) the process of racialisation, we began to get lyrical evocations of the resilience of black youth multicultures overcoming adversity to seize the time and storm the citadels of cultural power (Skelton and Valentine 1997; Mac an Ghail 1991).

It was perhaps the absence of a developed, empirically grounded theory of class articulation that rendered the problematic of new ethnicities so vulnerable to reductive misreadings. This lacuna was hardly surprising given the flight from class then going on in cultural studies, the bankruptcy of classical Marxist models of class consciousness, and the impasses of sociological theory around the structure–agency split (Archer 1995). The result was a serious underestimation of the impact that even limited amounts of sponsored and contested mobility were having on those who were not sponsored or who were in other ways losing out. These hidden wounds of race and class were not – and still are not – much considered.

If you are interpellated as young, gifted and Asian or black, but some of your friends are making it through to the middle class by whatever route while you are not, how do you explain that principle of selectivity or discrimination to yourself in a way that does not simply endorse racist constructions of failure? Clearly, reductive race and class theories of divide-and-rule may 'help' by providing a specious rationale with which to attack the success stories for being sell-outs, coconuts, Uncle Toms or what have you. Afrocentrism or Islamism may offer an alternative counter-hegemonic strategy of self-improvement that also salves wounded ethnic pride, especially by enabling young people to identify with an alternative set of role models. The forming of mixed-race relationships is another way through. So is the formation of street-gang communalism. In the last decade, black and Asian youth multicultures have encouraged a whole range of options to be explored for a time. But when you find you are in your late 20s, unemployed, and heading nowhere fast, no amount of mobile phoning, clubbing, or visiting the Gurdwara is likely to hide the fact that you are radically disconnected from the global 'network society', even and especially if you notionally belong to a diasporic community.

The social responses to the persistence, and indeed deepening, of race inequality in contemporary Britain cannot be neatly labelled in terms of old or new ethnicities, at least not in the simplistic renderings that have gained popular currency. We are dealing with truly hybrid forms, in negotiation simultaneously with cultural and structural aspects of racism, and thus not susceptible to analysis along only one dimension.

The split formation of the black and Asian intelligentsia has made it especially difficult to put the two sides of the story together. Cultural workers tend to view issues of race and racism through a cultural lens, while anti-racist professionals dealing with everyday issues of race discrimination in employment, housing and the law tend understandably to see things more in structural and institutional terms. How to connect those two perspectives and constituencies of concern continues to be central to the 'new ethnicities' project, and is indeed the test of its ultimate success or failure.

Many of the black and Asian artists and film-makers who pioneered the new cultural politics throughout the 1980s did in fact succeed brilliantly in making some of the more immediate connections through imaginative initiatives in the field of community arts (Gupta 1993). But for the generation of movers and shakers who came after them, emerging as a distinctive force in the mid 1990s, it was always going to be harder to address the predicament of those left behind in the economic and social margins that they had vacated in other than purely rhetorical terms (Feagin 1994). The coincidence of strenuous personal investment in career trajectories and a process of involution going on around identity politics meant that the kinds of solidarity that had supported earlier, more collective, phases of struggle were harder and harder to sustain (Hall 1999). In any case, in a market-place of ideas where last year's books are already past their sell-by date, what was there new to say about the old racisms?

In fact the 'old' racism showed a remarkable resilience and capacity to reinvent itself. Not only did white supremacist organisations wise up to the travelling story of transnational youth culture, but racial science took on a new lease of life as the eugenicist dream came ever closer to realisation, thanks to advances in genetic engineering (Kohn 1996). Depressingly, as we enter the new millennium, the resources and repertoires of racism, ethnicism and nationalism have never been so diverse, so ramified, so conflated and so versatile in their articulation (Cohen and Schwarz 1998).

After Stephen Lawrence

Given this situation, it could be argued that to hold on to binary oppositions between an 'old' biological and 'new' cultural racism, or between old organic and new hybridised ethnicity, or between backward-looking ethnic nationalism and forward-looking civic nationalism, is to beg a number of vital questions. It is to reintroduce ideal typical distinctions that no longer (if they ever did) correspond to the complexity of what is happening on the ground. At the very least these binarisms assume precisely what has to be explained: namely, the shifting forms and conditions of articulation of these categories. The question mark in the book's title is there to signal as much. But is there more to answering the question than simply making an inventory of changing semantics? Is it also a question about the role that different kinds of intelligentsia, or different kinds of intellectual strategy, play in defining the issues?

The Stephen Lawrence campaign has, amongst its many achievements, opened up a new style of engagement with the dominant discourses about racism. This was not a conventional grass-roots community campaign, based around a strategy of mass mobilisation; nor was it a liberal *cause célèbre* conducted through the columns of the press by famous public intellectuals or charismatic media personalities; nor did it constitue a new social movement. Instead the issue was fought by the family itself, assisted by a small group of dedicated and highly professional advisers drawn from a wide spectrum, including lawyers, journalists, academics, and political campaigners, who deployed state-of-the-art lobbying techniques to keep the momentum of the campaign going over a long period.

The campaign addressed and linked the problematics of new ethnicities and old racisms in a way that laid the foundations for the MacPherson Enquiry (MacPherson 1999). For the first time, an official government report brought the different sides of the story together, connecting the structural and cultural aspects of racism, the violence of racial hatreds acted out on the street and the subtle indifference that characterised the official response. The campaign not only brought the concerns of the older generation closer to those of the youth; within the youth constituency itself the issues worked to build bridges between the 'high fliers' who, like Stephen Lawrence, had set their sights on university, and those whose everyday lives are still ruled by what happens on the street and in the neighbourhood. Finally, as a result of the campaign, debates that had long been confined to race professionals and academics entered widely into popular consciousness. Yet at this crucial juncture the mediocracy stepped in to make a spectacle out of racism (and anti-racism) as if it was news from nowhere; this both endorsed a large section of public opinion that wanted to forget about the long duration of the issues, and confirmed the *plus ça change, plus c'est la même chose* pessimism of those for whom racism is, by default, always the same old story. The legislators were for once in place and ready to act. But where were the interpreters?

The Stephen Lawrence campaign has highlighted the importance of sustaining serious intellectual work, in a broad but focused way, around the issues it raises. One of the roles which the new universities can play, precisely because they draw students from such a broad social base and have strong local community links, is to take up agendas that are not being highlighted elsewhere and explore them. The fact that the University of East London is located in an area with a long history of popular racism, has one of the largest black and Asian student populations in the country, and a student culture in which Afrocentrism and Islamism are both important currents, means that the questions I have been discussing are very much on its front doorstep. As academics in the University, many of the contributors to this book have found themselves in the thick of debates about how the curriculum, pedagogy, and general ethos of the institution should be changed to something less 'Eurocentric' in order engage proactively with these new developments. In principle, everyone is in favour of an evolution towards a 'multicultural university'; yet in the context of the growing racialisation of higher education, there is very little agreement about what this might practically entail. Moreover, the issue cannot be divorced from a wider debate about the historical project of the Enlightenment and its intimate connection with both the humanism and scientism of the Western university and the traditional 'civilising mission' of intellectuals.

Lines of Thought

This book brings together a selection of work produced in the Centre for New Ethnicities Research (CNER), which was set up at the University in 1992. For some of us the priority has been to question received notions of multiculturalism and the postcolonial, or to explore the problematics of the 'postmodern turn'; for others the task was to rewrite and complicate histories of the nation to include hitherto marginalised racisms and sexisms. Another important focus of work has been on the changing geography of international migration as it impacts on the local/global city, especially with reference to the newly arrivant refugee communities (Somalians,

Kurds, Kosovans) of East London. A final major area of concern has been with developing new ways of understanding and tackling popular cultures of racism, as manifested in the mass media, sport, schooling and face-to-face community relations.

Each of these strands is represented in the book. It has not, however, been possible to cover every aspect of the Centre's work. I have not included material relating to our educational and cultural work with young people, or my own psychoanalytically informed approach to understanding imagined communities of race and nation. It is a good editorial rule never to be judge and jury in one's own case! For those readers who are interested, a checklist of the Centre's current publications is provided in an Appendix.

Running through all the chosen contributions is a common preoccupation with new ethnicities, white and black, emerging out of various inmixtures of cultural influence, and their relation to the racisms that continue to be reproduced through various forms of governance in the Western world. The style of engagement with these questions varies considerably. There are essays in high cultural theory and empirically grounded studies; there is sociological analysis and critical ethnography; literary studies run side by side with political commentary. This diversity of registers also relates to questions of intellectual strategy, whose terms I have briefly sketched.

Chapters 2 and 3 contribute directly to this wider debate. Phil Marfleet begins by considering the 'Clash of Civilisations' thesis advanced by Samuel Huntington, and charts the way it has been taken up by ideologues of the European Union. He documents the enthusiasm of European politicians for notions of cultural essentialism, and their attempts to integrate Huntington's ideas on 'civilisational conflict' into their construction of a 'Fortress Europe'. He argues that new definitions of Europe which facilitate racist exclusion of non-Europeans have the effect of heightening notions of racial difference within Europe and strengthening ideologies of the Right. While EU politicians may have seized upon the 'clash thesis' instrumentally, it is now playing a part in deepening notions of immutable difference in the discourse of domestic politics within European societies.

In Chapter 3, Couze Venn sets this debate about the limits and conditions of European identity in a wider and more explicitly theoretical account of the complex correlations between modernity, colonialism and the formations of the 'sovereign subject'. His central argument is that the colonial space was historically and discursively necessary for the establishment of a modern form of individualised subjectivity. The hegemony of the 'West' and its attendant questions of power and ideology are then reconsidered in the light of globalisation theory and the current crisis in the project of modernity. The chapter concludes by arguing that the critique of occidentalism should be a core agenda for problematising the terms of the current debate about the postcolonial and postmodern world.

The importance of developing a historical and comparative perspective in understanding the peculiarities of multiracist Britain has been a core concern of the Centre's research programme. The next section of the book examines 'histories of the interior', focusing on aspects of racialised discourse that have been neglected both by historians and by theorists of racism. Reina Lewis intervenes in current debates about gender and postcoloniality by attending to the particularities of memoirs, travel writing and popular fiction written in English by Ottoman women writers, especially in relation to issues of female emancipation in Turkey, Europe and North America. All these women were, in different ways, concerned with the transformative effects of feminism. Their English-language writing can be seen as a reverse discourse in which the usually silenced 'oriental' woman writes back against dominant Western stereotypes. At the same time, their work's circulation in the Middle East during a period of accelerated social change contributed to internal debates about changing gender relations within these societies. The different readerships constructed by and for these texts are also assessed in relation to Western popular fiction and autobiography of the period.

John Marriot's contribution shifts the axis of racial articulation from gender to class. He shows how, in the course of the 19th century, the metropolitan poor were constructed as a race apart – a process which located them firmly within a discourse of nation and empire. Around 1840, public preoccupation with the curious, bizarre and criminal propensities of the underworld was displaced by perspectives which, although diverse, were embedded in theorizations of the innate superiority of the bourgeois Anglo-Saxon subject over colonial and class others. The chapter discusses a number of key texts in which images of dirt, disease and degradation are deployed to create a versatile means of transcoding physical difference into a moral and cultural geography of quasi-racial exclusion. Through these case studies, it becomes clear that race was not an anterior category augmenting the inventory of élite concerns about social order, citizenship and empire, but was from the outset integral to ways in which these problems were defined and perceived.

The book then turns to an area of contemporary concern that has been crucial to the development of the Centre's postgraduate programme – refugee studies. In Chapter 6, Patricia Tuitt tells a prototypical story about the late-twentieth-century refugee, permanently in transit, unable to produce positive proof of identity and detained pending an investigation of the case. The narrative recreation of this situation is counterpointed by a legal commentary on two notable decisions by the UK courts, in order to look at how official constructions of refugee status render invisible the situation of refugees. It is not just a question of creating a more inclusive definition of refugee status; as this chapter shows, the structures of representation that make this possible are precisely the structures that are put into question by the position of those whom they exclude.

In the following chapter, Alice Bloch examines the material and social conditions that refugee communities have to face in multiracist Britain. Drawing on data from her recent survey of refugees in Newham, she shows how patterns of refugee settlement are variously shaped by government policy, migration, family networks, language and literacy, and access to the labour market. The chapter as a whole presents a detailed case-study of the micropolitics of immigration control and the way it works to exclude refugees from full participation in civil society.

The book then turns to a field that has been one of the most distinctive and productive aspects of the Centre's work, namely a critical ethnographic approach to tackling popular cultures of racism. In an area dominated by moral assertion and political posturing, the importance of grounding explanations and policies in a 'thick description' of actual contexts and conjunctures needs to be continually emphasised. In Chapter 9, Ian MacDonald and Sharda Ugra draw on a collaborative study into cricketing cultures in Essex and East London, carried out on behalf of the Essex County Cricket Board. The study sets out to look at the some of the deeper, underlying reasons why Asian and Afro-Caribbean players do not affiliate to the established, white-dominated structures of the game, but rather organise themselves into separate clubs and leagues. Drawing on a survey of over two hundred clubs, and including in-depth interviews with players and officials, the chapter looks at how the culture of 'little England-ism' is being reproduced and challenged at the level of local sporting practice. The structures which govern unequal access to sporting amenities are examined in detail, along with prevailing attitudes and feelings towards the concept of multicultural cricket. The chapter concludes by looking at policies designed to improve equal opportunities in cricket, at a local, regional and national level.

When the report on which this chapter is based was first published, it raised a predictable storm of controversy. Questions were asked in the House of Commons, and at the seminar we organised as part of the launch, attended by senior figures from all levels of the game, strategies of dis-avowal were much in evidence. The same may well prove true of the research project carried out jointly by the CNER and the Centre for Urban and Community Research (CUCR) into young peoples' landscapes of community safety and racial danger, reported here by Les Back and Michael Keith.

In their chapter we move from the refined prejudices of the English cricketing establishment to the more brutal 'in your face' racism enacted on the streets and neighbourhoods of the working-class city. Nevertheless the links between dominant and subordinated discourses of racism remain, as always, to be unravelled. The chapter explores the ways in which the language of civil 'rights and wrongs', so much a part of our established political lexicon, provides a mechanism to racialise conflicts and generate moral panic about Asian gang violence within an East London context. The analysis brings out the importance of understanding how white working-class claims about unfairness and discrimination become the means through which a specific language of popular racism operates to both erase and elide the history of minority experiences of racial violence. The chapter concludes by arguing for the need for a new language, which can both acknowledge the grievances of white working-class communities and simultaneously avoid perpetuating moral panics about 'Asian crime'.

The need to renew the theory as well as the practice of multiculturalism has been at the forefront of the Centre's work from the very beginning. This has resulted in the development of new curricula and pedagogies in schools, and an extended series of youth and community arts projects in East London, culminating in the Rich Mix Exhibition Centre, being constructed as this book is published. It is fitting then that the final section of the book contains two chapters that explore what might be entailed in rethinking multiculturalism in the light of new developments in postcolonial and poststructuralist theory. Jayne Ifekwunigwe engages with one of the buzzwords of current intellectual debate – hybridity. The origins of the term are traced back to their problematic beginnings in nineteenth-century racial science, especially anthropology. She goes on to examine the work of contemporary cultural theorists who reframe 'race' as 'difference(s)'. Finally, the testimonies of contemporary *métis(se)* ('mixed-race') women, collected during two years' ethnographic research in Bristol, provide necessary context and content for a discussion of the continuities between theories predicated on so-called biological 'race' science and 'postmodernist' cultural explanations. The chapter finishes by arguing that contemporary *métisse* identities delimit and transgress 'bi-racialist' discourses and point the way towards a profound re-alignment of thinking about race and ethnicity as we hobble into the new millennium.

In the penultimate chapter, Barnor Hesse brings this debate home to roost by showing how the landscape of British identities has been profoundly transformed during the twentieth century. First, a colonial relation was re-articulated as a relation of migration. Second, the racialised political and cultural histories of Britain have multiplied and are threatened by recurrent revision. The chapter goes on to suggest that the crisis of late

Western multiculturalism is registered on at least three levels: the dislocation of British nationalism; the emergence of discrepant imaginations of the West; and the affirmation of political ethnicities no longer based on territorial affiliations but involving attachments to different 'virtual communities', ethnicities that are transactional, dialogical and transnational in their orientation. The implications of this analysis for the contemporary politics of race are briefly drawn out.

Despite the abstract theoretical language in which these questions are sometimes addressed, the issues involved are far from academic, as Desirée Ntolo shows in her moving postscript to the book. She provides a dramatic first-person account of what happens when someone challenges the narrow limits and conditions of official 'tolerance' for what is recognised as 'cultural diversity'. Mrs Ntolo belongs to the Essene Community, a group of black Jews who settled in Africa after the fall of the first Temple, and who have been practising a unique syncretic form of Judaism ever since. Part of the requirement of her religion is that certain observances should be carried out in an oracle built on specially consecrated ground outside the house, in a way which allows the observant to be in physical contact with the earth. As Mrs Ntolo describes here, putting up such a structure in your own back yard in a white working-class suburb like Dagenham pitches you on to the front line of confrontation with the forces of the local state, the law, popular racism and the mass media. Everything in her garden might have been lovely as far as she was concerned, but it was seen by others as an affront to the principle of order in variety (the English provide the order, the 'others, the variety'), which continues to rule the official cartographies of this white unpleasant land.

Mrs Ntolo's story brings together many of the strands of the book and of the Centre's work. It points to the shifting urban geographies of racial conflict, in which local and global ethnoscapes are intimately linked. It highlights the persistence of national insularities within a still 'racially superior' sense of the play of difference in the making of postcolonial Anglo–Britishness. And it exposes the limitations of official multiculturalism. The 'danger' of the oracle lay not only in its mixing together of sacred and profane, purification and syncretism, but its construction by someone whose authority derived from a 'wild', unassimilable form of diasporic identity that did not fit neatly into the pigeon-holes created by the race relations industry. It is because so much of what makes this country an interesting and exciting place demands another kind of map that we believe it is important to continue the intellectual project whose beginnings are traced in this book. Whatever the differences in perspective and priority between the contributors, this much is common ground.

Note

1. An earlier version of this text was presented as a paper to an editorial discussion group of the journal *Soundings*. I am very grateful for the comments made on that occasion, especially those by Stuart Hall and Doreen Massey. I have subsequently revised the text extensively in the light of these criticisms, and also after further discussion with members of CNER. None of the above should be held responsible for the line of argument developed here, which is that of the author alone.

Bibliography

Archer, M. (1995) *Realist Social Theory*, Cambridge: Cambridge University Press.

Back, L. (1997) *New Ethnicities and Urban Multicultures*, London: UCL Press.

Barker, M. (1981) *The New Racism*, London: Junction Books.

Beiner, R. (ed.) (1999) *Theorizing Nationalism*, New York: Albany.

Brah, A. (1996) *Cartographies of Diaspora*, London: Routledge.

Cambridge, A. and S. Feuchtwang (1991) *Anti-Racist Strategies*, Aldershot: Avebury.

Cannadine, D. (1999) *Class in Britain*, New Haven, Conn: Yale University Press.

Clifford, J. (1998) *Routes: travel and translation in the late 20th century*, London: Harvard University Press.

Cohen, P. (1994) 'Yesterday's Words, Tomorrow's Children', in Gaber and Aldridge.

— and H.S. Bains (1988) *Multiracist Britain*, Basingstoke: Macmillan.

Cohen, P. and W. Schwarz (eds) (1998) 'Front Lines Back Yards', *New Formations*, 33, Lawrence and Wishart.

Debray, R. (1981) *Teachers, Writers, Celebrities*, London: Verso.

Donald, J. and A. Rattansi (eds)(1991) *Race, Culture, Difference*, London: Sage.

Feagin, J. (1994) *Living with Racism – the Black Middle-Class Experience*, Boston: Beacon.

Featherstone, M. (ed.) (1990) *Global Culture*, London: Sage.

Fieldstein, R. (1990) *Political Correctness*, Minneapolis: University of Minnesota Press.

Gabriel, J. (1994) *Racism, Culture, Markets*, London: Routledge.

Gaber, I. and J. Aldridge (1994) *Culture, Identity and Transracial Adoption*, London: Free Association Books.

Gilroy, P. (1993) *The Black Atlantic*, London: Verso.

Gordon, P. (1989) *New Right, New Racism*, London: Searchlight.

Gupta, S. (1993) *Disrupted Borders*, London: Oram.

Hall, S. (1996) 'New Ethnicities', in Morley and Hsing Chen.

Hirschfield, L. (1996) *Race in the Making*, London: MIT Press.

Ignatieff, M. (1994) *Blood and Belonging*, London: Vintage.

Institute of Race Relations (1989) *Racism and the Press in Thatcher's Britain*, London: IRR.

Kellas,. J. (1988) *The Politics of Nationalism and Ethnicity*, Basingstoke: Macmillan.

Kohn, M. (1996) *The Race Gallery*, London: Vintage.

Lévi-Strauss, C. (1977) *Structural Anthropology*, London: Allen Lane.

Mac an Ghaill, M. (1991) *Young, Gifted and Black*, London: Routledge.

Macdonald, I. (1989) *Murder in the Playground*, London: Longsight.

MacPherson (1999) *The Stephen Lawrence Enquiry*, London: HMSO.

Malik, K. (1996) *The Meaning of Race*, Basingstoke: Macmillan.

Morley, D. and K. Hsing Chen (1996) *Stuart Hall – Critical Dialogues in Cultural Studies*, London: Routledge.

Rorty, R. (1991) *Contingency, Irony and Solidarity*, Cambridge: Cambridge University Press.

Rutherford, J. (1998) *Forever England*, London: Lawrence and Wishart.

Sassen, S. (1991) *The Global City*, Princeton NJ: Princeton University Press.

Sharma, S. *et al.* (eds) (1997) *Disorienting Rhythms*, London: Zed Books.

Skelton, T. and G. Valentine (1998) *Cool Places*, London: Routledge.

Smith, A.D. (1991) *National Identity*, Harmondsworth: Penguin.

Sollors, W. (ed.) (1989) *The Invention of Ethnicity*, Oxford: Oxford University Press.

Solomos, J. (1993) *Race and Racism in Britain*, Basingstoke: Macmillan.

Taylor, C. (1994) *Multiculturalism and the Politics of Recognition*, Princeton NJ: Princeton University Press.

Werbner, P. and T. Modood (eds) (1997) *Debating Cultural Hybridity*, London: Zed Books.

Wright, W.D. (1997) *Black Intellectuals, Black Cognition, Black Aesthetics*, London: Praeger.

Europe's Civilising Mission

Phil Marfleet

Progress towards a unified Europe has invariably been described as an assertion of internationalism.[1] Pro-European politicians depict the European Union (EU) as a positive challenge to narrow nationalist perspectives, to ideologies of separation and of difference. As a boundary-spanning unity, the EU is said to offer the prospect of close collaboration among member states, while its citizens are to enjoy prosperity and common legal rights which may realise genuine pan-continental harmony. There are alternative perspectives, however. As one recent analysis observes: 'any discussion of integration is also in fact, inseparably, a discussion of disintegration' (Crowley 1996: 151). This chapter argues that the attempt to construct a unified Europe has heightened ideas about cultural difference across the continent and that the EU is already a means of celebrating such difference within Europe and between Europe and 'non-Europe'.

This chapter also argues that the efforts of European politicians and EU officials to define these differences have borrowed from recent theories of global conflict which depict a 'clash' of cultures as inevitable and destructive. In particular, in accepting implicitly the notion of a 'clash of civilisations', some influential European politicians have provided a rationale for a racist celebration of difference.

American international relations theorist Samuel Huntington produced his 'clash' theory in 1993. He described a world in which, with nation-states of decreasing influence, global politics is to be shaped by relations between cultural 'blocs'. Such relations will be fundamentally hostile, he argued, for the blocs are already separated by deep 'fault lines' which mark ancient boundaries between civilisations. According to Huntington (1993: 25), 'differences between civilizations are not only real; they are basic ... far more fundamental than differences among political ideologies and political regimes'. It is these differences, he maintains, that will generate prolonged and violent conflict between blocs that are to dominate the global order.

This deeply pessimistic thesis has generated an extraordinarily intense debate among academics and politicians. One critic comments that it has been the subject of more controversy than any other single article written in almost 50 years, since Kennan argued for United States guardianship of the post-war world (Qadir 1998: 149). Huntington's original article, and a book published on the same theme in 1996, have produced responses worldwide. Some are in the form of celebratory or highly critical reviews; others both praise and damn the piece.[2] At the same time, the 'clash' thesis appears to have entered the consciousness of some political figures who have mobilised it within particular perspectives and strategies. Among these are European leaders, EU officials ('Eurocrats'), and various ideologues of European unity, for whom it appears to provide a rationale for their own quest for 'Europeanness' – a pan-continental identity which can complement the EU's project of economic unification and political 'solidarisation'.

The search for 'Europe' has become increasingly urgent. For ideologues of the EU, Martiniello (1994: 39) argues, 'the cultural construction of Europe should follow the same pattern as the economic one'. Here, the drive towards economic integration should be accompanied by the creation of a 'common European cultural space' (ibid). Within this space are to reside those said to possess the characteristics of 'Europeanness': those deemed to bear the values of a specific cultural heritage. Europe is to be the place of *homo europus*: equally, it is to be the place from which those judged not 'European' will be excluded. The notion of European culture as a European 'civilisation' which stands against the cultures of others has become a critical issue.

Integration

The idea of economic collaboration in Europe lay in attempts to rescue those states of the region which had been seriously affected by the Second World War and faced perceived new threats from the Communist bloc. As Milward (1992) makes clear, the European Community (EC) was conceived primarily as a means of assuring the future of capitalism in France and Germany – it constituted a 'rescue of the European nation-state'. This was consistent with US efforts to promote European integration in the context of growing Cold War hostilities. But the project took on other dimensions. From the 1980s, the major concern of the Community, later the Union, was to forge an economic integration that might operate effectively within a perceived 'global' economy.

Martiniello (1994: 33) comments that the priority of the EC/EU has been 'to complete the internal market as soon as possible and to assure the conditions of its efficiency'. Delanty (1995: 143) spells out the broader picture:

One should not be deluded into believing that the Europe of the European Union has come about because of its inherent value. *The ideas of elites are promoted for their functional value in maintaining or pursuing a system of power.* In the case of the European Union this is a matter of securing the optimal conditions for the accumulation and free flow of capital and to make Western European capitalism competitive on a global level. (emphasis added)

It is in this context that efforts are being made to establish positive visions of European unity. The project is intensely difficult, largely because the national ideologies of member states have long been premised upon ideas about the distinctness of each *vis-à-vis* 'rival' European entities. Hence the EU has itself been a forum for competition between politicians of member states who wish to prove their vigour by championing specific national agendas around all manner of issues – exchange rates, agricultural quotas, fishing rights, commercial standards, military relations. One result has been cynicism and chaos at the centre of a notionally integrating European entity, summed up by the former Eurocrat Bernard Connolly (1995) as 'The Rotten Heart of Europe'. This milieu has been fertile ground for the extreme right, which has viewed the Union as an arena for the assertion of populist national projects. A host of right-wing parties has attempted to direct mass energies into hostility towards other European national or regional groups, perceived as privileged by the EU, or those they characterise as parasitic upon it.

In this context the ideology of a unified Europe has often looked fragile. In effect, the EU suffers from an ideological deficit; as Waever and Kelstrup (1993: 66) note, 'worried Eurocrats ... fear that there are limits as to how far one can push integration in the political and economic spheres unless people feel sufficiently European'. And such feeling, leading EU politicians have argued, must be more than mere recognition of the EU's claim to economic significance: as Jacques Delors observed memorably, 'people do not fall in love with an Inner Market' (ibid). There has therefore been an urgent exploration of 'Europeanness' – of notions of Europe which can be a basis for identification with the EU. In effect, ideologues of Europe wish to simulate ideologies of the nation state. They wish the 'community of nations' said to constitute the EU to possess some of the attributes of 'imagined community' (Anderson 1983). By such means they hope to generate among its population a mood of consent to their increasingly centralised initiatives.

As Delanty points out, this demands more than a rallying call to the European ideal. He observes: 'Europeanism is not a fixed set of ideas and ideals which can be unilaterally aspired to as an alternative to national chauvinism and xenophobia' (Delanty 1995: 143). It must draw upon traditions within which national loyalties, 'chauvinism and xenophobia' are integral. At the same time, ideologues of an integrated Europe have been compelled to shape a pan-continental identity which can *contain* conflicting nationalisms. After a series of halting and unsuccessful efforts, they appear to have settled upon the theme of cultural heritage. This, they argue, confers 'Europeanness' upon citizens of the continent, and with it a host of benefits which can make the EU an object of positive popular concern.

'New' Europeans

For forty years 'Europe' was identified differently. From the 1940s the architects of the Community depicted it overwhelmingly as Western Europe – the portion of Europe that was of the West and with America in its Cold War conflicts. In the late 1940s a new 'eastern' frontier had been constructed along the western territorial borders of Poland and Czechoslovakia, abandoning 'Central Europe' to the malign forces of the East. Within the borders of Western Europe, it was argued, the traditions of democratic pluralism would be nurtured and societies which had earlier fallen to one brand of dangerous authoritarianism would be protected from another. This Europe and these processes were to be guaranteed by a protective elder brother – 'Europe had in effect become America's eastern frontier' (Delanty 1995: 121).

This definition of Europe was made problematic by the rapid processes of change that culminated in the collapse of the Stalinist ruling class in the late 1980s. The EC was confronted with requests for membership from states which had been regarded earlier as alien, but now sought, with Gorbachev, a place in the 'common European home'. New definitions of Europe were required and increasingly these were built upon notions of a common European cultural heritage. As a result, contemporary attitudes to Europe are less those of a place which confronts an alienated East than of a continent *in itself*, within which the inhabitants share cultural traits which make them 'European'.

For ideologues of pan-Europeanism, Smith argues, 'there has always been a European culture and identity, however vague and difficult to pin down and formulate' (Smith 1995: 129). The problem in the past has been the difficulty of asserting such identity, for conflicts within the continent have intervened, preventing its realisation. 'Although [pan-Europeans] may speak of a new European culture and the new Europeans, they see both as modern versions of something that existed in the past but was destroyed by internecine wars and must now be recovered and restored' (ibid.). For today's pan-Europeans, the continent at last has an opportunity to contain the national traditions which have disrupted its past. It can do so, they argue, by asserting values which are said to reside in all Europeans, qualities evident even when they are in conflict. One prominent British Europhile asserts that such qualities are unique.

> The peoples of Europe share humane principles which are not found in other parts of the world ... Christian Europeans are as ancient Greeks used to be: they may go to war with each other, but despite these conflicts they do observe the proprieties ... that a Frenchman and an Englishman and a German when they meet often seem as if they were born in the same town. (Radice 1992: 123)

Europeans are said to be kin: indeed, the metaphor of family recurs in recent analyses of European politics. According to Kapteyn (1996: 171), for example, it is now 'brotherly love' that assures co-operation across the continent.

It is here that the approach of the European 'internationalist', who wishes to supersede national differences, draws on ideas which also provide ideological materials for the extreme right. Europeans, it is argued, share qualities denied to others. In effect, it is the character of non-Europeans – those who do not hold the continent's 'humane principles' – that informs Europeans about who they really are. It is a small step to declare that these others do not have a place in the continental coherence. Thus the fascist Republican Party in Germany uses the notion of 'living space' mobilised by the Nazis in an earlier era; its leader, Franz Schönhuber, argues that such 'space' must be defended against 'others': 'We're not a welfare office for the Mediterranean ... We want to protect the German people's eco-logical living space against foreign infiltration' (Evans 1996: 47). In a similar vein, Jean-Marie Le Pen of the French National Front maintains that 'We must act ... by occupying our vital space, because nature has a horror of space and if we do not occupy it, others will occupy it in our place' (Evans 1996: 49).

Invariably the notion of defending Europe against others is based on ideas of a threatening East. But this East is not the one observed across the Iron Curtain of an earlier era. Rather it is one glimpsed across an imagined 'fault line' said to divide European civilisation from other cultures to the south, primarily (as for Schönhuber and Le Pen) from 'Islam'. It is in this sense that, although 'the East' has remained a focus of European hostility, the 'East' has been transferred southwards (Delanty 1995: 150). And it is in this context that the notion of civilisational conflict has entered the discourse of Europeanness.

Fault Lines

According to Huntington and his co-thinkers, religious identities are the most essential of human qualities. They define 'civilisation', an aspect of human interaction almost as important as the physical characteristics which distinguish *homo sapiens* from other species (Huntington 1993: 24). As important as the fact of civilisation, however, are the differences associated with it. And such differences, Huntington argues, are enduring. Placing 'relations between God and man' at the head of a list of civilisational attributes, he asserts:

> The people of different civilizations have different views on the relations between God and man, the individual and the group, the citizen and the state, parents and children, husband and wife, as well as differing views on the relative importance of rights and responsibilities, liberty and authority, equality and hierarchy. These differences are the product of centuries. They will not soon disappear. (Huntington 1993: 25)

It is these notions of cultural essentialism and historical continuity that underlie an approach characterised by Sakamoto (1995: 135) as 'civilizational determinism'.

In a world which is being made smaller by technological change, 'civilisations' are now being thrust closer together, Huntington maintains. The sense of difference between cultural blocs is being intensified, and, as the nation-state weakens, religion is emerging as the focal point for the assertion of identity. This process is inevitable, he argues, because, unlike nation states or the ideologies associated with them, religious heritage is immutable. At a global level the historic significance of civilisation is being asserted anew.

Today there are 'seven or eight' major world civilisations, Huntington argues: Western, Confucian, Japanese, Islamic, Hindu, Slavic–Orthodox, Latin American and 'possibly' African (Huntington 1993: 25). Within each, 'civilization-consciousness' is based upon 'kin-country' loyalty, of which the most important component is awareness of religious heritage. In a globalising world this is of ever greater importance, he maintains. The geographical distribution of believers has always identified 'fault lines' between cultural blocs, but now these are thrown into sharper relief. It is across such frontiers that new world conflicts are to take place.

The most significant blocs are said to be those centred upon the 'Judaeo-Christian' West, the 'Confucianism/Buddhism' of East Asia, and Islam, based in the Middle East (Huntington 1993: 23). Among these, the most persistent tensions and conflicts have been those presented to the West by Islam – a bloc marked by its 'bloody borders'. Islam has been an 'ancient rival' of the West, and is likely to remain a menacing presence. It will constitute the key threat to world order (Huntington 1993: 34).

These notions are far from original. Huntington pursues a theme which had been gaining currency among American strategic analysts since the Iranian revolution of 1979. For a decade after these events the US foreign policy establishment and associated academics exerted enormous efforts to identify Islam as a key threat to world order. Muslims, their traditions and institutions were homogenised. Muslims from all regions and a host of persuasions (various movements, sects and currents) were deemed part of a 'fundamentalist' bloc, of which the chief characteristics were 'rage, extremism, fanaticism, terrorism' (Esposito 1992: 173). Writing in 1989, Patrick Buchanan summed up this approach: the Islamic threat was ubiquitous – nothing less than a 'global challenge' to the West (Esposito 1992: 175).

Such attitudes were sharpened by the collapse of Communist regimes in Russia and Eastern Europe. Rather than prompting a relaxation of American relations with the wider world, these events stimulated a search for new enemies, which promptly fixed upon Islam. One of Huntington's leading collaborators, Charles Krauthammer, argued that at the very moment of America's triumph *vis-à-vis* its old Communist rivals an 'Islamic uprising' was under way. Krauthammer saw 'a new "arc of crisis" ... another great movement is going on ... a global intifada' (Esposito 1992: 175), which must be confronted.

The switch in focus from a Communist 'East' to an Islamic 'East' was entirely consistent, argued Daniel Pipes, another of Huntington's colleagues. Muslims were little different from the authoritarian, anti-democratic and – most important – anti-Western forces represented by Communism, he maintained. 'Fundamentalist' Islam, he insisted, is

> closer in spirit to other such movements (communism, fascism) than to traditional religion. ... By nature anti-democratic and aggressive, anti-semitic and anti-Western, it has great plans. Indeed spokesmen for funda-mentalist Islam see their movement standing in direct competition to Western civilization and challenging it for global supremacy. (Salla 1997: 733)

Huntington himself has spelt out what is implicit in such comments. He has noted that the history of the United States – which he so often makes synonymous with 'the West' – has been a history of national identification against 'others'. In the eighteenth century, the movement for American independence defined its project against British colonialism; for much of the twentieth century the relevant 'other' was communism. Such mobil-isation of an American national consciousness against a succession of enemies has not been merely conjunctural. Rather, the coherence of a major national capitalism has demanded such an arrangement, especially within a state marked by sharp class differences and repeated traumatic political upheavals. Huntington makes a rhetorical enquiry on behalf of the American state: 'How will we know who we are if we don't know who we are against?' (O'Hagan 1995: 28). In effect, the idea of civilisational conflict has been mobilised as a means of ideological coherence within and for a nation state which remains economically unequal, culturally diverse and socially volatile.

Huntington anticipates conflict *between* imagined blocs, never within them, and never within the national society which is, in effect, the real subject of his concerns. After half a century of orientation by America's rulers upon the Soviet threat, by the 1980s the need to synthesise a new Communism was urgent. O'Hagan (1995: 28) comments that 'Losing an enemy could ... be perceived as a threat to the constitution of national identity.' Huntington has all but recognised that his project consists in what O'Hagan (1995: 35) calls '"looking for enemies", trying to locate and justify the next threat'. It is in this sense that the 'clash' theory should be seen as ideological in the classic Marxist sense. It can be seen as an attempt to discover 'who we are against' – to generate a means of renewing national community.

A New Iron Curtain

It is the 'clash' theory, rather than Huntington's revealing musings on American identity, that has attracted attention in Europe. According to some writers on ethnic relations, emergence of the theory has been timely, assisting those who wish to develop their own ideas about external threat, which in the European case are focused primarily on the imagined menace posed by the 'South', principally Islam. Bjorgo writes of developments in Scandinavia, where Muslims are increasingly depicted as bent upon 'conspiracy' against the West.

> Islamic conspiracy theories may appear more credible to larger segments of the public ... due to the fact that even among political elites, Islam is more and more replacing communism as the perceived main threat to Western civilization. One expression of this trend was Samuel P. Huntington's 'The Clash of Civilizations?' in which he asserted that 'the fault lines between civilizations will be the battle lines of the future'. (Bjorgo 1997: 67)

Huntington's ideas have been seized upon by the extreme right: Bjorgo also notes (ibid.) how the clash theory is easily assimilated by the type of nationalist discourse prompted by the Front National (FN) in France, the new right in England, and Scandinavian anti-immigration activists. In France, the relative strength of the FN has given Le Pen licence to air publicly a particularly vulgar racism. Evans (1996: 50) describes Le Pen's attempts to develop an 'apocalyptic scenario', insisting that French national identity has two choices: 'either it will survive or it will be replaced by Islam'. Here the notion of an essential cultural conflict – an idea which long predates Huntington's intervention – receives endorsement from theories which not only appear to set the 'clash' in a universal context but also generate sustained discussion in universities, academic journals, and the corridors of power, and which provide welcome 'official' endorsement.

European fascists' embrace of the 'clash' thesis is not remarkable. More striking is the endorsement offered by very prominent European politicians viewed as being of the political mainstream, some of whom have been centrally involved in EU policy-making. Former Belgian Prime Minister Willy Claes (from the centre-right of European politics) has made a series of statements to the effect that Islam has emerged as the Western world's number one menace (Vertovic and Peach 1997: 4; Bjorgo 1997: 67). Javier Solana, former Spanish foreign minister (from the centre-left), has commented on the historic significance of conflicts between 'Europe' and 'Islam' – what he calls 'an unhappy history' (Independent, 8 February 1995). The timing of these comments is significant: Solana spoke as host at the 1995 Barcelona Summit, a forum within which EU foreign ministers met their counterparts from Middle Eastern countries to discuss cross-Mediterranean collaboration. Well-briefed European media described the EU's agenda as focused upon the Mediterranean as '"the new fault line" that has replaced the old iron curtain' (Independent, 8 February 1995). Here the vocabulary of the 'clash' discourse is mobilised quite precisely within a European context.

These examples bear out the observation that a perspective within which Muslims are viewed as a problem or a threat is not confined to the political fringe 'but is prominent in some elite discourses' (Modood 1997: 3). Bjorno (1997: 68) suggests that images of an Islamic enemy may appeal to certain sections of popular opinion and 'may even gain a foothold within sections of the political and military establishment'. In fact, I suggest, these institutions are actively engaged in promoting such views. They are being mobilised instrumentally as part of the attempt to develop a coherent pan-European project and help induce a popular ideology of 'Europeanness'.

Building the 'Fortress'

How is an integrated Europe to be constructed at the level of popular consciousness? Reviewing the debate on 'Europeanness', Waever and

Kelstrup (1993: 66) note leading Eurocrats' conviction that 'there has to be more culture in the EC'. During the 1970s and 1980s, the Community attempted a 'balloons and flags' strategy designed to induce 'popular loyalty and affection' for Europe (Waever and Kelstrup 1993: 67). There was a systematic effort to introduce the EC symbol and EC flags, to regularise passports, and especially to establish institutions such as those which promoted the idea of European linkages at the cultural level.

Delanty suggests that these initiatives were doomed to failure:

> Most attempts to create a European cultural identity are pathetic exercises in cultural engineering: the Eurovision Song Contest, Euro-Disney, the Ecu, the Annual European City of Culture and the cultural apparatus of the new institutions was not the stuff out of which new symbolic structures could be built. (Delanty 1995: 128)

Delanty maintains that, in attempting to mimic the ideological constructions of the nation-state, Eurocrats mobilised inappropriate materials. They focused mainly upon symbols of 'bourgeois high culture', rather than on matters of language and on the rural nostalgias with which national identities have been mainly concerned. One result, it can be argued, is that the EU's ideological deficit has been more marked. As Europe moved towards economic integration and political 'solidarisation', its populations remained unmoved by the European idea: belonging to Europe was an abstraction, being a 'European' hardly meaningful. Yet the apparatus which supervised economic and political integration required increased legitimacy among 'its' 350 million citizens.

It is unthinkable that the ideologues of Europe should challenge the structures of the nation state itself. Internationalist ideas, such as those which promote unity from below on the basis of class identification, and contest the national idea, cannot be the stuff of their supranational project. Europeanisation is a project supervised from above, which must work through the rulers and bureaucratic structures of EU member states. It is therefore more than the nation state but never detached from it.

Smith notes some of the problems which necessarily emerge. A host of physical symbols linked to myths and memories of nation remind citizens of the EU member states of their local allegiance. At the same time, at the supranational level, they remain unengaged: 'Without shared memories and meaning, without common symbols and myths, without shrines and ceremonies and monuments, except the bitter reminders of recent holocausts and wars, who will feel European in the depths of their being?' (Smith 1995: 139). In fact Smith goes too far in asking 'who will die for Europe?' Pan-Europeanism does not need to mimic the nation state in ways that *replace* its communities of the imagination with a supranational structure that can 'be' a nation. Nevertheless, the problem of operational legitimacy for the EU remains, in the sense that the Union requires a form of authority which can draw on a hegemonic definition of Europe. If the EU is in some sense 'to be' Europe, what is Europe to be?

By the late 1980s this problem was becoming intensely difficult, reflected in Eurocrats' anxiety that people 'should feel sufficiently European'. It was resolved in part by collapse of the old framework for defining Europe. When the Communist East disintegrated, the Eurocrats' anxiety could, paradoxically, be eased somewhat, for now there were opportunities to modify the definition of Europe in relation to a new imagined border. This saw the continent less as 'Western Europe' than as a culturally delineated Europe, a coherence that derived its meaning from Europe's perceived status in a wider world.

Since the early 1990s there has been an unprecedented series of legal reforms across the EU, putting in place a system of exclusion – 'Fortress Europe' – *vis-à-vis* migrants from the Third World. Officially, this is an intervention aimed at confronting problems of 'over-population' outside the continent. On this view, there has been development of a 'demographic gradient', along which vast numbers of people from the Third World seek to move towards a thinly populated but prosperous Europe. I have argued elsewhere (Marfleet 1998) that this scenario, a contemporary Malthusianism, raises imagined threats which can be mobilised against the problem of explaining and confronting instability in a world of uneven development and crisis. This is especially important in the face of the profound crises which for twenty years have affected Africa, Asia, Latin America and the Middle East. Large numbers of forced migrants have emerged from the most seriously affected regions, a minority of whom have sought asylum in Europe, where they have been greeted with rising hostility. Such migrants have become, in effect, the vision of threat around which pan-Europeans wish to mobilise.

Collinson describes precisely how, from the late 1980s, European strategists reoriented from Eastern Europe to the 'South', especially towards the Middle East and North Africa, and the perceived threats of demographic crisis and Islamic insurgency. She notes (Collinson 1996: 39) that, as the Communist threat evaporated, it took with it many of the old certainties, not least Western Europe's sense of control over national borders. European policy-makers began to focus on what they termed 'soft' security issues located elsewhere, notably the problem of immigration. In 1991 the Western European Union (WEU) produced a report on security in the Mediterranean, in which it warned:

Europe can no longer view its security solely in terms of the establishment of peace on the continent of Europe; it must also bear in mind that its relations with its southern neighbours also concern its security and involve risks which at first sight are probably not of a military nature but affect its internal stability and the conduct of its economy and, if allowed to develop, might in the long run jeopardise what now seems to have been acquired in terms of peace. (Collinson 1996: 39)

Among these 'security' concerns, Collinson notes, immigration appeared to top the list. 'Apocalyptic images of a Europe under siege' (Collinson 1996: 40) fed a paranoia in which threats from Islam were most prominent. These were not only threats to jobs and livelihoods, 'but also to the very foundations and identities of the nation states concerned – and a threat to be controlled' (ibid). The control of people, and the related question of definition of their cultural heritage, now became key issues on the agenda of Europeanisation.

EU states had already been engaged in a series of largely secret meetings at which agreement had been reached on principles for harmonisation of migration and asylum policies. From the early 1990s these took on much greater importance. They were conducted against a background of rising activity by the extreme right and of accommodation to the latter's racist agenda by national governments. In France, for example, de Wenden noted a shift of emphasis in migration policies. Such policies were no longer placed in the context of economic objectives, or 'clothed in technocratic discourse', she observed:

> Immigration policies are now formed in response to the collective insecurities and imaginings governing public opinion; the clampdown on illegal immigrants, the need for tighter border controls, the threat of delinquency and of religious fundamentalism, the perceived loss of French identity, and fears of demographic invasion are characteristic reactions. (de Wenden 1991: 100)

Across Europe, government attitudes to migration turned increasingly around the notion of the legality of migrants. In France the term 'clandestine' appeared in official discourse; in Britain the notion of 'bogus' migrants, especially asylum-seekers, entered the official vocabulary. The more immigration became a question of control and legitimacy, the more earlier generations of migrants – often long-established – came to be seen as problematic. An external enemy which could be a focus for all governments of the EU helped to define an internal presence which, by association with the threatening non-Europeans, became subject to increased hostility.

Racism was hardly new to European national societies, but now it was being given a continental dimension. Castles notes how long-established terms used with a pejorative connotation – '*Arabe*' in France, or '*Auslander*' in Germany – were now complemented by the Italian '*extracomunitario*', widely used to describe immigrants from outside the EU. He notes: 'it is a way of homogenizing difference in exclusionary terms, whereby the core of difference is non-belonging to a (new) imagined community' (Castles 1993:29). These developments fed into the Europe-wide agenda on which Eurocrats found it increasingly easy to assert themselves as guardians of both national and continental integrity. After all the intra-European disputes of earlier decades, it now seemed much easier to develop a pan-continental project, albeit one that aggressively defined 'Europe' by identifying and excluding those deemed not of Europe.

A Christian Club

During the 1990s the EU has moved somewhat closer to attaining an inward coherence. It has done so almost solely on the basis of a culture of exclusion. In an earlier era, Europe asserted itself by preparing for military confrontation with a threatening East; today it projects the ideology of cultural incompatibility.

For those engaged in advancing this project a universal theory of cultural difference is of some importance. Huntington's vision of an essentialised world provides a useful framework, especially when its author also goes to some trouble to place the European experience quite precisely within his thesis. For Huntington, economic regionalism is an expression of the re-emergence of civilisation from the era of the nation state. But such regionalism can succeed only when the civilisational element is most fully expressed, he argues: 'On the one hand, successful economic regionalism will reinforce civilization-consciousness. On the other hand, economic regionalism may succeed only when it is rooted in a common civilization. The European Community rests on the shared foundation of European culture and Western Christianity' (Huntington 1993: 27).

For the EU to succeed, therefore, the cultural 'foundation' of Europe must be more fully understood, and foundational values must be demonstrated and asserted. The consequences in terms of intensified racist difference are understood, and are dismissed. Huntington is sanguine about the relationship between harmonisation of European migration regimes and increased levels of racism, including the 'political reactions and violence … against migrants' which, he notes, has increased since 1990 (Huntington 1993: 27).

Not content with identifying 'fault lines' such as that of the Mediterranean, Huntington depicts 'torn countries', of which 'the most obvious and prototypical' is Turkey. A predominantly Muslim state, but one on the 'edge' of the European bloc, Turkey should be firmly excluded from the EU, he maintains. Holmes (1997: 7) sums up Huntington's view: 'the European Union is, and should be, a Christian club ... to bolster the West's inward coherence, we need to slam the door in Turkey's face.' The EU continues to do just that, firmly excluding Turkey and hardening the outer walls of its fortress.

Such official exclusion of Turkey from the EU by member states, based on thinly disguised recognition of cultural 'incompatibility', gives greater confidence to those who wish to confront internal enemies, those who are not to be of 'the club'. In France, the FN demonises North Africans as bearers of a religious impulse which drives them to attempt the subordination of French national culture. Assaults on people of North African origin are given legitimacy by an official discourse of difference which speaks of the incompatibility of Europeans with those from across the 'Mediterranean fault line'. Similarly in Germany, the fascist German People's Union (DVU) has drawn strength from the exclusionary policies being adopted by regional authorities. The DVU, believed to have played a leading role in a series of murderous attacks on foreigners (notably the 'Rostock pogrom' of August 1992 [Evans 1996: 49]), has recently campaigned successfully for the expulsion from Germany of 'non-Europeans'.[3]

The German case provides a good example of the process by which exclusionary policies implemented at the supranational level assist parties of the right which make claims in defence of the nation. One outcome is that 'the center-right is beginning to join the extreme right as a mouthpiece of antiforeigner nationalism. Nor should we forget that the left (as in France) is also endowed with a nationalistic faction' (Suleiman 1995: 82).

In Britain, meanwhile, there has been enough alarm at the recent rise of anti-Muslim feeling to prompt a special report on 'Islamophobia'. The Runnymede Trust describes 'a national epidemic' of anti-Muslim sentiment, partly as a function of prejudicial coverage of Islam in the media. Among key features of Islamophobia, the report argues, are claims that Islamic cultures are 'wholly different from other cultures' and that Islam is 'implacably threatening'. The report observes that Islamophobic discourse mentions Islam as a successor to Nazism and communism, and contains imagery of both invasion and infiltration. It concludes that 'The expression of anti-Muslim ideas and sentiments is increasingly respectable' (*Independent*, 21 February 1997).

Formally, the EU is not concerned with ethnicity or 'race'. But, as MacEwan notes, the migration and asylum regime that it supervises in the form of Fortress Europe has had a serious impact in these areas. He adds that 'there has been little institutional concern' on the part of the Union (MacEwan 1995: 13). The EU is indeed unmoved by the ways in which its strategy of exclusion helps to formalise notions of racist difference within member states. It continues to reinforce the Fortress provisions, notably by strengthening 'permeable' borders of southern states such as Greece, Italy and Spain. The Mediterranean is seen as a border which must be policed with great vigour: it is in this sense that 'Europe is becoming a fortress with the Straits of Gibraltar and the Bosporus as moats' (Delanty 1995: 150).

The notion of a cultural 'fault line' is all but recognised in official EU discourse and is now used routinely by leading European strategists. In an extensive review of migration as a factor in recent EU–Maghreb relations, Collinson (1996: 42) concludes that in the EU perspective, an older East–West divide 'has been replaced by a North–South religious divide running through the Mediterranean'; she adds, significantly, 'as argued by Samuel Huntington in his essay "The Clash of Civilizations?"'.

Conclusion

Huntington and his co-thinkers have succeeded in advancing their ideas of cultural conflict into the mainstream of public debate. Their search for new enemies has been congenial to European strategists engaged in their own project of integration. This development can of course be seen as a confirmation of the 'clash' theory: a European assertion of 'civilisation-consciousness' made necessary by global changes, especially by changes to the status of the nation state. But this is to credit Huntington with far too much. The clash theory has a specific origin. As Huntington has in effect admitted, it is less an explanation of global affairs than an attempt to refurbish the notion of American national coherence against threatening external enemies: 'How will we know who we are if we don't know who we are against?' Its utility to ideologues of pan-Europe lies precisely in its mobilisation of ideas about difference which are rooted in ideologies of national society. Hence the 'civilisation-consciousness' Huntington wishes to promote in 'the West' (a synonym for the US) proves congenial to those in Europe who hope to mobilise a pan-continental entity which can contain specific national ideologies rather than contest them.

The turn to theories of 'clash' has been entirely instrumental. Like all attempts to construct national, or nation-like ideologies, it seeks to provide a rationale for coherence which conceals inequality and operates to minimise social conflict. Here the project reveals a telling contradiction, for although Fortress Europe is essentially a racist construction it does not exclude all people of 'non-European' status. Huntington himself has noted that class relations cut across his cultural blocs. In an aside which subverts the essentialist thesis, he comments baldly that 'elites of non-Western societies are often better able to communicate with Westerners and with each other than with the people of their own [*sic*] society' (Holmes 1997: 10). In fact, it is not merely a matter of 'communication': those with wealth and privilege have well-established links with those of their class elsewhere, including Europe. Their right to unhindered movement is seldom in question and they usually travel untroubled across 'cultural' boundaries.

Miles identifies this situation precisely, as an expression of 'class logic':

> If it is a fortress that is being constructed, it is intended to deny entry to almost all of those seeking a buyer for their semi- and unskilled labour power, as well as those seeking sanctuary from civil conflict and state repression ... there is a predominant class logic to the structure of exclusion. (Miles 1993: 18)

Such 'logic' is a primary element in constructions of national identity. In the case of Europeanism, it is a critical factor, often ignored in the anxiety about racist exclusion expressed by those hostile to the Fortress legislation.

Matters of class are intimately related to those of 'race'. Thus Delanty (1995: 154) identifies the idea of unified Europe as 'a racism of the wealthy'. By speaking less of 'race' and more of cultural boundaries, Europeanism is able to disguise itself as an internationalism. This, on the one hand, permits the embrace of national identity and of 'Europeanness' and, on the other hand, promotes heightened awareness of difference *within* European national societies. Its architects hope that it can contain the more troublesome expressions of national rivalry and operate against solidarities of class that may emerge from below.

This is not an abstract anxiety. There is a long (albeit inconsistent) tradition of internationalism that has been able to construct class solidarities from below, challenging national states, their rivalries and their collaborations. In 1997 this took a contemporary turn when automobile workers from across Europe challenged policies associated with the 'liberalisation' of the EU's economic regime – what they termed 'sweatshop Europe' (*Guardian*, 12 March 1997). Following a widespread strike in support of sacked Renault employees in Belgium, car workers from many countries and a host of companies demonstrated in Paris – an exemplary action which may have caused alarm in corporate boardrooms and in European capitals. The mobilisations were prompted both by corporate 'downsizing' and by attacks on living standards across EU states which have been closely linked to the agenda for monetary integration (Callinicos 1997). Prominent among participants were many workers of 'ethnic minority' groups – those of African, Asian, and Middle Eastern origin often placed outside 'European culture'. The *Guardian* (12 March 1997) commented that 'the Euro-demo is born': it is appropriate to add that this was not the expression of Euro-identity envisaged by the ideologues of pan-Europeanism.

Such events are testimony to the cultural complexity of modern European states and to the increasing difficulties faced by those pressing for continental integration. They also point up the obvious – glaring – inadequacies of the 'clash' theory, with its homogenisation of vast regions on the basis of imagined civilisational attributes. The theory is an unoriginal attempt to define the hegemonic status of the United States (and 'the West') at a moment of increased world disorder. The alacrity with which it has been embraced says less of Huntington than of the absence of coherent perspectives which might challenge Washington and its allies, including academic partisans of the new 'global order' in the US, Europe and elsewhere.

For the moment the big conflicts envisaged by Huntington remain 'conflicts of the mind, translated only occasionally into horrid acts' (Axford 1995: 194). Those who embrace and embroider the theory are already helping to generate increased conflict: for Huntington, this miserable outcome would be a prophecy fulfilled.

Notes

1. Thanks to Adrian Budd of South Bank University and to Phil Cohen of the Centre for New Ethnicities Research at the University of East London for their comments on this chapter.

2. See, for example, Tarock 1995, O'Hagan 1995, Mottahedeh 1995, McNeill 1997, Holmes 1997.

3. Following its electoral success in Bavaria in April 1998, the DVU secured from the regional government a decision to deport a Turkish family resident in Munich for thirty years, on the basis of the alleged 'criminality' of a boy aged 13. The boy was said to represent 'a massive risk to public security and order' (*Guardian*, 1 May 1998).

Bibliography

Anderson, Benedict (1983) *Imagined Communities*, London: Verso.

Axford, Barrie (1995) *The Global System: Economics, Politics and Culture*, Cambridge: Polity.

Bjorgo, Tore (1997) '"The Invaders", "the traitors" and "the Resistance Movement"': The Extreme Right's Conceptualisation of Opponents and Self in Scandinavia', in T. Modood and P. Werbner (eds), *The Politics of Multiculturalism in the New Europe*, London: Zed.

Callinicos, Alex (1997) 'Europe: the mounting crisis', in *International Socialism* 2 (74).

Castles, Stephen (1993) 'Migrations and Minorities in Europe. Perspectives for the 1990s: Eleven Hypotheses', in J. Wrench and J. Solomos, *Racism and Migration in Western Europe*, Oxford: Berg.

Collinson, Sarah (1996) *Shore to Shore: The Politics of Migration in Euro-Arab Relations*, London: Royal Institute of International Affairs.

Connolly, Bernard (1995) *The Rotten Heart of Europe*, London: Faber.

Crowley, John (1996) 'European Integration: Sociological Process or Political Project?', in *Innovation* 9 (2): 149–60.

Delanty, Gerard (1995) *Inventing Europe*, Basingstoke: Macmillan.

De Wenden, Catherine Withol (1991) 'North African Immigration and the French Political Imaginary', in M. Silverman (ed.), *Race, Discourse and Power in France*, Aldershot: Avebury.

Esposito, John (1992) *The Islamic Threat: Myth or Reality?*, New York: Oxford University Press.

Evans, Martin (1996) 'Languages of Racism within Contemporary Europe', in B. Jenkins and S. Sofos, *Nation and Identity in Contemporary Europe*, London: Routledge.

Holmes, Stephen (1997) 'In Search of New Enemies', in *London Review of Books*, 24 April.

Huntington, Samuel (1993) 'The Clash of Civilizations?' in *Foreign Affairs*, Summer: 22–49.

Huntington, Samuel (1996) *The Clash of Civilizations and the Remaking of World Order*, New York: Simon and Schuster.

Kapteyn, Paul (1996) *The Stateless Market*, London: Routledge.

MacEwan, Martin (1995) *Tackling Racism in Europe*, Oxford: Berg.

McNeill W.H. (1997) 'Decline of the West?', in *New York Review of Books*, 9 January: 11–22.

Marfleet, Philip (1998) 'Migration and the Refugee Experience', in R. Kiely and P. Marfleet, *Globalisation and the Third World*, London: Routledge.

Martiniello, Marco (1994) 'Citizenship of the European Union: A Critical View', in R. Baubock (ed.), *From Aliens to Citizens: Redefining the Status of Immigrants in Europe*, Aldershot: Avebury.

Miles, Robert (1991) *Racism after Race Relations*, London: Routledge.

Milward, Alan (1992) *The European Rescue of the Nation State*, London: Routledge.

Modood, Tariq (1997) 'The Politics of Multiculturalism in the New Europe', in T. Modood and P. Werbner (eds), *The Politics of Multiculturalism in the New Europe*, London: Zed.

Mottahedeh, Roy (1995) 'The clash of civilizations: an Islamicist's critique', in *Harvard Middle Eastern and Islamic Review* 2 (2).

O'Hagan, Jacinta (1995) 'Civilisational conflict? Looking for cultural enemies', in *Third World Quarterly* 18 (1): 19–38.

Qadir, Shahid (1998) 'Civilisational Clashes: surveying the faultlines', in *Third World Quarterly* 19 (1): 149–52.

Radice, Giles (1992) *Offshore: Britain and the European Idea*, London: I.B. Tauris.

Runnymede Trust (1997) *Islamophobia: a challenge for us all*, London: Runnymede Trust.

Sakamoto, Yoshikazu (1995) 'Democratization, Social Movements and World Order', in R. Cox *et al.* (eds), *International Political Economy: Understanding Global Disorder*, London: Zed.

Salla, Michael (1997) 'Political Islam and the West: A new Cold War or convergence?' in *Third World Quarterly* 18 (4): 729–42.

Smith, Anthony (1995) *Nations and Nationalism in a Global Era*, Cambridge: Polity.

Suleiman, Ezra (1995) 'Is Democratic Supranationalism a Danger?', in C. Kupchan (ed.), *Nationalism and Nationalities in the New Europe*, Ithaca: Cornell University Press.

Tarock, Adam (1995) 'Civilisational conflict? Fighting the enemy under a new banner', in *Third World Quarterly* 18 (1): 5–18.

Vertovic, Steven and Ceri Peach (1997) 'Islam in Europe and the Politics of Religion and Community', in S. Vertovic and C. Peach (eds), *Islam in Europe: the Politics of Religion and Community*, Basingstoke: Macmillan.

Waever, Ole and Morten Kelstrup (1993) 'Europe and its nations: political and cultural identities', in O. Waever, B. Buzan, M. Kelstrup and P. Lemaitre, *Identity, Migration and the New Security Agenda in Europe*, London: Pinter.

3

Occidentalism and Its Discontents

Couze Venn

My exploration of the question of occidentalism begins from the conviction that culture plays a central role in processes of domination and resistance, that it does so through the authority of certain kinds of narratives about ourselves and the world and through the effects of these narratives on 'identity' and subjectivity. The underlying proposition that runs through this chapter is that a particular narrative of the human being became established with modernity and continues to direct our vision of the good society and the desirable life. A central part of my argument is that because the project of modernity was a universal one, sustained and disseminated through colonialism, the world is still, to various degrees, framed by it. Furthermore, I think that with the loss of faith in the grand narratives of modernity, several tendencies have appeared in the postmodern and post-colonial world which convert the violence intrinsic to the previous period into new, equally destructive, forms. The corollary of my position is that a new understanding of these narratives and of modernity is necessary for the construction of new visions and new 'identities'.

In that sense, my return to modernity is a return not to an origin or a cause but an event. By 'event' I mean a change in history, the effects of which are initially indeterminate but are conditioned by a complex of other events which combine to set limits to its possible trajectory. An event is a ripple in history. It is a return because I want to re-examine modernity in the light of what has happened since, that is to say everything that now leads to the threshold of the postmodern, including the theoretical elaborations that have sought not only to make sense of the history of modernity but indeed to envisage and describe its unfolding. I have in mind the kinds of explanation posed in terms of the periodisations of 'progress', supported by the development of reason, or making appeal to the transformative becoming of a reflective consciousness; all of these feed the idea of the forward march of 'civilisation' carrying the whole world on its surge. The intervening events include the critiques that have targeted modernity because its founding discourses excluded women, non-Europeans and anyone who falls outside the norms of the rational and the 'civilised', which these discourses themselves construct and which have become normative and authoritative through their alliance with power. In other words, these critiques have demonstrated the ideological functioning of these discourses in support of patriarchal, masculinist and colonial domination. One of the crucial effects of the discourses sustaining modernity has been through their functioning in the formation of subjects, in the West and elsewhere. This will be the particular focus of my analysis.

Nothing testifies more eloquently to the anxious insecurities of post-colonial 'identities' and subjectivities than the proliferation of collective names – black, African-American, third world and many more – which chart the will to erase the marks of dispossession inflicted by colonialism and imperialism. They are names that, once uttered, are soon inadequate to the complexity of politics and existence in the 'hybrid' cultures of postmodernity. True enough, they assert new differences and solidarities, yet they cannot help but remake new divisions and exclusions. Often they imply a return to the fixity of origin and type, or consign us to a place and a geography carved out by the vagaries of colonialism. India, Africa, Latin America are European constructs, laden with the ambivalences of colonial history. On the one hand, they mark out the space of the 'worlding of the Third World' (Spivak 1985: 128) adequate to the appropriating gaze of colonisers; on the other hand, they symbolise the rescued imagined homelands, and function as signs of belonging for those once dispossessed. We know, however, that these signs signify differently for real people, their multi-accentuality having to do with longer histories of community and blood and with the specificities of place and context. Our different belongings – say, someone who is at once Tamil and black and Indian and third world – together with continuing political struggles where other stakes are involved, mean that the borders of 'identity' and subjectivity are messy and not easily crossed. The 'hybridity' of identities in the diaspora is admirably expressed by the jazz artist Courtney Pine, who explained that the plurality of sources and references in his work communicates his attempt to be an 'African West Indian Westerner' (*Guardian*, 19 October 1992). A simple enough statement on the face of it, yet invoking several narratives about postcolonial identity which have surfaced in black politics, namely about reclaiming an origin, about recognising the specificity of geography in the formation of subjectivity and acknowledging the indelible marks of Western culture on the way we are. It is, too, a statement that seeks to dissolve 'hybridity' by fusing it into the transformed being of 'postcoloniality'.

The other side of hybridity is the sense of belonging to the West and to a specific third world community, 'without being completely of either one or the other', as Edward Said (1993) expressed it in *Culture and Imperialism*. Said's interrogation of the place of empire in the formation of metropolitan culture and globalisation demonstrates the 'contrapuntal' character of the relationship between the West and 'its others'; that is to say, a dynamic interplay in which sometimes the metropolitan and sometimes the 'peripheral' culture and history determine the patterns.

A background element in discussions of subjectivity and identity, and one which has become vociferous in current politics, is the extent to which the concept of nation is at stake in struggles around hegemony and domination and in strategies for autonomy and recognition. The problem is that the discourse of a national or supranational entity, such as India or the West, belongs to a different time and space from that of everyday life, although the two cross each other. Their meeting has to be staged to enable the ghostly, uncanny reality of the national to appear on the mundane quotidian scene, clothed in the emblematic habits of tradition, ceremonies, regalia, flags: a theatre of illusion which makes present the space of the imagined community. Homi Bhabha has put is thus: 'Nations, like narratives, lose their origins in the myths of time and only fully realize their horizons in the mind's eye' (Bhabha 1990: 1). But how then does the national enter and affect everyday life? It could be argued that the discourse of the national and the everyday meet through the narrative structure of myth and repetition; the process would be similar to that of ideology; as such it has effects for subjectivity and identity.

To explain this I must first deal with the fact that because cultures are 'hybrid, heterogenous, extraordinarily differentiated, and unmonolithic' (Said 1993: xxix), the imagined community that validates the unity of the nation is sustained in narratives that constantly fragment into the multiple realities of existence. Thus, someone who identifies herself as Indian in relation to the French or in official documents may feel that the category Tamil or Sikh has, from the point of view of cultural belongingness and home, greater existential density than geographical designation. It is this heterogeneity of cultures locked into the ambivalence of narratives of unity that undermines attempts to establish new communities and identities that cross and unite disparate groups in some common interest. Yet alliances are possible, provided there is commitment and faith in some (grand) narrative or common purpose, for example, Marxism or liberalism or ecological politics, which found the principles of their unity and solidarity. These principles function as the signifiers of the becoming or future of the people or the community. For instance, it could be argued that some kind of common understanding existed in the 1960s and early 1970s in the uneasy alliances of Black Power, socialist politics and feminism, when a number of positions shared the recognition that capitalism and imperialism were the bases for the diverse oppressions against which common struggles could be fought. In the present moment of suspicion towards grand narratives and utopian visions, signs that cemented solidarity have become loosened from their historical and discursive moorings and are now the objects of a struggle for their appropriation in a pluralist political universe. It is in such periods of crisis that the multi-accentuality of the sign becomes evident, as Mercer (1992) demonstrates in his study of the re-codings of the concept 'black' in relation to the politics of the 1950s, 1960s and 1980s. During these periods, 'black' was symbolically counterposed as a marker of positive difference, denying its previous connotation of non-white and inferior, such that it could function as a trope of pride and autonomy. The term 'black' transcended biological differences, forging a new solidarity based not on categories derived from white narratives of race but on new 'myths' of belonging, spoken in the new voice of those who knew they were engaged in the struggle 'to decolonize inherited models of subjectivity' (Mercer 1992: 434).

The problem is not merely a terminological one. At the level of theory, we live in a time of the problematisation of almost everything that had acquired the status of undisputed truth. It is now taken for granted that general concepts like race, the West, Africa, the third world, postcolonialism and so on are discursively constituted objects that provide a temporary grip on entities and processes which evade our attempts to find precise signifiers for them. Thus, 'third world' appears to unify a disparate collection of countries with quite different colonial histories, different economies and geographies, different cultures – for example, Brazil, Algeria, the Philippines – and, in this way, can misguide analysis into drawing general conclusions that have little bearing on the reality of this heterogeneous world. At the same time, 'third world' is the sign that has come to stand for the history of exploitative relationships with the old imperial states of Europe and the USA, relationships that continue in neo-imperial forms. By that token, it can be the index of a consciousness that fashions a solidarity out of the common ground of oppression, as when Jean Binta Breeze writes 'how third world my blues / of oceans bending backwards / to make ends meet / ... of mothers / patching pieces of sky / to cover the winded bellies / of their babies' cry / how third world my blues' (Breeze 1988: 38), signifying the shared experience of oppression and gauging the immeasurable cost of that oppression.

Another example: Africa, in the singular, constitutes as a homogeneous territory a space which is the product of Western cartographical imagination – itself a formulation that contains the idea of the West as a unitary subject and subordinating centre, from which the diversity and difference of other spaces and cultures are seen as inferior, alien blocs, unified by reference to its norms. It is but a short step from this conceptual framework to assertions about African philosophy – or Asian mentality, Oriental despotism and so on – irrespective of whether or not these common characteristics exist across the cultural mix which constitutes African or Asian cultural spaces. Again this is not a way of saying that the claim to be, say, African–American does not have an important political and counter-ideological purchase. My point is to suggest caution about the applicability of such general entities, while recognising the fact that they are the coinage and the stake in diverse ideological manoeuvres intrinsic to strategies of resistance and power and, therefore, strategies of subjectification and subjection.

To return to the question of narrativity and subjectivity, let us start with Bhabha's view that the political unity of the nation is constructed through the 'displacement of its irredeemably plural modern space, bounded by different, even hostile nations, into a signifying space that is archaic and mythical, paradoxically representing the nation's modern territoriality in the patriotic, atavistic temporality of Traditionalism' (Bhabha 1990: 300). Furthermore, counter-narratives of the nation 'continually evoke and erase its totalising boundaries ... disturb those ideological manoeuvres through which "imagined communities" are given essentialist identities' (Bhabha 1990: 300). Faye (1972) has analysed this process in the case of France, demonstrating how the repetition of a mythical narration of origin works to confirm, citationally, the identity of the modern state. It does so by validating the myth of authenticity and ethnic identity – the Frank = the French – articulating it in the narration of a history in which events and dates are assigned the value of truths of which the narration itself is the only source. Its enunciative structure is that of repetition. Equally, it authenticates the story of a beginning which privileges a particular time and a particular geographical place, as the temporal and spatial demarcation of the arena in which the nation state is enacted, through particular events and statements which at once constitute and express the people, and which have become inscribed as the nation's originary icons. Thus the modern state superimposes a narrative of becoming, a story of the nation-in-being, upon an archaic discursive template, not erasing it but writing over it while drawing support from its illegible presence. This stratagem works as long as the national project remains dynamic and delivers what it promises, especially in the case of relatively new states that must silence the rumour of older communities with the clamour of brighter and more fulfilling futures. The disruption of the project – by external intervention, for example, or by loss of faith in the principles guaranteeing the development and welfare of the nation state, by a decline in resources, and so on –

releases all the archaic forces of traditionalism. Such forces can take the form of the monster of Nazi cynicism, 'a modern archaic politics of humanity, a politics of origins passing for the politics of the ideal future' (Lyotard 1983: 31). Lyotard designates Auschwitz as the place of silence from which justice cannot return, because there is no way for the injustice it signifies to be redeemed. We can today add other places where similar archaic forces crossing the crises of modernisation result in ethnic cleansing or fundamentalist purification. These are not forces of stability or continuity, for the narratives that sustain them belong to a different space and time, buried in an irrevocable past. Nor are they the memory of resistance that has long dreamt of future victory over an oppressive power. They are the forces that seek an older territory, the mythical or symbolic spaces that can be re-appropriated only via ethnic cleansing: history washed away with blood. It could be argued that the break-up of the USSR and of Yugoslavia and the crisis of identity and governance in India and Algeria in recent years illustrate responses of this kind. We should remember what these crises are responses to: changes in economic and geo-political reality, shifts in the Cold War and the global economy and their diverse, unpredictable effects in different countries.

Ania Loomba's (1991) analysis of post-colonial identity and neo-colonialism illustrates these processes in contemporary Indian politics. She focuses on the representations of colonial history in the general elections of November 1989. The government's media campaign attempted to weld together the themes of modernisation, nationalism and anti-imperialism, projecting a new, post-colonial identity. The strategy combined two elements. The first was the appropriation of a history of resistance to British rule through representations of key events such as the Rani of Jhansi's role in the 1857 uprising and Mahatma Gandhi's Dandi march, both represented as events enacting the nation, constituting the people and its leaders in a seeming unity of will and purpose. In the second, the divisions of class, gender, caste and religion in Indian society were dissolved in images of India as a 'happy family' in order to construct a sense of unity in diversity that covered 'the jagged edges of nationhood' (Loomba 1991: 169). These representations tried to fuse the present with the past, for example, by splicing archive footage of Mahatma Gandhi on the Dandi march with those of Rajiv Gandhi's re-enactment of these events. It sought to abolish the tensions between the signs 'women' and 'nation', and between the images of India as modern, post-colonial and democratic, and those of feudal or colonial India. The point is made that 'post-colonial authority is legitimated by a specific and reductive evocation of the spectre of colonialism and a frozen moment of confrontation' (Loomba 1991: 169).

Colonialism remains the sign of the greatest threat to the nation, yet it encompassed the time of the making of the state by the colonisers. Its ending announced the beginning of the reconstituted state – as nation state – yet the nation invokes a more ancient past temporarily disrupted by the moment of colonialism. It is the history over which the modern nation must write.

Loomba makes a central point which helps us to understand how the ambivalences in colonial discourse are resolved at the level of signifying process. She refers to Partha Chatterjee's argument about how nationalism has attempted to derive its authority by identifying itself with the spiritual-ised domain of culture, which is claimed to be superior to and undominated by the West. In this way, it could concede the claims of Western civilisation in the material sphere, and so continue to promote Western education, while holding on to the idea of Indian cultural superiority. The coupling of the old and the new, the traditional and the modern, the closure of archaic time and the open temporality of modernity is discursively brought about through the figure of the Indian woman. She is projected as the emblematic incarnation of the doctrine, the extraordinary subject who, although educated in the Western mode, nevertheless remains spiritually Indian, the unconquered bearer of the truth and authenticity of the nation. The Indian woman thus carries the burden of authenticating Indian cultural identity and vindicating its superiority and survival in spite of colonialism. The destruction of the mosque at Ayodhya in December 1992 by Hindu fundamentalists and the ensuing inter-ethnic violence show the failure of these attempts to forge new identities without resolving deep-seated inequalities and injustices, those intransigent 'differends' (Lyotard 1983). The repressed returns in the dystopian eruption and repetition of archaic, primal violence.

Identities and subjectivities are caught up in these ways of telling the nation or the community. If we consider that 'history is above all a narration' (Faye 1972: 15), it follows that it is not a question of going beyond narration but of producing both a critical narration of the history already told and a (utopian) narrative of the future. Clearly such critiques belong to the space of relations of representations, as Hall (1992) has argued, and therefore bring up the question of the relations of power. However, the knowledge that power never leaves the scene of representation does not tell us what drama is unfolding, nor our place in it. We cannot avoid the part we have to play, nor the fact that we have to act and, in acting, constitute ourselves beyond the innocence of already constituted or essential 'identities' and roles.

Let us consider the way in which the production of a narration of the past indicates how history comes to have effects in the present, in the form of a memory and in the manner in which this memory relates to subjectivity.

The process refers to the argument that 'narration binds' (Faye 1972: 9) and that, in relation to the 'material base' of society, narration 'not only relates to history but effectively engenders it' (Faye 1972: 107). It binds previous narrations, which it thereby renews in the service of a new or continuing interest. A historical narration – for example, relating to the role of the Rani of Jhansi in the events of 1857 in India – is ideological. This means that the deployment of historical narratives on the side of different interests takes place in a space of contestation. So, the formation of subjectivity and identity always takes place in an agonistic space. For example, the story of Black Power in the US belongs either to the dominant official history – of insurrection and violence against the democratic, legal process – or to a history of resistance to oppression and injustice. At the same time, it locates the narrator as a particular subject, on one or other side of the struggle, who identifies him or herself in relation to 'blackness'. Each retelling is a particular appropriation and a re-memorization of the events, as in Spike Lee's film of Malcolm X. The film and its effects demonstrate too the contestatory aspect of the process, engaged on the side of antagonistic goals, for '[t]o give people back a memory is also to give them back a future' (Ricoeur 1984: 26).

Ricoeur has argued that the narrative structure of history and the story operate 'to create new forms of human time, and therefore new forms of human community' and that 'to live in human time is to live between the private time of our mortality and the public time of language' (Ricoeur 1984:20). Both dimensions are woven of narratives of the past that make sense of both the past and the future. The question of who has the power and authority to be narrator, who tells our stories, becomes crucial for identity and for the future, for 'the structure of narrativity demonstrates that it is by trying to put order on our past, by retelling and recounting what has been, that we acquire an identity' (Ricoeur 1984: 21).

This has been amply demonstrated in the history of resistance to patriarchal and masculinist domination and to Eurocentrism and cultural imperialism. When third world peoples continue to see in the West the image of the future, they cannot properly retell and repossess their past, wrestled from them by colonial history. Equally, the history of the subaltern cannot be written in the idiom of élite historiography, as the Subaltern Studies Group has shown (Guha and Spivak 1988).

But what does it mean, to turn away from the 'West' and from its vision of modernity, especially if one wants to avoid the temptation of seeking a future in archaic forms of being, thereby courting the danger of trying to repeat a past whose time has vanished? Is it not a question of settling accounts and coming to terms with a legacy which continues to shape our material world and, importantly, to shape the critiques that nourish the decolonisation of mind? Between Westernisation and fundamentalism, is there what Homi Bhabha calls a 'third space' of becoming, framed by a critical interrogation of the 'West' and colonial discourse, and accepting that all cultures are now hybrid, heterogeneous, and interdependent?

Let me explore this through an interrogation of the view that too many third world intellectuals are still in thrall to Western cultural hegemony. Tim Brennan, for example, upbraids third world cosmopolitan celebrities who are 'spokespersons for a kind of perennial immigration, valorised by a rhetoric of wandering, and rife with allusions to the all-seeing eye of the nomadic sensibility' (Brennan 1989: 2), intellectuals for whom exile and unbelonging have become the trademark for a literary and cultural production that locates itself within a global culture. The objection of Brennan – and others who share his position – is that these cosmopolitan intellectuals do not contribute to the formation of 'national cultures', although most of them claim to be speaking from the side of third world communities. The songlines in their writings do not meet the literature of resistance produced by indigenous (organic?) intellectuals. Indeed, this cosmopolitan writing supplies 'sceptical readings of national liberation struggles from the comfort of the observation tower' (Brennan 1989: 16); it is not so much heteroglossia as speaking with forked tongue. This echoes the supicion that too many third world intellectuals have effectively become lost to the enemy, even as they denounce the ravages of neo- and post-colonialism. Although some people fit the description, there are two kinds of misunderstanding in this view: first, about the resilience and invisibility of the legacy of colonialism and imperialism; second, about the conceptual space of critique and the (im)possibility of unconquered or pure cultural territory from which critique may develop.

Let me take each in turn. A central feature of the process of securing Western hegemony has been assimilation and Europeanisation founded on the constant reiteration of the explicit superiority of the West. This ceaseless repetition, that the colonised needed the tutelage of the imperial powers because of their presumed barbarity or underdevelopment, occurring throughout colonial discourse and in Western intellectual discourse, has left deep wounds in the psyche that still hurt well after Fanon described their symptoms in the period of dying colonialism. The longevity of these effects can be explained by reference to the means employed in colonial subjection. Abdul Jan Mohamed makes the interesting point that colonialist discourse represents the colonised as so irremediably backward in relation to Europeans that 'the process of civilizing the natives can continue in-definitely' (Jan Mohamed 1986: 87). The cognitive framework for this is a Manichean allegory, 'a field of diverse yet interchangeable oppositions between white and black, good and evil, superiority and inferiority, civilization and savagery, intelligence and emotion, rationality and sensuality, self and other, subject and object' (Jan Mohamed 1986: 82). If we think of the diversity and mobility of representations of the other in the texts of the colonisers, from novels and films to cartoons and anthropological studies, we can see how the allegory functions as a grid of intelligibility framing the knowledge of the other that it already harbours within it, awaiting a kind of revelation which is a verification, repeated in every encounter, fictional or real. The other is always already what the coloniser had imagined s/he would be. If reality does not fit, no matter; it can be invented or imagined, as in countless travellers' tales, for the descriptions are guaranteed to appear true to the imagined reality that the grid already secretes. In the discourse of modernity, what does not fit can always be neutralised in the form of the exotic, commodified for the 'tourist gaze' (Urry 1990) and the consuming pleasures of Western culture, gratified through cultural products like Flaubert's Salambo, Verdi's Aida and, more recently, in hundreds of films and tourist brochures.

Interestingly, the fetishisation of an abstract notion of otherness in some studies of colonial discourse, through 'altericist readings' (Suleri 1992), end up reinscribing the exotic and the presumption of the un-knowable other into narratives of colonial relations. The effects of these developments for the third world have been a complex, unstable com-bination of these sensibilities – I say sensibilities rather than culture or ideology because I want to keep open the issue of the mechanisms of formation of subjects involved in this complex. There is an intellectual élite imbued with humanist and modernist aspirations, often westernised to the point of becoming 'mimic' persons, though many share the critical dimension interior to humanist and modernist discourses, working at the 'contradictions' which the material reality of oppression and exploitation force into visibility .

Overlapping with this élite is a technical and administrative cadre for whom the norms of Western instrumental rationality have acquired the authority of a common sense which is all the more persuasive and seductive because it coincides with the models of 'modernisation' in 'advanced' economies. Alongside these groups is the majority of the people, for whom the sense of place and the time of indigenous cultures and identities are rooted in the inter-subjective space of mundane reality, where 'tradi-tionalism' provides a security of belonging, constantly threatened by the machinery of modernisation. If we inspect most ex-colonial countries for signs of the presence of the West, we cannot fail to notice the extent and variety of this presence, though most of it has acquired the naturalised character of the mundane. Take the built environment, particularly in urban areas, in which buildings, roads, a whole infrastructure, especially in the more affluent areas and in administrative and business centres, increasingly resemble towns and cities anywhere in the world. This is not surprising, since they are often the planned result of modernisation, advised by experts hired from Western countries and, in any case, conceived by people trained to see with Western eyes and think with Western minds. Nothing is left to the untutored imagination, not even the system of traffic-lights and road-markings. If we extend our view to the construction and physical organisation of factories and offices, the homogeneity is striking. Even more interesting are the effects of this technology of production and regulation on the division of labour and on the social relations of production and of administration – that is, structuring the time and space of people in countless routine activities across the social body. These are not necessary effects of technology. The structural homogeneity exists not because it is determined by the technology, but because it is anchored in a specific concept of modernisation. In the Third world, what is elusively described as the 'West' is inscribed in the scientific and disciplinary knowledges institutionalised in the apparatuses of education, the judiciary, health, commerce, production, administration and communication, such that little is untouched, directly or indirectly. It is not simply a matter of 'flows' of technology, information and knowledge, of people and commodities. The site of production and circulation is irrelevant when they take place within the already established and policed discursive space characteristic of occidentalism. For example, within that space, to modernise administrative practices means to reorganize according to the cybernetic logic of computer systems and information technology and all their implications. Today, globalisation builds upon the structures of colonialism, preserved by neo-colonialism or by the failure to decolonise the mind, as Ngugi wa Thiong'o demonstrated in the case of literature and the humanities syllabus in post-independence Kenya. My point is that the old metropolitan centres continue to have profound effects at all levels in the ex-colonies and the third world generally, including in the apparatuses that form and regulate subjects. This hegemony is often unrecognised, and remains invisible because many of its mechanisms appear in the neutral colours of an unquestioned instrumental rationality, functioning as common sense or weighted with the solidity of postcolonial reality.

I do not want to give the impression that the presence of the West is everywhere unmediated or simply overwhelming. Differences in local interests and goals and different histories of colonial domination result in significant variations, as Appadurai (1990) has argued in relation to 'ethnoscapes', 'mediascapes' and 'ideoscapes'. It is, however, a question of the parameters of these variations. Power and authoritative discourses are two of the determining parameters, which means that the problem of unequal

access to the machineries of power, both within a country and at the geo-
political level, must remain foregrounded in any analysis of the effects of
the West on modernisation and globalisation. None of this is particularly
surprising, since I am rephrasing well-rehearsed arguments, developed in
various forms by radical third world intellectuals from Ngugi to García
Márquez, who have often paid a high price for their readiness to dig under
the surface of postcolonial reality. I am trying to understand the resilience
of the authority of Western discourses, their seductive and normative
power. The fact that subjectivity, postcolonial or Western, is caught up in
this whole process is a thought that informs my examination of occidentalism. Most of us are divided among these spaces, further complicated by
what class, religion, gender, age and other categories contribute to the
equation. Hybridity, today as well as in previous periods, is as much the
effect of these processes as it is that of the colonialist discourses which
cross them. The crisis in modernity called postmodernity throws into
turmoil the ambivalences and dissonances in this complex; indeed, the
'contradictions' in the complex I have described have reciprocal effects on
the first world.

Colonialist discourse has not gone unchallenged, either at the level of
textual analysis or in terms of the massive production of a counter-
discourse and an artistic culture than now speak the 'other' in all its
diversity and wealth. Today, the narratives which denigrate the 'black'
person as 'a problem', outside the norm, needing correction or development
is everywhere countered by texts that disrupt and attempt to put an end
to oppressive representations of otherness. For example, in England, works
such as *Handsworth Songs* (Black Audio Film Collective, 1985) appeal to a
different truth, valorising feelings and experiences which are represented
in official discourse as belonging to a history of inadequacy or as refractory
backwardness, but which 'black' people can recognise as an expression of
the complicated experience of what it feels like to be denied respect and
autonomy and to fight back. An important body of texts now contributes
to the vocabulary that makes it possible for those side-tracked into invisibility and silence to articulate their presence, for example in the writing
of Buchi Emecheta, Salman Rushdie, Ben Okri, Naguib Mahfouz and
Toni Morrison, in films by a long list of third world directors, in painting
and music: in short, in the 'black arts' of resistance.

Sadly, the majority of the peoples of the third world and of the
postcolonial diaspora, for a variety of reasons, are denied access to this
transgressive, subversive culture. They continue to be exposed to a barrage
of narratives and representations of the West and its others through the
mass culture of popular films, television, video, music, magazines, realist
writings and other commodities in which the values and world view of

occidentalism have become naturalised. One has only to inspect the bestseller lists of books and music and films in places as far apart as Tokyo and Calcutta to verify the global character of mass culture. In spite of the mediations that occur, as I noted already, one cannot deny their effects on subjectivity. They add to the technical, scientific and administrative practices and knowledges in which the West and its claimed superiority are inscribed, and which the whole world accepts as normative. Together they combine to constitute a discursive economy which binds and constitutes all those who fall within its sphere of effectivity to and in the same logos.

The rest of this chapter will develop a critique of that economy, locating the challenge to its authority, and reading into it the elements that enable us to move beyond its terrain. First, I want to examine an example which illustrates some of the things I have been discussing. On a recent visit to my native Mauritius, I dropped in unexpectedly on a friend. He was a rebellious character, living a clandestine existence in the margins of the tourist industry, providing the mainly white clientele with a variety of services. His house was a chaotic place, shared with his mother and his sister, two rooms serving the needs of the three adults and an assortment of animals. It was furnished with whatever had come to hand to cater for bare necessities. As in other poor people's homes on the island, the careful clutter left little space for the merely decorative or the luxurious, the adornments of status and prestige. Each room crossed functional borders, mixing sleeping areas with cooking, sitting and work areas. There were no books that I could see; García Márquez, Morrison, Rushdie, Ngugi had no place there. My westernised gaze was amused by the presence of chickens everywhere, walking around unconcerned, one rooster cockily asserting its share of the bed in which my friend's sister was asleep. There was a television in pride of place, that being the one possession for which many families endured every privation to acquire. There were some pictures on the wall, family snaps and famous Mauritian landmarks. Alongside these were adverts for non-stick pots and pans, and for fridges: the stuff of dreams, cut out of some English magazine. Above them all hung a picture of the Virgin Mary and two framed postcards of Paris, fading snaps of the Eiffel Tower and Montmartre. They stood there as the signs of what would abolish the drabness of life, gateway to the place of fantasies, representing the greatest hope. In this room, with its chickens strolling around, one person asleep while several sat and talked, a pot boiling on a stove in a corner, amongst the hybrid and heterogeneous space of casual poverty, my friend talked about being both Creole and Indian, feeling part Catholic and part Hindu, relating his escapades in touristland, talking about the sega – the Mauritian ' roots' music – he performed for tourists on the beach, and his greatest desire: to go and make a living in Paris. He was not a unique case by any means. It admirably illustrates the mingling and interpenetration of cultures and 'scapes' constituting the heterogeneous space of daily existence in most third world countries.

What is interesting is the sense of a hierarchy of values, whereby the signs of the West are privileged, and the economy of desire which compels the gaze to be fixed towards the occident. This fetishisation of Western objects is reinforced by international 'image markets' (Mattelart *et al.* 1984) and by the identities that have been constructed in the space between modernisation and westernisation, traditionalism and backwardness, realised in the apparatuses, infrastructure and institutions of production, administration, education and regulation. What Zukin (1992) calls 'post-modernization' invests the private space of the vernacular with the cultural power of a public, commercialised fantasy driven by the market. He claims that even place has become a simulacrum, the copy of what the image markets represent as 'roots' culture. This is especially so in more affluent areas, that is, in certain kinds of 'ethnoscapes'. Poorer and relatively more traditional spaces escape the regulatory logics of centralised states and late capitalism, though increasingly the shock waves of cultural and socio-economic transformation in the urban and metropolitan areas shatter the infrastructure of local cultures. A stark example is the extent to which village communities have been degraded in Thailand, where a whole younger generation has been sucked into the sweated labour and soul-destroying business of prostitution and the clothing industry, leaving villages dependent on the income gained in the urban jungle and destitute of the means to sustain the local culture for much longer, establishing destructive vicious circles. Attempts to resist these processes can take the form of a cultural re-mix, whereby the signifying narratives of the market are filtered and mediated through older narratives of community. These counter-appropriations sometimes feed racism through 'the racialization of place' (Cohen 1992: 92), a response to the insecurity and alienation that people thrown into the maelstrom of new ethnoscapes must experience.

Is it a surprise that the rejection of Westernisation, with its attachment to neocolonialism, should so easily slide into fundamentalism? The theoretical problem is that of accounting for how such a subjectivity as I have described is lived, what might capture it for a different project or future, what part occidentalism plays in its formation.

The Critique of Logocentrism

The argument initiated by Fanon and developed in the work of Said and other analysts of colonial discourse, that colonialism constituted the West, finds increasing support amongst historians, for example Pagden

(1993). What is not clear are the intellectual reasons for the hegemonic domination that the West has exercised for such a considerable time, and why some elements of occidentalism are still pervasively authoritative. The question turns, therefore, around an understanding of occidentalism itself. I have already pointed to the one crucial element which reappears at every corner of diverse analyses of colonialism and imperialism, namely, the particular form of the subject which emerged with modernity (although its genealogy extends, as Derrida has argued, to Judeo-Christian and Greek ontology and metaphysics).

The discourse of the modern subject not only characterises how one is to conceptualise identity, but has specific effects for the real subjects at two levels. First, at the general level, it enables the systematic exclusion of whole categories from specific rights, privileges and practices and access to certain forms of power, for example women, the insane and children, in addition to non-white, non-Western communities. Second, at the level of face-to-face encounters, it enables the objectivisation of the other as 'other' (often less, or worse, than oneself: as merely a body), in relation to whom the normative subject need not have an ethical relation based on the obligation to treat the other like oneself. The discourse is what Levinas calls egology, that is to say a subject-centred philosophy which legitimises the exclusion of the other, whose otherness it performatively produces as part of its own speech. The connection with occidentalism is that in the space opened up by colonial conditions, egology found its proof and its measure. At the same time, its discourse, from Descartes, becomes progressively secularised, vested in a specific notion of rationality; it is naturalised in the discourse of social Darwinism.

What is specific about the logocentric discourse of the subject that has destined it to play such a crucial role in the Western enterprise of empire and subjugation? My analysis tries to show that the troubled concept of a self-centred subject holds together not only by virtue of the philosophical discourse underpinning it, but also by virtue of what it has cast out: the other, principally in the shape of the non-white, non-European, non-masculine non-being whose invisibility as subject became a condition for the apparent facticity of Western 'man', the mirage of his self-presence.

In his reflection on the work of Levinas, Derrida asks whether '[i]t is possible to wonder if history itself does not begin with this relation to the other which for Levinas transcends history' (Derrida 1967a: 139). My critique of the self-centred subject searches around this proposition, examining it in the specific contexts of the birth of modernity and, in this way, interrogates the manner in which logocentrism in the 'ego's era'[1] has been sustained by the conditions which have accompanied colonialism and capitalism. It is the complex, dynamic co-articulation of these phenomena in the history of modern times which frames my argument that the form of subjectivity which appeared with Descartes is founded on the systematic disavowal of the primacy of the relation to the other and the denial of the difference of the other. It could be argued, indeed, that the crisis in modernity, signalled by the troubled concept of the postmodern, is mirrored in the current vicissitudes of the subject, a subject clinging still to the debris of grand narratives, yet finding little purchase in the dissolution of the foundations which, until now, had harboured the signs of secure identities: race, nation, reason, progress and History itself. My argument is that it is not possible to imagine new foundations except by way of overcoming the metaphysics of presence that has crossed the discourses which constitute the autonomous, rational, unitary subject whose end we might be able to envisage in the midst of the 'morbid symptoms' of 'late capitalism' (Jameson 1984).

The different history of the subject which this implies proceeds from the view that resistance to oppression and the changing of circumstances are dependent on a politics which valorises, but does not essentialise, difference and is informed by the rewriting of histories from the side of the oppressed and the dispossessed. It could be argued that the elements of such a history already exists, for example, in the important work which the political economy of exploitation has accumulated concerning the mechanisms and capillary ramifications of neo-colonialism and global or transnational capitalism. The weakening of the Marxist frameworks which have shaped these analyses and the resilience of forms of oppression throughout the world have provoked theoretical insecurities that dilute prescriptive scenarios for curing the ills of the world. On the credit side, one must acknowledge the greater conceptual openness towards questions of power and its exercise. Power operates on the basis of both domination and seduction, and is not uniform but heterogeneous, such that sections of otherwise oppressed groups collude in its efficacious exercise, for instance, postcolonial industrial élites and the new 'kleptocracies'. For this reason, the problem of the formation of subjects and all the classic debates about ideology need to be rethought beyond reductionist or essentialist models, which have all but abolished the reality and meaningfulness of human lives.

We cannot, however, resolve these theoretical problems merely by way of a strategic switch to the point of view of the other. I explained earlier the extent to which the expectation of a pure or innocent space of alterity is an illusion; yet critique requires a strategic switch to the position and gaze of those consigned to the invisibility of the dispossessed. There are snares in this move, for instance the temptation to ascribe a unified consciousness, will or agency to those located as subaltern in the plays of power, and the way this strategic reversal of the hegemonic narratives of (neo)-colonialist masters or dominant groups can reinscribe a humanist self-centred subject or agent at the core of the process of history. This might seem to be objectionable only from the point of view of 'First World anti-humanist post-Marxism', as G.C. Spivak (1988) notes. But the objection must be tempered by the injustice of condemning the subaltern to the 'unpresentability' which is already the mark of oppression and a feature of the 'epistemic violence that constituted/effaced a subject that was obliged to cathect [occupy in response to a desire] the space of the imperialists' self-consolidating other' (Spivak 1988: 209). It is not a dilemma that one can avoid by by-passing the terrain of poststructuralism or, indeed, Western theorisations of subjectivity and history. We are not outside occidentalism, we have to work our way through it to the other side.

So how does one rethink agency without privileging either history – and thus the structural determinations at work in social formations – or the humanist subject and its substitutes as origin of history? And how does one secure a space for the other to reinvent itself, an other whose assumed otherness is already defined by reference to the Western norm of subjectivity or identity? These are questions which we can re-examine in the light of several correlated developments.

First, we must take account of the critiques developed within structuralism and poststructuralism which target the key concepts that underwrite subject-centred accounts of history and culture. Derrida's deconstruction of the place of the logocentric subject is particularly useful to the extent that it destabilises the Western ratio that has legitimated and authorised Europe's expansion; it indirectly reinstates a project of subjective becoming which follows Levinas in prioritising the ethical dimension in the subject's relation to the other. Second, the Lacanian re-reading of Freud has provided some conceptual tools for historicising the process of the constitution of subjects and for thinking through the mechanisms by which the individual comes to be inscribed in the order of culture. Third, the work which interrogates colonial discourse from the side of the 'other', by people such as Fanon, Said, Spivak, Gilroy and Bhabha, has demonstrated the erasures and ambivalences, the psychic and epistemic violence, the suppressions and phantasies that have participated in the subjugative project of the modern subject. This work has blown the cover of this would-be master of the universe and has opened the way for rewriting the history of Europe's others. Feminist challenges to the authority of masculinist social relations and thought, as well as crises arising from the violence inflicted on nature and the human spirit through exploitative systems, add to the urgency and the possibility of thinking otherwise the history of humanity and its future.

Historical context The challenge to the founding principles of dominant

Western consciousness has gathered momentum during a period which it is difficult to characterise except negatively by way of the. 'post' of postmodern. If we add to that the sense of a discontinuity conveyed in associated terms – postcolonial, post-industrial, post-capitalist, post-humanist – we are returned to the co-ordinates which framed the period of emergence of logocentrism and bourgeois individualism in the context of the formation of modernity. In the wake of poststructuralist critiques, no one finds shocking the claim that the grand narratives of modernity died with colonial liberation, with the ending of Europe's tragic Faustian adventure in the theatre of the world. Berman (1984), in his meditation on modernity, returns to Goethe's figure of Faust to highlight the fact that the overdevelopment of Faust is paid for by the underdevelopment of others, a scenario which aptly describes the relationship between Europe and its others under colonialism. Yet Sartre appeared particularly provocative when, thirty years ago, in the preface to Fanon's *The Wretched of the Earth*, he accused the whole of Europe of participation in the exploitation of the dispossessed and of guilt for the crimes against humanity which were integral to the advancement of the West: 'with us there is nothing more consistent than a racist humanism since the European has only been able to become a man through creating slaves and monsters' (Sartre 1967: 22).

Today Robert Young (1990) can invoke Derrida, Levinas, Foucault and Jameson alongside Sartre as participants in the grand critique of the 'white mythologies' of modernity. It is tempting with hindsight to announce, as he does, that poststructuralism is not so much the product of May 1968 as it is that of the struggle for decolonisation. We should remind ourselves though that the intellectual climate on the left was rather more complex than Young implies in his reference to the recognition of Hegelianism and Eurocentrism in much Western intellectual work. For even that recognition was in the name of a broad Marxism, whilst the critiques of the subject were aimed at the ideology of bourgeois individualism. It is true that the dreams of the (Kantian) 'long march of progress' faltered in the realities of the post-Second World War reassessment amongst the intellectual left, yet the aim remained Marx's call for the changing of circumstances to enable the emergence of the 'whole man, whom Europe has been incapable of bringing to triumphant birth' (Fanon 1967: 252).

Nineteen-sixty-eight, and not just May '68, proved a turning point because it deepened the disenchantment provoked by the realisation that the longevity of the systematic inhumanity and irrationality of capitalism and imperialism owes its tenacity to certain features interior to the modern logos itself. It is a malaise that the marginalised felt more deeply in the bone than those who were persuaded that they had never had it so good.

The prospect of changing the world dimmed as the revolutionary lights went out, or were snuffed out, throughout Europe and elsewhere. It is not poststructuralism itself that has occasioned the re-evaluation of modernity, nor is it the theoretical response to the crisis of modernity in any simple way. We need to bear in mind that a whole series of failures from the time of Nietzsche culminate in the postmodern condition. For Lyotard (1986), Auschwitz has come to stand for the sign of the collapse of the project of modernity; one could add Hiroshima, Algiers, the Gulag, Vietnam and much else. One feature of this condition is the existential crisis lived as a certain lack of being, whose angst, for many, is assuaged in the compulsions and delights of consumerism. The Western individual – who is not a geographical entity – is no longer called upon to prove and redeem 'himself' in the project of becoming called 'history', but turns upon himself with a mixture of narcissism and disgust. In these circumstances – variously understood by writers such as Lyotard, Baudrillard, Jameson – the re-assessment of the modern period has been drawn towards a critique of what Lacan called the 'ego's era'. This era coincides with modernity and inaugurates an 'egology' which, for Levinas (1987), is the index of an ontological error. The connection with decolonisation arises from the argument, proposed by Derrida, that the self-centred epistemology which supports 'egology' feeds into the 'appropriating narcissism of the West' (Derrida 1967a: 11), as I shall explain below. It is a thought which directs us to the theme of 'otherness' and the struggle to break free from Europe's subjugating enterprise.

One other major ingredient of the historical context is the denunciation of the 'man of reason', inscribed as the authoritative subject at the heart of the discourses which claim to speak the truth of being everywhere and in every time. The rewriting of women's history and critiques of the patriarchal social order have made impossible the discursive recuperation of such a concept of the subject. At the same time, there is no clear conceptualisation of the subject which is not simply an inversion, and thus a repetition, of a subject-centred ontology. There is thus a clear enough case establishing the affiliations between logocentrism, ethnocentrism, phallocentrism and Western colonialism in the constitution of the specific form of subjectivity that has functioned to sustain modernity. A first step in moving away from this terrain is a critical engagement with the founding narratives which support that form of subjectivity.

Towards a Poetics of Dis/orientation

The history of colonialism, as I discussed at the beginning of this chapter, is an exemplary illustration of the fractures and costs of the 'white mythologies' of occidentalism. The making of difference in the context of colonial subjugation is marked by a process of distortion, displacement and repetition that must be understood against the repressed knowledge of the violence of subjugation. Repression in the colonial instance motivated the displacement of this knowledge in the narrative of representation of the coloniser, such that colonial presence appears split between its representation as original and authoritative and its articulation in forms of repetition and difference.[2] This is exemplified in the practice of history and narrative in the implantation of the Bible and the English language in India in the nineteenth century, as Viswanathan (1990) has shown; Homi Bhabha (1985) makes this economy visible through his interrogation of the texts, putting to work the Freudian concept of *Enstellung* – distortion as in dreamwork. This term, as Lyotard (1983b) reminds us, is charged with the force of repression and desire at work in dreamwork, and thus with the violence of censorship and wish.

In colonial discourse what is repressed in the other scene of the stereotype of the colonised is invested in the tropes of savagery, anarchy, lust. They become the elements that construct the signs of both identification and alienation, desire and fear for coloniser and colonised. Bhabha (1983) has analysed the play of recognition and disavowal of cultural and racial difference in terms of the stereotype functioning as fetish, explaining how it works to effect a closure in the space of the representation of difference. He argues that the disavowal of difference in the midst of its reality in the stratagems of colonial power produces ambivalence. What is disavowed is not repressed 'but repeated as something different – a mutation, a hybrid' (Bhabha 1985: 96, 97). Hybridity, however, is a 'metonymy of presence' (Bhabha 1984: 130), which means that it 'terrorises authority with the ruse of recognition, its mimicry' (Bhabha 1985: 100). Thus mimicry is both 'resemblance and menace' (Bhabha 1984: 127); it produces a caricatured image of the coloniser which disturbs and disrupts the unitary gaze of surveillance in the exercise of power. The hybridity it produces repeats differently, and returns a gaze which resists subjugation, and so undermines colonial authority by participating in the 'strategic reversal of the process of domination' (Bhabha 1985: 103).

It is possible, then, to understand a response such as mimicry as a mode of appropriation of colonial authority whereby the colonised or subaltern camouflages his or her resistance in the guise of an elusive sameness. It is here a tactic of power intrinsic to antagonistic relations within an agonistic space of signification. Power, besides, is seductive, inducing and promising pleasures, so that the masquerade of mimicry can be equally a veiled homage, a demand for recognition in the returned gaze of the powerful. This scene, however, is ever open to the frustrations of mistaken identity.

For there is this other specular misrecognition whereby the gaze of the colonised is fixed upon and transfixed by the imagined and desired identification with the other. It is only the reality, the presence of the other's challenging gaze – who/what do you think you are? – that interrupts the play of identification in the imaginary, introducing the alterity of power and provoking the violence of thwarted plenitude. Let us explore this through Lacan and Fanon.

Lacan's discussion of the basis of the subject's frustration relates it to the triadic binds of frustration, aggression, regression and more interestingly, to the theme of the empty word and the full word, the theme that returns us to the duality of *béance* and *jouissance*, that is, to the experience of lack or void and to the desired plenitude of being. Lacan, we know, was speaking about the silence of the analyst emptying out the discourse of the subject, but does not a similar silence confront the (ex)colonised when his or her westernised discourse, seeking recognition from the knowing gaze of the (ex)coloniser, fails to find confirmation there and meets instead the equivocation of the 'not-quite' of hybridity? The colonised subjectivity disappears into the *béance* that measures the enormity of his or her dispossession, a double dispossession since there is, in any case, no adequate reply to the subject's discourse of being: 'We are the hollow men'. Thus to every word that participates in the play of misrecognition is added the disappointment of mistaken identity, and becomes marked as the sign of the other's rejection and the insufficiency, indeed the castration and 'fading',[3] of the colonised as subject. Here is Lacan's explanation:

> Does the subject not become engaged in an ever increasing dispossession of that being of his, whereby ... he ends up with the recognition that this being has never been anything more than his own construct in the imaginary and that this construct disappoints all his certainties? For, in the work he does to reconstruct this construct for an other, he finds again the fundamental alienation which made him construct it in the image of an other, and which has always destined it to be stripped from him by an other. (Lacan 1966: 125)

We can understand why, when the mask of westernised identity is pulled off, self-disgust follows, and violence erupts, as Fanon perceptively described. Fanon argued that in a white world the black man's behaviour is oriented toward 'the Other in the guise of the white man, for the Other alone can give him worth' (Fanon 1970: 109). Or again: 'the native never ceases to dream of putting himself in the place of the settler ... [but] he is never sure whether or not he has crossed the frontier' (Fanon 1967: 41). Fanon explains that 'thwarted aggressivity' and the 'accumulated libido' are canalised and worked through in the ecstasy of collective dance or the transformative violence of uprisings. The body as the site of this working out is a fundamental insight which has remained underdeveloped. A good deal of work within phenomenological discourse stresses the centrality of the corporeal and the sensuous, something which (in the wake of Heidegger, Merleau-Ponty, Lacan and Levinas) writers like Luce Irigaray, Judith Butler or Elizabeth Grosz have been developing. This is consistent with Fanon's argument that skin, through the 'epidermal schema', may be as fundamental in the process of the formation of subjects as the Oedipal sexualisation of the body. The two, of course, are conjoined, for 'as soon as I desire I am asking to be considered' (Fanon 1967: 155). It is not surprising that Fanon declares that: '[h]e who is reluctant to recognize me opposes me. In a savage struggle, I am willing to accept convulsions of death, invincible dissolution, but also the possibility of the impossible' (Fanon 1967: 155).

We know from the history of colonial subjugation and liberation that this is not merely rhetorical violence, for colonial history is a catalogue of excess. Today the new names of that excess, like Angola, Indonesia, Cambodia, Rwanda and so many more, extend the list in the name of modernisation/Westernisation or fundamentalist returns to origins, often acting as cover for continuing dispossession and exploitation. In one way or another annihilation, fantasised or not, prowls around the hybrid being produced by colonial discourse and the material conditions of the formation of subject in (post)colonial spaces.

Not all colonised or subordinate subjects are caught to the same degree in these prisms. A subjugating power does not have to invest the whole of the colonial space for its authority or domination to be effective. It is often enough to 'govern the governors'. Often a degree of collusion emerges such that the space is the site of multiple dominations and coercions and 'multiple subjectivities'. Spivak's (1985, 1988) critique of the double oppression of women, subject to colonial domination and to that of masculinist indigenous cultures, is a case in point .

Resistance finds an anchorage in the places which a territorialising power either leaves untouched or has been unable to subvert. There are several examples one could cite: Guha's (1988) counter-narrative of insurrection in India, reconstructed from accounts of the Basarat uprising of 1831 and the Santal rebellion of 1855, and Panday's (1988) examination of peasant revolt in the context of the Indian nationalist movement, illustrate the discursive manoeuvres of power and resistance, the dodging and weaving, the tagging from one cultural lifeworld to another whereby struggles are relayed and interconnected, and spaces and identitites defended and preserved or altered.

When we come to analyse concrete historical events, we now need to acknowledge that subject positions exceed the places – gender, class, epistemic, ethnic – allowed in the enunciative positions constructed in totalising theories or in language generally. If the subject as centre is an effect sustained in the imaginary representations of self and other, and if the relation to the other is in fact primary and constitutive in the formation of identity, then we can recognise the different belongings into which we are seduced or compelled by the conditions and different temporalities of modernity.

Additionally, the analysis of subjectivity is complicated by the fact that the discourses of power, sexuality, desire, identity and the narratives that reconstruct their relationships and their lived reality establish rhizomic[4] signifying networks that are difficult to disentangle or apprehend because we are all caught up in them in our being. This means that if we wish to avoid being ensnared within the specular maze of the philosophy of the subject, we need to take the standpoint of the other. This involves the 'affirmative deconstruction' of the texts of colonialism and the reconstitution of a history of resistance to the epistemic and psychic violence of colonialism, through a narrativisation of history – that is, a refiguration and a re-memorisation (Morrison 1987) that repairs the place and the space of otherness. In this way, we engage with the conceptualization of the process of subjectification in the ego's era as a process constituting both self and other, coloniser and colonised, the occidental and its others as subjects belonging together but differently to modernity.

For the moment we are left with the fact that, because the other functions as supplement in the discourse of mastery and domination, 'affirmative deconstruction' and 'restorative genealogy' (Spivak 1988) can contribute to the destabilisation of narratives of power and superiority. They do so because, on the one hand, they affirm the agency of the dispossessed in an (unfinished) history of insurgency and resistance and, on the other, they can join with the work of re-memorisation, that is, the re-narrativisation of the monuments that Lacan talks about, to constitute a poetics of dis/orientation. What I have in mind are the kind of textual practices which harbour the liminal presence of the place of desire and the space of the sublime – the co-ordinates of subjectivity and ideology – and which can loosen our certainties and cognitive frames ready for transfiguration in the context of political struggles. They may, thus, be affiliated to other narratives which support counter-ideological discourses and practices for which other subject positions and other options for the future find their conditions of possibility.

In the urban environment of 'postmodernity', the counterpart of the instabilities threatening identity is the securing of spaces at the margins, which counter-cultures can defend from colonization – for example through the play of masquerade and the incessant remaking of these imagined 'homelands', as Stuart Hall and Phil Cohen, among others, explore.

In many parts of the world, the goals of the advancement of liberty and equality and justice, which was part of the project of Enlightenment humanism, has given way to totalitarianisms founded in 'a universally true and scientific discourse of politics' (Ricoeur 1984: 27), or in despotisms. Often the abandonment of these goals is masked by a rhetoric of the modernist utopia pressed into service for legitimating exploitation. One form of this discourse is tied up with the new political realism that claims that the status quo is preferable to other more risky options and is the best deal we can get. A 'secularised version of utopia' (Ricoeur 1984: 34), peddled by the state functioning as a totalising agency, has legitimated pernicious forms of power presented in terms of the victory of 'reason' over ideology, marking the 'end of history', circumscribed in the rationalisations of the 'last man'.

For all these reasons I am arguing that a new political and theoretical agenda beckons for both the 'first world' and the 'third world', namely occidentalism itself, its genealogy and its future. It is a more specific question than that of the modern and the postmodern which it enfolds and re-places in its problematisation of modernity. It is framed by the recognition that the destiny of the West and its others has been enmeshed for several centuries and is likely to remain so for a considerable time. It recognises too that the relationship between Europe and its others has been far more transformative for both than is usually acknowledged. In particular, it proposes that the co-articulation of capitalism, colonialism and subject-centred philosophies does not express a necessary epochal rupture engendering modernity but is an event, perhaps overdetermined, yet indeterminate, open to chance and probabilities. The space of this co-articulation is the ideological and epistemological space in which modernity and the modern form of subjectivity are enacted. I call occidentalism the discursive network which maps that space.

Notes

1. See Lacan's discussion in *Écrits* where he argues that modernity begins with a decisive shift in European culture, marked by the privilege granted to the human subject as centre of a new system of understanding and feeling. An obsessive concern for oneself and for one's individuality becomes the passionate emblem of this, the ego's era. The other side of this obsession is the neglect of the inter-subjective sphere from the point of view of the foundation of epistemic confidence.

2. Bhabha has illuminatingly explored the range of issues involved in this statement, putting to work psychoanalytic and poststructuralist tools to open up new ways of interrogating the effects of colonialism.

3. I think we can understand fading (aphanisis) to include both the covering of the subject by another and the forgetting of the subject in the other. See Lacan (1979: 207, 208).

4. Deleuze and Guattari explain rhizome by reference to some root-like network, that is to say, a dispersed and chaotic arrangement that, nevertheless, forms a complex system, (1976: 21).

Bibliography

Appadurai, A. (1990) 'Disjuncture and difference in the global economy', in M. Featherstone (ed.), *Global Culture, Nationalism, Globalization and Modernity*, London: Sage.

Barker, F. (ed.) (1983) *The Politics of Theory*, Colchester: University of Essex.

— (ed.) (1985) *Europe and its Others*, vols. 1 and 2, Colchester: University of Essex.

Berman, M. (1984) *All That Is Solid Melts Into Air*, London: Verso.

Bhabha, H. (1983) 'The other question – the stereotype and colonial discourse', in *Screen*, vol. 24, no. 6: 18–36.

— (1984) 'Of mimicry and man', in *October*, no.28: 125–33.

— (1985) 'Signs taken for wonders: Questions of ambivalence and authority under a tree outside Delhi, May 1817', in Barker 1985 (vol. 1): 89–127.

— (ed.) (1990) *Nation and Narration*, London: Routledge.

Breeze, J.B. (1988) *Riddym Ravings*, London: Race Today Publications.

Brennan, T. (1989) 'Cosmopolitans and celebrities', in *Race and Class*, vol. 31, no. 1.

Chatterjee, P. (1989) 'The nationalist resolution of the women's question', cited in Loomba 1991.

Cohen, P. (1992) 'It's racism what dunnit: hidden narratives in theories of racism', in J. Donald and A. Rattansi (eds), *'Race', Culture, Difference*, London: Sage.

Collits, T. (1989) 'Imperialism, Marxism, Conrad: a political reading of Victory', in *Textual Practice*, vol. 3, no. 3:303–22.

Derrida, J. (1967a) *L'Écriture et la Différence*, Paris: Editions du Seuil.

— (1967b) *De la Grammatologie*, Paris: Les Editions de Minuit.

Deleuze, G. (1983) *Nietzsche and Philosophy*, London: Athlone Press.

— and F. Guattari (1976) *Rhizome*, Paris: Editions de Minuit.

Fanon, F. (1967) *The Wretched of the Earth*, Harmondsworth: Penguin.

— (1970) *Black Skin White Masks*, London: Paladin.

Faye, J-P. (1972) *La Théorie du Récit*, Paris: Hermann.

Gates, H. L. (ed.) (1986) *'Race', Writing and Difference*, Chicago: University of Chicago Press.

Guha, R. and G.C. Spivak (eds) (1988) *Selected Subaltern Studies*, New York and Oxford: Oxford University Press.

Hall, S. (1992) 'New Ethnicities', in J. Donald and A. Rattansi, *'Race', Culture and Difference*, London: Sage.

Hegel, G. (1977) *Phenomenology of the Spirit*, trans. A.V. Miller, Oxford: Oxford University Press.

Hulme, P. (1985) 'Polytropic man: tropes of sexuality and mobility in early colonial discourse', in Barker 1985 (vol. 1).

Jameson, F. (1984) 'Post-modernism, or the cultural logic of late capitalism', in *New Left Review*, no. 146.

Jan Mohamed, A. (1986) 'The economy of Manichean aesthetics', in Gates 1986.

Kristeva, J. (1974) *La révolution du langage poétique*, Paris: Editions du Seuil.

Lacan, J. (1966) *Écrits I*, Paris: Editions du Seuil.

— (1979) *Four Fundamental Concepts of Psychoanalysis*, Harmondsworth: Penguin.

Laplanche, J. and J-B. Pontalis (1980) *The Language of Psychoanalysis*, London: Hogarth Press.

Levinas, E. (1987) *Collected Philosophical Papers*, trans. A. Lingis, Dordrecht/Boston/ Lancaster: Martinus Nijhoff Publishers.

Loomba, A. (1991) 'Overworlding the "third world"', in *Oxford Literary Review*, vol. 13, nos. 1, 2.

Lyotard, J-F. (1983a) *Le Différend*, Paris: Editions de Minuit.

— (1983b) 'The dream-work does not think', in *Oxford Literary Review*, vol. 6, no. 1.

— (1984) *The Postmodern Condition*, Manchester: Manchester University Press.

— (1986) 'Defining the postmodern', in *ICA Documents*, no. 4.

Mattelart, A., X. Delcourt and M. Mattelart (1984) *La culture contre la démocratie*, Paris: La Decouverte.

Mercer, K. (1992) '"1968": Periodising politics and identity', in L. Grossberg, C. Nelson and P. Treichler (eds), *Cultural Studies*, New York and London: Routledge.

Morrison, T. (1987) *Beloved*, New York: Plume.

Pagden, A. (1993) *European Encounters With the New World*, New Haven, Conn.: Yale University Press.

Panday, G. (1988) 'Peasant revolt and Indian nationalism', in Guha and Spivak.

Ricoeur, P. (1984) 'Dialogue with Kearney', in Kearney, *Dialogues with Contemporary Continental Thinkers*.

Said, E. (1978) *Orientalism*, London: Routledge.

— (1993) *Culture and Imperialism*, London: Chatto and Windus.

Sartre, J-P. (1967) Preface to Fanon 1967.

Spivak, G.C. (1985) 'The Rani of Sirmur', in Barker 1985 (vol. 1).

— (1988) *In Other Worlds: Essays in cultural politics*, London: Routledge.

Suleri, S. (1992) *The Rhetoric of English India*, Chicago: University of Chicago Press.

Urry, J. (1990) *The Tourist Gaze*, London: Sage.

Viswanathan, G. (1990) *Masks of Conquest*, London: Faber and Faber.

Wilden, A. (1981) *Speech and Language in Psychoanalysis*, Baltimore: Johns Hopkins University Press.

Young, R. (1990) *White Mythologies*, London: Routledge.

Zukin, S. (1992) 'Postmodern urban landscapes', in S. Lash and Friedman (eds) *Modernity and Identity*, Oxford: Blackwell.

4

Writing the Racialised Self? Ottoman Women Writers and Western Feminism

Reina Lewis

For centuries, the image of the secluded, polygamous Oriental woman has fascinated the West. The masculinist vision of the harem as a sexualised realm of deviance, cruelty and excess has animated some of the West's best-known examples of dominant Orientalism, from fine art to popular literature, while for nineteenth-century feminists the plight of the harem inmate functioned as a metaphor for women's oppression in Britain (Zonana 1993, Lewis 1996). But the veiled, secluded Oriental woman was not always represented as a hapless victim.

Some Western sources, women travellers in particular, were concerned to debunk such stereotypes: from Lady Mary Wortley Montagu in 1763 onwards, there was a strain of women's writing that explained the relative freedoms available to women within a segregated world, freedoms, such as the ability to own property, that sometimes outweighed the rights of their European contemporaries (Melman 1992). While the real or imagined status of Oriental woman came to operate as an index of female liberation for Western discussions of emancipation, Oriental women themselves were, of course, actively concerned with their own status and liberation. This chapter is concerned with how Oriental women, Ottoman Turkish women in particular, presented their struggle for emancipation to these Western onlookers. In dialogue with these, I shall be referring to the writings of the British feminist and journalist Grace Ellison, notably her book *An English Woman in a Turkish Harem* (1915).

All these accounts of Oriental female life were designed to counteract prevalent assumptions. The sources I shall be discussing were written in English by self-identified 'Oriental' women and were intended primarily for an Occidental European and North American audience. Their writings provide what is in effect a reverse or counter discourse; an insider account of segregated life, written for an audience of outsiders. The texts construct an addressee who is assumed to be familiar with and informed by dominant

Orientalist knowledges and stereotypes. But this is not to say that I think that we should read these sources simply as the realistic transcripts of an untroubled authorial intent, speaking 'authentically' from a usually silenced position. Rather, I want to look at how the struggle to create a narrative voice that can speak as an Oriental and as a woman, without being subsumed under the various stereotypes in operation, is itself part of the political fight for emancipation at home and understanding abroad.

The three authors I am concentrating on were all Ottoman subjects and hailed initially from Istanbul, but their life experiences and politics were very different. I have discussed elsewhere the non-fixity of the designation 'Oriental woman' (Lewis 1999); this is a shifting term whose geographical terrain varies for the West according to different periods and geo-political interests. All the sources I am covering name themselves as Oriental women, and this is my starting point. This shifting classification is important here, as we shall see, in relation to the internal, local differentiations between Oriental women, which these authors often assume will be invisible, unless explained, to their Western readers.

Halide Adivar Edib, who identifies herself as Oriental, is a Turkish Muslim who started life as an Ottoman subject and became a Turkish citizen with the establishment of the Republic in 1923. Halide came from an élite background and was given a Western education by her progressive-minded father. As a child she was dressed in European clothes, although by and large she moved in a segregated world. Her two volumes of memoirs were published in London in 1926 and 1928. My second author, Demetra Vaka Brown, also called herself Oriental and Ottoman yet she, though born and raised in Turkey, was of Greek Christian descent. Although Vaka Brown professed great affinity with segregated life, she was not Muslim and knew segregated society only as a visitor to Muslim houses. Vaka Brown wrote two volumes about Turkish women, both penned on the occasion of protracted visits back to Turkey after her emigration to America. The first, *Some Pages from the Life of Turkish Women*, published in 1909, is largely an account of her reunions with childhood friends and their circle, including an Istanbul feminist group. The second, *The Unveiled Ladies of Stamboul*, was published in 1923 after her second return visit. This second volume documents the changes in gender relations, already visible in the new Turkish republic, that mark the beginning of a period of accelerated social change. My third author, or authors, are the sisters who styled themselves Melek and Zeyneb Hanum, who travelled to Europe in 1906. Their correspondence with Grace Ellison was published under Ellison's editorship in 1913 as *A Turkish Woman's European Impressions*.[1]

While Vaka Brown presents herself to her Occidental readership as an authentic and reliable source, Halide Adivar disputes her version of harem life and her romanticization of polygamy. Writing bitterly of the misery that polygamy brought to her childhood when her father took a second wife, Halide says

> Although this dramatic introduction of polygamy may seem to promise the sugared life of harems pictured in the 'Haremlik' [the American title of *Some Pages*] of Mrs Kenneth [Vaka] Brown, it was not so in the least. ... On my own childhood, polygamy and its results produced a very ugly and distressing impression. (Adivar 1926: 144–5)

Halide Adivar includes this in the first volume of her memoirs, written while in exile in Britain, having fallen out of favour with the Ataturk regime. Adivar's authority rests on her experience of segregated life and her involvement in revolutionary politics. For her, the problem of being close enough to the object of study without being rendered unreliable by a lack of objectivity (see Melman 1992) is resolved through her obvious contribution to changing sexual politics in Turkey: other women are represented as retaining allegiances to outmoded customs, but not she. Her journey towards emancipation – which she, like Vaka Brown, stresses must be developed in specifically Turkish terms – chronicles her changing consciousness. In 1908, even as she was writing for the radical unionist (i.e. constitutionalist) newspaper *Tanine*, she was still 'not emancipated enough to go to the newspaper office' (Adivar 1926: 265).

Rewriting the Harem

The condition of Oriental women was inevitably discussed in relation to the harem. This system of segregated living was for a long time common to many different ethnic communities in the Middle East, but by the last decades of the Ottoman Empire it had come to be associated in the minds of the West almost entirely with Islam. Segregated life was central to both the dominant Western Orientalist fantasy and the challenges to it provided by Oriental women. There are four reasons for this. First, the mythic sexualised harem was the pivot of a well-established Western fantasy of Oriental depravity, that was both proof of the Oriental's inferiority and source of much pleasurable and envious contemplation. Second, this was well known to Oriental women, whether or not they identified as feminist, who in their various ways set out to debunk this myth and present the harem as a home, not a brothel (see for example Said-Ruete 1888). The primacy of the harem myth is illustrated by Grace Ellison's determination to challenge the Orientalist rarefication of the term. Arguing that the 'Turkish woman is not what Europe generally imagines her to be' (Ellison 1915: 16) she cites the philanthropic and educational activities of Turkish women as they move towards their own version of modernity. She writes specifically about how 'harem' operates as a sign within Orientalist discourse, giving this account of her first discussion with Halide Adivar, by then an acknowledged leader of the emerging Turkish feminist movement:

> I asked Halide-Hanum, perhaps the most active and best known of modern Turkish women, in the name of one of our prominent suffrage societies, how we English women could help the Turkish women in their advancement. 'Ask them', she said, 'to delete for ever that misunderstood word "harem", and speak of us in our Turkish "homes". Ask them to try and dispel the nasty atmosphere which a wrong meaning of that word has cast over our lives. Tell them what our existence really is.' (Ellison 1915: 17)

Third, it is clear that while the phantasmagorical harem plagued Oriental women in their dealings with the West (witness Melek Hanum in 1872 and Said-Ruete 1888) the harem as an experiential domestic system of segregated living was the very real terrain on which Turkish women fought for liberation. So when Ottoman women write about their domestic lives in English they are simultaneously trying to encode themselves as Oriental women in a way that wrests their image back from the 'misrepresentations' of dominant Orientalism *and* to argue their case against the forces of conservatism at home. The construction of an alternative female Oriental subject is thus a project of reincarnation that has a dual axis: in the struggle for self-definition and autonomy the Oriental woman is contesting her subordinated position in relation to both Western imperialist knowledges and local Oriental gender relations.

Fourth, the harem system in particular and the status of women in general had, since the Tanzimat reforms of the nineteenth century (1839–76), become a central issue in the fight for modernisation, against the Sultanate and in the subsequent national liberation struggle. As in many national and development struggles, all sides tried to make the status of women their particular property. Attitudes to female emancipation shifted regularly in the intense factionalism of Turkish politics between the Tanzimat, the second Constitutional period instigated by the Young Turk revolution in 1908 and the formation of the republic. For intellectuals and politicians of quite diverse political persuasions, the West featured large in discussions of modernity, of which female emancipation was considered an element, whether the Western model were to be emulated, adapted or rejected.[2] It is important to read women's discussions of changes in female life in relation to this wider intellectual and political current.

The initially pro-Western thrust of Tanzimat modernising reforms shifted in the late nineteenth century as Islamists developed a defence of Islamic law and custom regarding women (that was more or less apologist) and pan-Turanism constructed an imagined past that figured female emancipation as an indigenous, pre-Islamic Turkic tradition (Kandiyoti 1991). Niyazi Berkes characterises the rule of Sultan Abdulhamit II (1876–1909) as a period in which imperial policy tried to adopt elements of Western modernity that it could consider 'material', such as electricity and locomotives, without being tainted by what it considered 'moral', or rather immoral, such as prostitution, divorce and so on (Berkes 1964). During the second constitutional period (1908–19), Young Turk policy was increasingly influenced by Ziya Gökalp's Turkist sociology and his theories on gender equality and the modern family. When Mustafa Kemal (Ataturk) emerged as a visible leader with the collapse of the Ottoman empire in 1918, the Hamidians' imaginary division between the material and the moral was discarded, as he forged ahead with a policy of nation-building and modernisation that specifically emulated a secular Western model, within the context of an emerging Turkish nationalism (Berkes 1964). Predictably, the religious leaders who had already opposed the reforms of the Young Turks' Family Code in 1917 continued to oppose the newer reforms of the National Assembly and the adoption of the Swiss Civil Code in 1926.[3] The Civil Code made marriage a purely civil matter, gave equal divorce rights to men and women, and specifically prohibited polygamy, something which had only been discouraged in the 1917 Family Code. But Kemalism was not without internal divisions, and significant criticism was raised in relation to both Westernist and secularist policies (Berkes 1964).

It is within this matrix of competing definitions of what was truly Oriental, Ottoman and Turkish, and how to ameliorate women's conditions, that nineteenth- and twentieth-century Ottoman women writers represented the old and new woman of what came to be called Turkey.

The Problems of the New Woman

The conservative Vaka Brown and the revolutionary Halide Adivar have quite different politics, but both stress the need for a specifically Oriental route to female emancipation. Simply copying the West will not do. This view is shared by Melek and Zeyneb Hanum.

Whatever their political differences, all these writers begin by challenging the stereotype of the Oriental woman as docile, ignorant, inactive and uneducated. Writing from élite backgrounds, they are all at pains to stress the noble characteristics of Turkish womanhood: they may be unlike their European or North American sisters in many ways, but the difference may often be to the Orientals' advantage. Without denying the disadvantages of the Oriental attitude of fatalism and *mektoub* (tomorrow will do, everything is god's will) these writers emphasise Oriental women's active role in philanthropy (Halide), their legendary hospitality (Vaka Brown and Ellison) and great 'natural' nobility. Vaka Brown, in particular, poses the natural grandeur and justice of the Oriental woman against the false sophistication and misguided passions of the over-educated European new woman. Her cruel characterisation of the Occidental feminist grows as the book develops:

> There was so much of the sublime in them [Turkish women], which is so lacking in our European civilization. I felt petty and trivial every time I found myself facing one of those conditions which they understood so well. It is true that in Europe and America there are, and have been, women who sacrifice their lives for big causes. But as a rule it is a cause to which glory is attached, or else some tremendous thing they half understand, and to which they give themselves blindly because of its appeal to that sentimentality which is so colossal in European women. And through their self-abnegation they [Turkish women] were reaching heights unknown to us of the Western world. (Vaka Brown 1909: 128)

The image of the Western 'new woman' recurs again and again in all these sources. For Vaka Brown, the Occidental new woman is often depicted as intemperate, over-educated and misguided, with all the advantages accruing to her more natural Oriental sister. The pitfalls of blindly mimicking the American way are indicated in the account of her meeting with Houlmé, an élite Ottoman woman who was given an 'enlightened' Western-style education, only to find that she could not settle for a segregated life. Raised by her grandfather, 'a Turk of the new school, which believes women ought to be educated to be the companions of men' (Vaka Brown 1909: 137), Houlmé was betrothed to her cousin Murak, with whom she had played and been educated until she took the *tcharchaf* (veil) at 14. Promised to him as his only wife, she none the less begs her grandfather to send him away to Europe for three years so that she may really be sure that, having seen the world, he chooses only her. Now, of course, she is missing him desperately and feels all the evils of her transitional situation, caught between Western ideas and Eastern life. 'Since they let us share your studies they ought to let us lead your lives and if this cannot be done, then they ought not to let us study and know other ways but our own' (Vaka Brown 1909: 147). Houlmé's problem is that she now thinks that a man 'must be to his wife what she is to him, all in all. Is this not what Occidental love is? I did not use to think this way till I read your books. I wish I had never, never known' (Vaka Brown 1909: 148).

The impact of Western books, notably novels and romantic fiction, is illustrated by the contrast provided by Houlmé's sister Djimlah who, though also raised with a Western education, seems unaffected by it. To this point Houlmé responds, ' True ... my sister is educated as far as speaking European languages goes but she has never been touched by European thought; [she still believes that] her husband is her lord, the giver of her children'. It is not knowledge of Western languages, then, that are the problem so much as familiarity with Western literature. Vaka Brown repeatedly limits the impact on Turkish women of Western ideas to a concern with men and romance. While this fits in with her support for the refusal to export American feminism wholesale in favour of an indigenous development over time, it also allows her to trivialise Turkish women's aspirations somewhat. By keeping discussion of liberation firmly within the bounds of the domesticated realm of romance, Vaka Brown is able to appear marvellously contemporary and journalistic (a selling point) while simultaneously weaving a popular narrative of love stories. She thus captures the market both for popular romance and the exotica of harem travelogues.

Although I think that Vaka Brown presents this obsession with romantic love as a childish distraction from the real issues of female emancipation and social change, opposition to arranged marriages was indeed something that greatly concerned progressive Turkish men and women in the years prior to 1908. The complex signification of love as an ideological idea, even if not matched by actual practice, shifted, as Alan Duben and Cem Behar have shown, in the years between the Tanzimat and the formation of the republic. The individualism spawned by the liberal ideas of the Tanzimat led to a valorisation of love among the political élite in the 1860s and 1870s. During the years of Abdulhamit's rule, when political expression was severely censored, many opponents of the Hamidian regime turned to the expression of personal liberty, often focused on the issue of free as opposed to arranged marriages, as a substitute for the political self-expression they were denied. The role of Western, mainly French, literature in the development of this political discourse cannot be ignored .

> Love, or *amour*, as it was often referred to by privileged Ottomans [after the French literary and political writings that inspired them], came to stand for so much more than just an intense personal relationship. It came to be associated with a political passion ... *Amour* and *liberté*, then, went hand in hand in a wave of intellectual liberalism. (Duben and Behar 1991: 88)

Despite Vaka Brown's critical overlay, the pull of romantic love evidenced by the Turkish women in her account marks, I think, the legacy of this earlier period, especially as I would date her visit back to 1900 or 1901.[4] The women that Vaka Brown interviews are depicted as her contemporaries in age (she was born in 1877), and would have been, therefore, young enough to have spent their pre-marital years in the repressive Hamidian

era when love 'was often a euphemism, perhaps one might say a displacement, for liberty' (Duben and Behar, 1991: 92). So they can be
expected to have experienced the heightened trauma of the conflict between
modernising expectations and traditional practices. Houlmé, who as we
shall see shortly is relatively conservative in her attitude to changing gender
roles, does not believe that the Westernising experiment leads to personal
happiness. When Vaka Brown asks her how she would raise any daughters
she were to have, Houlmé's response calls for moderation – attempting to
make the change in one generation is too fast.

> I do not think Turkish parents have any right to experiment with their
> children. I should not like to give my daughters this burden of unrest. I
> should like to bring them up as true Osmanli women. *Then you disapprove*
> *of the modern system, of education that is creeping into the harems? Were you to*
> *be free to see men and choose your husbands would you still disapprove?* Yes. It
> took you many generations to come to where you are ... we ought to have
> [the new thought] come to us slowly and through our own efforts. Mus-
> sulman women, with the help of Mahomet, ought to work out their own
> salvation, and borrow nothing from the West. We are a race apart, with
> different traditions and associations. (Vaka Brown 1909: 148–50)

In contrast to Houlmé's conservatism, her other friends are ardent feminists
who want 'immediate freedom' and look upon her 'with mistrust as if
[she] were a traitor' (Vaka Brown 1909: 150). Their urgency is evidenced
by their choice of the French anarchist Louise Michel, after whom they
name their group (Vaka Brown 1909: 151–2).

Houlmé takes Vaka Brown to a meeting of the 'suffragettes of the
harem' and Vaka Brown is quite scathing. The women's plans are, in her
opinion, ill-thought and immature and betray more about the potential of
bored young women for self-dramatisation than any grasp of real world
politics. With dripping sarcasm she notes that the women arrive wearing
grey veils – to symbolise the new dawn – only to unveil and change into
contemporary French fashions the minute the meeting ends. Clearly, the
veils are simply there to create a gratifying sense of mystery and conspiracy
(Vaka Brown 1909: 167). After giving the whispered password, 'Twilight',
Vaka Brown and Houlmé are ushered into the meeting room:

> In a large hall stood the rest of the gray [*sic*] symbols of dawn all so closely
> veiled as to be unrecognizable ... It was all very mysterious and conspirator-
> like. The nine windows of the room were tightly shuttered, that no un-
> romantic sunlight should fall upon the forerunners of the new epoch. ... I
> was utterly disgusted at the whole meeting. I might just as well have been
> in one of those silly clubs in New York where women congregate to read

their immature compositions. These were totally lacking the sincerity, the
spontaneity, and the frankness which usually characterizes Turkish women.
(Vaka Brown 1909: 163–6)

After the meeting, at which point most of the women reappear in Paris
fashions for lunch, the discussion continues and Vaka Brown is asked for
her views. Again, much of the discussion centres on the relations between
the sexes. Vaka Brown starts by challenging their illusions about the
liberated lifestyle of American women, telling them that young American
women are also chaperoned, and that while divorce may be legally available,
it is none the less avoided by respectable women. On the subject of the
non-polygamous man, she challenges their vision of the romantic Western
hero who meets every female need.

> 'Few men are women's companions intellectually,' I said ... 'The only men
> who are the companions of intellectual women are half-baked poets, sopho-
> mores, and degenerates. Normal men, nice men, intelligent men, never talk
> the tomfoolery women want to talk about. They are too busy with things
> worthwhile to sit down and ponder over the gyrations of their souls. In fact,
> they don't have to worry over their souls at all. They are strong and healthy,
> and live useful lives without taking time to store their heads with all the
> nonsense women do.'
> Those forty women breathed heavily. To them I represented freedom
> and intellectual advancement and here I was smashing their ideals unmerci-
> fully. I pretended not to notice the effect of my words and continued: 'If
> you expect real men of any nationality to sit down and talk to you about
> your souls, you will find them disappointing. As for American women, they
> are as different from you as a dog from a bird. Whatever they do cannot
> affect you. They are a different stock altogether.' (Vaka Brown 1909: 169)

Vaka Brown repeatedly emphasises that the differences between Occidental
and Oriental women mean that their liberation must follow a separate
path. Picking up the lament of Houlmé that her unrealistic expectations
and subsequent suffering were prompted by the uncritical consumption of
Western fiction, Vaka Brown stresses that Occidental liberation is not
always as easy as it appears to be in French novels, from which, she
deduces, the suffragettes have derived many of their immature ideas. As
an antidote to this literary 'malady', she recommends them to take advantage of the benefits offered to women by Islam and to go about campaigning
for change in a more moderate and 'sensible way'.

> Then, instead of closeting yourselves together behaving like imitation French
> anarchists, you ought to have your meetings in the open. Since you all wear
> your veils, you can invite the men who are sympathetic to your movement,

to take an interest in it. Little by little, more men will come, and also more women. ... What you want is to be free to mingle with men. Since you want it, you had better have it, though you are overrating the privilege. There is a great deal of poetry and a great deal of charm in your system; but if you don't like it, you don't like it. (Vaka Brown 1909: 175–6)

Now, as we shall see, other women note the constraints and deficits of the so-called freedom in the West, but I want to stop for a moment and think about Vaka Brown's admiration for the traditional harem system. This is a woman who lives in America, at that time not yet married, and who works as a teacher, journalist and editor of Greek- and English-language American papers. She went on to travel and write political journalism (some with her husband) about the Middle East and the Balkans, as well as to be a prominent member of several American-based Greek relief and philanthropic organisations. Yet she treasures the luxury and grace of élite harem life. Although she is quick to note that she could not stay in the Orient – 'he who tastes of American bustle can never again live for long without it' (Vaka Brown 1909: 221) – she cannot condemn it out of hand. Her fondness for *konak* life (the grand wooden houses typical of the multiple/extended family of the Istanbul élite) means that she cannot recognise the predilection for romance as a burgeoning discourse of individual rights.[5] In contrast to the pro-Westernism of many progressives, Vaka Brown's need to commodify the East as a recognisable Orient for her Western readers in conjunction with her own mainly conservative politics works against a recognition of the value of social and political change. Although Westernisation was contested by many who also opposed Hamidian autocracy, there is something very peculiar about Vaka Brown's need to defend a system which her American modernism might well render unappealing. This resistance is driven by her investment in elements of Orientalism (Lewis 1999). While part of her selling-power is her ability to reveal the inside of harem life to an Occidental audience, and although, as a self-identified Oriental woman, she clearly has an investment in challenging some negative Orientalist stereotypes, Vaka Brown does not really want to see change in harem life. Her critique of the Turkish feminists' idealisation of romantic love, while also an accurate indication of the idealisation of the West typical of many strands of Turkish Westernism in the late Ottoman period (Berkes 1964), allows her to patronise her Turkish hosts and assert a Western superiority to which she, as a hybrid subject, can subscribe. As we shall see shortly, Turkish women were also critical of the limits of Western 'liberation', but Vaka Brown's rendition of the feminist meeting allows no such sophistication to those who wish to end their *konak* lifestyle.

In contrast to Vaka Brown's nostalgia for the charm and luxury of the élite harem, Halide presents it as a stifling environment. She left her first husband when he took a second wife, and challenges all romanticisation of polygamy. 'I have heard polygamy discussed as a future possibility in Europe in recent years by sincere and intellectual people of both sexes. "As there is informal polygamy and man is polygamous by nature, why not have the sanction of the law?" they say' (Adivar 1926: 144). Without stinting in her criticism of the supposed superiority of Western Christian marriage, Halide rejects this idea. While she also wants to assert the benefits of a specifically Oriental emancipatory politics, and has no objection to the export of valuable Oriental qualities or habits (selflessness, patriotism, lack of élitism), polygamy is not an example she would have the world follow. Notably, she removes polygamy from the privatised realm of individuated romance and locates it within the social unit of the household, which includes children, servants and relations. Here, the hurt is even worse than the injury done to a wife who shares her husband with a 'temporary mistress'.

Whatever theories people may hold as to what should or should not be the ideal tendencies as regards the family constitution, there remains one ir- refutable fact about the human heart, to whichever sex it may belong. It is almost organic in us to suffer when we have to share the object of our love, whether that love be sexual or otherwise. I believe indeed that there are as many degrees and forms of jealousy as there are degrees and forms of human affection. But even supposing that time and education are able to tone down this very elemental feeling, the family problem will still not be solved; for the family is the primary unit of human society, and it is the integrity of this smallest division which is, as a matter of fact, in question. The nature and consequences of the suffering of a wife, who in the same house shares a husband lawfully with a second and equal partner, differs both in kind and in degree from that of the woman who shares him with a temporary mistress. In the former case, it must also be borne in mind, the suffering extends to two very often considerable groups of people – children, servants, and relations – two whole groups whose interests are from the very nature of the case more or less antagonistic, and who are living in a destructive atmo- sphere of mutual distrust and a struggle for supremacy.

On my own childhood, polygamy and its results produced a very ugly and distressing impression. The constant tension in our home made every simple family ceremony seem like a physical pain, and the consciousness of it hardly ever left me …

And my father too was suffering in more than one way. As a man of liberal and modern ideas, his marriage was very unfavorably regarded by his friends.... Among the household too he felt that he had fallen in general esteem, and he cast about for some justification of his conduct which would reinstate him. 'It was for Halide that I married her,' he used to say ...

The wives never quarreled, and they were always extremely polite, but one felt a deep and mutual hatred accumulating in their hearts, to which they gave vent only when each was alone with father. He wore the look of a man who was getting more than his just punishment now. (Adivar 1926: 144–7)

Halide Adivar clearly abhors polygamy, and has no allegiance to the veil. For her, Vaka Brown is dealing with fantasy, not reality. To Halide, represented as the voice of the 'new woman' of the Turkish Republic and writing some years after Vaka Brown's first publication, the harem produced a state of mind that was not healthy. The end of the old ways, which Vaka Brown sees as the sad Ottoman decline, Halide Adivar celebrates as a new, modernising order. But she is torn: she also wants to represent all that is best about Muslim women of the old order (their contribution to the war effort, and so on).

Halide was one of the founder members of the first women's club in Istanbul, but her presentation of Turkish feminism is very different from Vaka Brown's. For Halide, this momentous event in the annals of female emancipation is subsumed under the wider national crisis of the Balkan wars. Female emancipation is located almost entirely within the fight for a wider social and, crucially, national emancipation. In the winter of 1913, Istanbul was flooded with refugees and wounded troops as the Bulgarian army advanced south. Many families in her circle left the city, but Halide remained, having sent her servants and children to safety elsewhere. This is how she introduces the club:

I stayed in Fatih [Istanbul] at Nakie Hanum's house and worked with the women of the Taali-Nisvan Club for relief and nursing. We, with some teachers and some educated Turkish women, had formed that first women's club. Its ultimate object was the cultivation of its members. It had a small center where the members took lessons in French and English. It also opened classes for a limited number of Turkish women to study Turkish, domestic science, and the bringing up of children ... There was a feministic tendency in the club, but as a whole it kept within the bounds of usefulness and philanthropy, and we tried to maintain a quiet tone, avoiding propaganda, which becomes so ugly and loud and offers such an easy way to fame for any one who can make sufficient noise.

The club organized and opened a small hospital with thirty beds in Istamboul. A young surgeon and a chemist, both husbands of club members, volunteered to help; ... We took only privates. As the Balkan war saw

Turkish women nursing men for the first time, any little human incident became a tremendous scandal. (Adivar 1926: 334–5)

Halide's disapproval of attention-seeking feminists is in a register quite different from Vaka Brown's. For Halide, personal emancipation is presented as part of national emancipation, and seeking publicity might distract from that. Also, by the 1920s, when Halide was writing, an individualist emphasis on love had been recomplexioned as reactionary in favour of a view that registered the modern Western family as the foundational unit of the new republican society. Tracing the political travails of love, we can see how the nuclear family and individualism, which for late nineteenth-century Ottomans represented a progressive-minded attack on the old order and its associated repressive family and state structures, had shifted. By the time of the Young Turks in the early twentieth century, such individualism had come to 'be associated with anti-nationalism, moral corruption and even treason' (Duben and Behar 1991: 94). By the end of the First World War, the discursive terrain had shifted again, as the companionate nuclear family was reactivated by Kemalism as a national model.

It is worth considering how Halide's account is partly determined by the changing status of feminism in Kemalist politics. Women's emancipation was taken up as a cause in the fight for the republic, and was central to Ataturk's anti-religious social reforms. Some commentators have argued that Kemalism wanted to control the boundaries of feminism, too much of which would be seen as a distraction (Jayawardena 1986), and it would certainly seem that the early republic preferred a centralist 'state-sponsored' feminism to the development of an autonomous women's movement (Kandiyoti 1991: 42). One illustration of the repositioning of women's demands as part of a national, rather than only a gender, issue is Halide's endorsement of women's contribution to the world of work. This is in contrast to writers published in the early years of the century such as Vaka Brown and Zeyneb Hanum. Although most commentators agree that Turkish feminism began with élite and governmental initiatives, and not as a grassroots movement, women had already taken on a limited involvement in work outside the home before Ataturk emerged as a leader at the end of the First World War. He inherited measures permitting women's public labour from the Young Turk era, when Imperial decrees permitted women to work during the First World War in factories (munitions, textiles, food) and nursing, although their dress and demeanour was strictly policed (Kandiyoti 1991). Apart from the economically crucial nature of this female labour, modern, educated women were also a sign to the West of Turkey's progress. So, for the Kemalists, the cultural capital of women's new and, crucially, public working lives was immense, as was the primacy of women's role as mothers of the nation, and hence guardians of the new ways. In light of these changes, we can see the tensions in Halide's work between an overarching nationalist rationale, which provides an alibi for feminism, and a very personal account of her own response to the limitations of the old order and the sometimes frightening challenges of the new.

Status: Does Emancipation Require Lost of Class or Race Status

The West was central to women's consideration of female emancipation too, although it figured as a disappointment just as often as it did as a positive model. A clear exposition of how Turkish women perceived the constraints of Western liberation is given in Zeyneb Hanoum's account of their journey through Europe in 1906. The letters from Zeyneb quoted here make it clear that, like the feminists Vaka Brown represents in 1909, she and her sister started out with an elevated idea of European female life. But these illusions were soon challenged:

> It seems to me that we Orientals are children to whom fairy tales have been told for too long – fairy tales which have every appearance of truth. You hear so much of the mirage of the East, but what is that compared to the mirage of the West, to which all Orientals are attracted?
>
> They tell you fairy tales, too, you women of the West – fairy tales which, like ours, have all the appearances of truth. I wonder, when the English-women have really won their vote and the right to exercise all the tiring professions of men, what they will have gained? Their faces will be a little sadder, a little more weary, and they will have become wholly disillusioned ...
>
> When in Turkey we met together, and spoke of the Women of England, we imagined that they had nothing more to wish for in this world. But we had no idea of what the struggle for life meant to them, nor how terrible was this eternal search after happiness. Which is the harder struggle of the two? The latter is the only struggle we know in Turkey, and the same futile struggle goes on all the world over. (Zeyneb 1913: 186–8, letter dated 1908)

The emphasis on the tiring pursuit of dubious pleasures is constant in Zeyneb's letters. The sisters miss the quiet ease and companionship of Turkish social life, and are bemused by the ceaseless and, to them, pointless and graceless, activities of the European upper and middle classes (sports, skating, soirees, and so on). Their negative depiction of women's entry into the professions speaks to their privileged Oriental background which, formed without a northern Protestant work ethic, does not see wage labour as ennobling. This fits with much of what Vaka Brown, who is similarly conservative, reports from Istanbul's feminist meetings: that Turkish

women crave emancipation in terms of education, freedom of movement
and sexual politics, rather than for a right to work. The ways in which
Zeyneb's and Melek's gendered identifications are class- and race-specific
are highlighted by Zeyneb's next lines, where she argues that concepts of
happiness are culturally specific.

> Happiness – what a mirage! At best is it not a mere negation of pain, for
> each one's idea of happiness is so different? When I was fifteen years old
> they made me present of a little native from Central Africa. For her there
> was no greater torture than to wear garments of any kind, and her idea of
> happiness was to get back to the home on the borders of Lake Chad and the
> possibility of eating another roasted European. (Zeyneb 1913: 186–8, letter
> dated 1908)

Having previously discussed the myths or mirages that the East and the
West hold about each other, Zeyneb now deploys a stereotype about the
'South' that presumably transcends the East–West divide. The stereotype
of the primitive cannibalistic African was a staple of Western popular
imperialism by the late nineteenth and early twentieth centuries. In Oriental
sources, which make clear distinctions between Arab and non-Arab
Africans, reference to cannibalism also occurs, though infrequently. Halide
makes joking reference to being told such tales as a child, also in relation
to a young enslaved African (Adivar 1926: 166–8). Clearly, Zeyneb uses
this image tongue in cheek for her European audience, but it is also part
of her own Oriental lexicon of racialised division, something that she and
her Occidental readers can share. Tellingly, neither she nor her English
editor Ellison sees any need to remove or explain it (and Ellison does use
footnotes elsewhere to explain what she sees as Zeyneb's misapprehensions
about European life). The figure of the naked African cannibal does what
she is meant to do: she simultaneously exemplifies the non-universality of
human happiness, thus naturalising the different aspirations of Turkish
and English women, and also unites the Turks with the Europeans by
separating them from Africans. This supports Zeyneb's (and Ellison's)
argument for a separate Oriental route to female emancipation. But because
the African slave represents the worst of human depravity, the differences
between Occident and Orient are minimised: Turkish women, although
different from European women, are far more like them than they are like
the uncivilised savage. Although it is not clear whether for the purposes of
the cooking-pot a Turk would count as European, the story certainly serves
to separate Turkey from the more primitively coded others of imperial
Europe, without merging her with Europe. The humorous tone with which
the slave's cannibalism is invoked deflates the threat that such alleged
practices provide for Europeans and reinforces the African's subordinate

position. Enslaved, young and uncivilised, without the power to enact her revenge, the African's inferiority elevates and unites the Occidental readers and Oriental writer.

The need to be separated from these 'primitives' occurs infrequently in the text, but another separation – between herself and the European working class – is frequently constructed. It is clearly imperative for Zeyneb to be recognised as a lady and distinguished from a primitivised working class. She regularly remarks on Western activities that seem to her unladylike (exercise that leaves women with red cheeks and disordered clothes, for example) and is traumatised by the possibility of not being 'taken for a lady'. It is this potential loss of class status that colours her response to English feminists. In this account of a feminist meeting, differences of class rather than nationality are paramount.

Since I came here I have seen nothing but 'Votes for Women' chalked all over the pavements and walls of the town. These methods of propaganda are all so new to me. I went to a suffrage street-corner meeting the other night, and I can assure you I never want to go again. The speaker carried her little stool herself, another carried a flag, and yet a third woman a bundle of leaflets and papers to distribute to the crowd. After walking for a little while they placed the stool outside a dirty-looking public-house.... When the other lady began to speak, quite a big crowd of men and women assembled: degraded-looking ruffians they were, most of them, and a class of man I had not yet seen. All the time they interrupted her, but she went bravely on, returning their rudeness with sarcasm. What an insult to womanhood it seemed to me, to have to bandy words with this vulgar mob. One man told her that 'she was ugly'. Another asked 'if she had done her washing,' but most of the hateful remarks I could not understand, so different was their English from the English I had learned in Turkey.

Yet how I admired the courage of that woman! No physical pain could be more awful to me than not to be taken for a lady, and this speaker of such remarkable eloquence and culture was not taken for a lady by the crowd, seeing she was supposed 'to do her own washing' like any woman of the people.

The most pitiful part of it all to me is the blind faith these women have in their cause, and the confidence they have that in explaining their policy to the street ruffians, who cannot even understand that they are ladies, they will further their cause by half an inch. I was glad when the meeting was over, but sorry that such rhetoric should have been wasted on the half-intoxicated loungers who deigned to come of the public-house and listen. If this is what the women of your country have to bear in their fight for freedom, all honour to them, but I would rather groan in bondage. (Zeyneb 1913: 89–91, letter dated 1908)

Gender emerges as an identification calibrated by class. Changes in women's status achieved at the cost of losing the class-specific privileges of their position as ladies may not be worthwhile. As Zeyneb later concludes:

I do not pretend to understand the suffragettes or their 'window-smashing' policy, but I must say, I am even more surprised at the attitude of your Government. ... I cannot tell you the horrible impression it produces on the mind of a Turkish woman to learn that England not only imprisons but tortures women: to me it is the cataclysm of all my most cherished faiths. Ever since I can remember, England had been to me a kind of Paradise on earth, the land which welcomed to its big hospitable bosom all Europe's political refugees. It was the land of all lands I longed to visit, and now I hear a Liberal Government is torturing women. Somehow my mind will not accept this statement. (Zeyneb 1913: 236, letter dated 1912)

Conclusion

Compared to Europe, Turkey may not be so bad. It is clear that Oriental women writers evaluate female status in the West in relation to their own home conditions, just as European women had long looked East for a comparison or contrast. For Oriental women, the gaze is reversed as they examine European social mores in relation to their own changing situation. Since the nineteenth century, Oriental women had been puncturing myths about the relative evils of Occidental and Oriental marriage, even though the polygamy that so gripped the Western imagination was uncommon by the late nineteenth century and even rarer by the twentieth. In the twentieth century, while clearly still concerned with the practice and representation of polygamy, Oriental women widen the discussion to cover the conditions for the emergence of social and political emancipation in both East and West. And, as we have seen, the West does not always come out on top. In contrast to the negative treatment of suffragettes in England, ranging from rudeness to brutality, Turkish women have the advantage of substantial and active male support, something which Ellison, after her British experience, finds 'still almost incomprehensible' (Ellison 1915: 65). For the avowed feminist Ellison, the contrast with Turkey makes the limits of Western freedom all the more keenly felt.

I came here with perhaps just a little of the 'downtrodden woman of the East' fallacy left, but that has now completely vanished. To me, as an Englishwoman, there are sides of this life which would irritate me into open rebellion [the veil, separate transport, etc.] ... But then, after all, is not everything relative? ... If we in the West possess what is known as the 'joy of liberty', have not so many of us been deprived of the blessing of protection? If the Moslem women are 'possessions' they are 'cherished possessions' and treated as such. (Ellison 1915: 195–8)

Notes

1. Allegedly the inspiration for Pierre Loti's *Les Désenchantées*, the two women's real names were possibly Nouryé and Zennar; see Szyliowicz 1988.
2. For historical overviews and different interpretations of the political significance of Westernism see Berkes 1964, Shaw and Shaw 1994 and Kandiyoti 1991.
3. The Family Code of 1917 brought marriage under state regulation, rendering a religious ceremony alone insufficient for legal recognition. It also made limited provision for women to initiate divorce, notably in relation to polygamy, which a woman was now able to stipulate against and over which she was entitled to a divorce if her husband married again against her will.
4. Although the book was published in 1909, I estimate that the visit on which it is based occurred in 1900 or 1901, since Vaka Brown reflects back on her 'six years' in America. She emigrated in 1894, so this would put the visit to Istanbul at the start of the twentieth century. Further, references to her unmarried state also date the visit several years prior to publication and certainly no later than early 1904, in April of which she married Kenneth Brown. This puts her in Istanbul before the second constitutional period began in 1908.
5. Alan Duben and Cam Behar (1991) note how in Turkish novels of the period and in their interviews with elderly people in Istanbul the phrase 'the end of *konak* life' came to signify the end of an era, typified by gracious living and multiple-family dwellings. The emergence of a 'modern' nuclear family on a Western model, based on companionate love marriage, was not just about individual choice, it also drastically reordered the previously patriarchal and cross-generational structure of family and civic society.

References

Adivar, H. Edib (1926) *Memoirs of Halide Edib*, London: John Murray.

Berkes, N. (1964) *The Development of Secularism in Turkey*, Montreal: McGill University Press.

Duben, A. and C. Behar (1991) *Istanbul Households: Marriage, Family and Fertility, 1880–1940*, Cambridge: Cambridge University Press.

Ellison, G. (1915) *An Englishwoman in a Turkish Harem*, London: Methuen.

Jayawardena, K. (1986) *Feminism and Nationalism in the Third World*, London: Zed Books.

Kandiyoti, D. (ed.) (1991) *Women, Islam and the State*, Basingstoke: Macmillan.

Lewis, R. (1996) *Gendering Orientalism: Race, Femininity and Representation*, London: Routledge.

— (1999) 'Cross-Cultural Reiterations: Demetra Vaka Brown and the Performance of Racialised Female Beauty', in A. Jones and A. Stephenson (eds) *Performing the Body/Performing the Text*, London: Routledge.

Melek-Hanum (1872) *Thirty Years in the Harem: or the Autobiography of Melek-hanum, Wife of H.H. Kibrizli-Mehemet-Pasha*, second edition, Calcutta: Lewis and Co., 1888.

Melman, B. (1992) *Women's Orients: English Women and the Middle East, 1718–1918. Sexuality, Religion and Work*, Basingstoke: Macmillan.

Said-Ruete, E. (1888) *Memoirs of an Arabian Princess: Princess Salme bint Said ibn Sultan al-Bu Saidi of Oman and Zanzibar*, London: East-West Publications, 1981.

Shaw, S.J. and E.K. Shaw (1994) *History of the Ottoman Empire and Modern Turkey, vol. 2: Reform, Revolution and Republic*, Cambridge: Cambridge University Press, second edition.

Szyliowicz, I.R. (1988) *Pierre Loti and the Oriental Woman*, Basingstoke: Macmillan.

Vaka Brown, D. (1909) *Some Pages from the Life of Turkish Women*, London: Constable.

— (1911) *In The Shadow of Islam*, London: Constable.

— (1923) *The Unveiled Ladies of Stamboul*, Boston: Houghton Mifflin.

Zeyneb Hanoum (1913) *A Turkish Woman's European Impressions*, London: Seeley, Service Co.

Zonana, J. (1993) 'The Sultan and the Slave: Feminist Orientalisms and the Structure of *Jane Eyre*', in *Signs*, vol. 18, no. 3, Spring.

In Darkest England: the Poor, the Crowd and Race in the Nineteenth-century Metropolis

John Marriott

In the first half of the nineteenth century the metropolitan poor were constructed as a race apart.[1] Urban explorers and evangelical journalists, claiming distinct access to their object of inquiry, abandoned iconographies of the criminal, bizarre and grotesque to develop perspectives deeply embedded in theorisations of the innate superiority of the Anglo-Saxon subject over both poor and colonial others. These writers, however, rarely used racial theory with rigour and coherence. The pioneering Henry Mayhew borrowed freely from contemporary racial theory in writing the interpretive preface to his *London Labour and London Poor*, but any putative logic was undermined by the plurality of empirical material on the experience of the poor recorded in the corpus of his work. Nevertheless, the tradition of urban exploration that followed increasingly displayed an intensified concern with race. Around 1860, as fears of social disorder and imperial decline gripped the bourgeois imagination, writings of journalists such as James Greenwood took a sinister turn, manifest particularly in their use of symbolic repertoires of dirt and degeneration.

The Meaning of Dirt

Dirt featured prominently in the imaginative universe constructed around the nineteenth-century metropolitan and colonial poor. Consider, for example, the Revd Garratt, who in 1852 lectured to the London City Mission on the problem of the London Irish. While displaying admirable qualities of 'intellectual acuteness and imaginative glow', the Irish, he claimed, had another side to their character: 'The worst parts in the character of the Irish in London are that they are idle and dirty; that they are without that honourable independence of mind which is so valuable a feature of the English character.'[2] J. Hollingshead, a staff member of Dickens' *Household Words*, in a sociological flourish anticipating Beveridge by nearly a hundred years, talked of the poor as a population marked by the 'five great divisions ... of poverty, ignorance, dirt, immorality and crime'.[3] And James Greenwood, in a description typical of his writings, referred to 'Creatures that you know to be female by the length and raggedness of hair that makes their heads hideous, and by their high pitched voices, with bare red arms and their bodies bundled in a complication of dirty rags.[4]

This physicality was linked increasingly to urban topography. Phillips' 'Wild tribes of London' crouched in 'darkness, dirt, and disease',[5] Hollingshead's 'Ragged London' were 'half buried in black kitchens and sewer-like courts and alleys'.[6] In 1863, W. Cosens, Secretary of the Additional Curates Society, spelt out the necessary lessons: 'The purity of the moral atmosphere in which we live exercises over us an influence as real as the purity of the physical atmosphere. ... The parallel between the infection of disease and the infection of crime holds strictly; if we suffer pollution to remain unabashed in the hovel it will take its revenge on the palace.[7] Most influential, however, was G. Godwin, editor of *The Builder*, the most important architectural and building periodical of the time, who wrote prolifically on the relationship between living conditions and the social pathology of the poor. Although investigation was 'a task of no small danger and difficulty; it is necessary to brave the risks of fever and other injuries to health, and the contact of men and women often as lawless as the Arab or the Kaffir',[8] he persevered, and in the 1850s published a series of articles, collected later in *Town swamps and social bridges*.[9] Guided by the maxim 'As the homes, so the people', he described vividly the housing environments suffered by the poor in ways that were to become very familiar. By a Thames tributary, for example:

> Dwelling-houses are built on the sewer wall, and around it. The people living about here have, in most instances, sickly children, who in a measure resemble the poor plants observable in some of the windows about. Everything around is bad. The bank, when the tide goes out, is covered with filth; and when the number of the similar tributaries which flow to Father Thames, both night and day, is recollected, his state is not to be wondered at.[10]

Nineteenth-century discourses on the metropolis created an urban topography in which the slum, the sewer, the poor and the prostitute were effectively separated from the suburb. This separation enabled the social reformer, as part of a process of validation of the bourgeois imaginary, to survey and classify its *own antithesis*.[11] Dirt was crucial because while it moved readily across the symbolic domains it was always matter in the wrong place. Furthermore, the physical filth of the poor and the colonized became a metonym for moral defilement and impurity. Thus 'contagion' and 'contamination' were the tropes through which the imperial formation appropriated the metropolis and the colonies, and expressed fears that dismantling boundaries between suburb and slum, public and private would threaten class distinctions.[12]

These symbolic hierarchies, however, contained inherent contradictions. Filthy bodies and geographical spaces were held ambivalently between disgust and fascination, repugnance and desire in a way that suggested that the low was not a marginalised other, but lay as an 'eroticised constituent' at the centre of the bourgeois imaginary. Prostitutes, rookeries, the body of the poor, the lascar and other sources of contagion in the Victorian metropolis attracted a degree of attention incommensurate with their 'real' presence, thereby revealing the symbolic centrality of the socially and economically peripheral. The preoccupation with social reform, slumming, visits from the members of the Charity Organisation Society, urban exploration and prostitution was therefore in part an encoding of fascination with the transgressive qualities of the dirty, low other.

Important though this analysis is to an understanding of how dirt moves freely around symbolic domains, in focusing on the consolidation of *class*-based hierarchies certain limitations are exposed. In the imperial formation the category of class was articulated with gender and race in ways that denied any essential privileging; class, gender and race existed only as relational categories in a state of 'dynamic, shifting and intimate interdependence'.[13] This imparted a new range of meanings to dirt.

But even here, the nuanced repertoire of dirt is not grasped adequately. The dirt of manual labour was not the dirt of the metropolitan poor. Despite their enforced remoteness from the bourgeois imaginary, a cultural void existed between the 'honest', 'manufactured' dirt of the artisan – grease, sweat, oil, dust and grime – and the 'grotesque', 'faecal' dirt of the poor – filth, sewage, swamp, slime and putrefaction. This distinction was of considerable significance in interrelated ways: first, the vocabulary was used highly selectively; the coding of manual dirt was rarely deployed in descriptions of the poor. Second, as the dirt of the poor became subject to surveillance, so was it mapped in distinctive ways. 'Honest' dirt – matter in the right place – was to be found on the hands and the brow; 'grotesque' dirt was located on the whole body of the poor, and within the body of the metropolis that they inhabited. Third, it was specifically the dirt of the poor that entered the bourgeois psyche as a repugnant low other.

These processes never operated independently. In the construction of symbolic hierarchies of the body, for example, they were all in evidence:

> But whilst the 'low' of the bourgeois body becomes unmentionable, we hear an ever increasing garrulity about the *city's* 'low' – the slum, the rag-picker,

the prostitute, the sewer – the 'dirt' which is 'down there'. In other words, the axis of the body is transcoded through the axis of the city, and whilst the bodily low is 'forgotten', the city's low becomes a site of obsessive preoccupation, a preoccupation which is itself intimately conceptualized in terms of discourses of the body.[14]

Furthermore, dirt was colour coded; it was neither brown nor grey, but unambiguously black. This was no semantic or poetic device. This synonymic association was part of a structuring process through which a complex chain of signification was established in a series of binary oppositions: dirt/filth–cleanliness; unwashed–washed; darkness/shadow–light; impure/defiled–pure; black–white; low–high.[15]

Until the 1850s much of this coding was muted; for most Victorians heretofore, race described social rather than colour distinctions.[16] Thus in Grant's metropolis the poor lived in 'miserable hovels, many of them underneath the ground, without glass windows, or indeed without windows of any kind – the only light and air being admitted through the horizontal door'.[17] While Phillips guided the reader through the courts of St Giles: 'Let us cross the road, and pausing before that dark archway, that seems to have retreated from the ill-paved street, and slink, as it were, into the shadow of the wall, glance into the pandemonium which lies beyond. ... Such courts are the headquarters of filth and fever'.[18]

During the 1880s, however, the associations with 'black' became more direct. In the East End 'the angular meanness of the buildings is veiled by the dusk, and there stretches on either hand a hummocked wilderness of mysterious murk. ... In the by-streets the lamps are so few and dim the feeble flickering light they cast upon the house fronts is only less dark than the pitchy blackness that broods above the lonely-looking roofs'.[19] The Revd Rice-Jones visited the vicinity of St Giles Mission House: 'The walls are stained black with dirt; the passage and the stairs are thickly carpeted with dirt; and wherever you go, dirt reigns supreme'. While its inhabitants had 'bare black feet, as black as the hands and face; shapeless boots, ungartered hose falling over the instep; brimless hats, low-looking eared caps drawn athwart the wickedest little faces possible to imagine'.[20]

This black/white coding became a critical trope in the imperial formation of the late nineteenth century.[21] Stereotypical images based on physical characteristics, most notably skin colour, had existed ever since a black presence was known. But at determinate historical moments the coding took on particular forms. The wretched history of slavery provides abundant evidence of how virulent racist forms emerged as a means of validating the practice of enslavement, and were mobilised by pro-slavery interests when they felt threatened by the impulses of abolition and slave revolt. In India, the caste system, the internal boundaries of which were defined by precisely the same allegory, was reconstructed and rigidified by imperial intervention after 1850.[22] It was at this time that racial discourse, cultivated by scientific theory, shifted from the bestowal of arbitrary features to the systematic ascription of natural and essential signs.[23]

Faced with seemingly diverse, uncontrollable and unknowable low others, the imperial formation found in the allegory a versatile means of transforming physical difference into moral and cultural difference. The superiority of white over black was naturalised and thereby consolidated. Eventually, through improvised extensions, such allegorical forms dominated most spheres of the imperial formation, implicating sympathisers and critics alike.

Peculiar problems were created within the metropolis. Here the poor were for the most part white, that is, without the visual sign of otherness. The poor presented a radical disruption to racial order by forcing the conjunction of a culturally constituted whiteness with its own metaphors of difference;[24] they could be embraced within a symbolic dualism and hence resolved only by being constructed as black. The Irish, as both colonial subjects and urban poor, were doubly problematic, and it comes as no surprise to find that the most strident racial coding was deployed on them.

Carlyle's infamous epithet in *Sartor Resartus* of the Irish as 'white negroes', and Kingsley's impressions on his tour of Ireland in 1860 of being 'haunted by human chimpanzees' were isolated examples of a more general process through which the Irish were increasingly 'simianized'.[25] Between 1840 and 1890 visual representations of the Irish physiognomy gradually changed; the early 1860s was the critical period, for it was then that the early emphasis on big-mouthed and prognathous faces was displaced by stereotypes with ape-like features.[26] Cartoonists in popular periodicals such as *Punch*, *Judy* and *Puck*, drawing upon the earlier Francophobic anthropomorphisms of Gillray and Cruikshank, effectively invented the Irish ape in the aftermath of the explosions at Clerkenwell and Manchester when Fenians had attempted to liberate some of their leaders from police custody. A second wave of intense simianisation occurred during the 1880s following the Phoenix Park assassination, renewed land wars and the rise of Parnellite nationalism. Similarities between Tenniel's 1882 cartoon of the Irish Frankenstein and 1888 portrayal of the Ripper were striking and unambiguous.

Thus although simianisation may have been evident in depictions of other subjects, and the process was complex, the most virulent forms were retained for the Irish. Occasionally members of the English poor were endowed with ape-like features, but they were very much the exception. Even the brutal stereotypes of African 'savages' at the time did not 'come close in terms of monstrousness to the Irish and Irish American gorillas of the Fenian era'.[27]

Dirt therefore was a versatile metaphor that helped give meaning to shifting, complex fields of racial hierarchy. It assumed a distinct significance in the 1860s, when a peculiar conjunction of metropolitan and imperial crises forced a reconstitution of the racial order. The Indian revolt of 1857, Fenian bomb campaigns on the mainland during the 1860s, and the Morant Bay rebellion of 1865 shook the foundations of the imperial formation by demonstrating unequivocally that colonial subjects were no longer prepared to tolerate imperial authority or, in the aftermath of the abolition of slavery, the state of free wage labour, and that in mounting such challenges such subjects revealed the dangers of an endemic savagery out of control.[28] Across the Atlantic the course of the American Civil War – closely watched in this country – placed in sharp relief a kaleidoscopic range of racial tensions.

Meanwhile, the 1860s represented something of a watershed in metropolitan history. The collapse of traditional industry in East London cast tens of thousands of workers into the residuum, precipitating a series of bread riots, undermining the actuarial basis of poor relief, and threatening the moral and economic rationality upon which liberal utopian visions of the 'future of the race' were based.[29]

Degeneration and Desire

It was at this moment that notions of degeneration assailed the discursive realm of the metropolitan poor. Expressing certain anxieties about the stability of the social order in the face of revolutionary upheaval, such ideas had surfaced occasionally to influence post-enlightenment thought, but they remained relatively minor components within large theories of social and political evolution.[30] Now, at a time of an unprecedented loss of confidence in the idea of progress, degeneration took on dramatic new significance. The attractions were obvious. Degeneration was a fluid category; it shifted readily between the human sciences, fiction and social commentary, rendering it irreducible to any fixed theory and unidentifiable with any single political cause.[31] But in the second half of the nineteenth century, degeneration was increasingly articulated with race. Thus the pathological condition of the urban poor was seen as evidence of a degenerative process within the imperial race, and the savagery of colonial subjects as a characteristic degeneration from the ideal white race.[32] Both provided an ominous portent that could be mobilized to legitimate an extensive repertoire of repressive measures.

Theories of degeneration imparted a sinister and menacing twist to the racialisation of the poor. Social pathologies, it was argued, were due to characteristic hereditary factors, not to the social conditions that the poor inhabited. This effectively rendered their presence invisible, and even more of a threat. For while heredity encouraged the racial separation of the poor, their persistence – indeed, their increased presence within the bourgeois imaginary – suggested simultaneously that the poor constituted a degenerative and threatening strain within the Anglo-Saxon race. For many, this invisible enemy within posed a 'far greater problem than the racial inferiority of non-European peoples';[33] it also helped to explain why the racialisation of the metropolitan poor assumed its most pernicious forms after the 1860s, when the immediate crises in imperial rule precipitated by colonial insurrection had been superseded by fears that dissembling processes were operating at the heart of empire.

Robert Young has argued that in the troubled climate manifested in theories of degeneration, hybridity emerged as a key cultural signifier.[34] Drawing upon examples from animal and plant kingdoms, racial theorists of the nineteenth century surmised that because hybrid offspring had diminishing fertility, sexual unions between people from two different races threatened the propagation of the human species. In the worst scenario, the intermixing of races gave rise to a raceless mass, a chaos of indiscrimination that threatened to contaminate and hence subvert the vigour of the pure race with which it came into contact. At the core of emergent racial theory, therefore, 'hybridity also maps out its most anxious, vulnerable site: a fulcrum at its edge and centre where its dialectics of injustice, hatred and oppression can find themselves effaced and expunged'.[35] But this preoccupation with hybridity betrayed an ambivalence between desire and repulsion, thereby revealing the centrality of sexuality in race and culture, and suggested that racial theories were deeply implicated in theories of desire. A dialectic existed between a structure of covert colonial desire promoting racial intermixing and a structure of repulsion in which racial antagonisms were perpetuated.

Parallels with contemporary discourses about the metropolitan poor were unmistakable. As we have seen, the same dialectic between fascination and disgust informed the imaginary relationship with the low other. Equally significantly, the trope of degeneration assumed a new salience from the 1860s, as the presence of the poor and colonial others – seen as part of an internal orient – became subject to urgent concern and surveillance.[36] J. Salter, Missionary to the Asiatics in England, concluded from a survey undertaken into the effect of a visit to a Christian country on 'Hindoos, Chinamen, Negroes, and other heathens in the streets of London' that 'the treatment they had received had evidently produced upon their minds the very reverse of a favourable impression of the Christian religion'.[37]

The profound neglect they suffered, forcing them to associate with the depraved poor, served only to build a dangerous moral isolation:

> The heathens of the heathen land associate here with the heathens of Christian London; and, truly, they both dwell in the valley of the shadow of death. Between these waifs from the banks of the Indus and Ganges, and the reputable white man brought up on the banks of the Thames, there is a great gulf fixed, and this gulf is crossed by very few. The difficulty of colloquial communication is one barrier that stands in the way; but far more formidable, as a division, is the foul atmosphere of human depravity in which these Orientals live and suffer. ... The heathen mind is dark, and the vices of the various heathen systems in which the Asiatic is so brought up, as to form part of his nature, are bad enough when unmingled with European sin in his own land of superstition; but here is an interchange of sin and an unholy compound of both.[38]

This sense of impenetrable isolation combined with cultural fantasies redolent of De Quincey constructed the opium den as *the* site of orientalist disgust and desire, hybridity and degradation. Accounts of the metropolitan poor came routinely to include descriptions of dens and their inhabitants. In 'Tiger Bay' (Brunswick St, Wapping) was discovered a cellar in which

> four lascars roll their yellow and black eyes upon us as they glare silently at each other, and smoke from one bamboo pipe. ... The two wretched women who are cooking some rice at a scanty fire are English, but so degraded, even below the degradation of such a neighbourhood, that they answer only with ghastly grins and a cringing paucity of words. ... Rooms where dark-skinned, snake-like Hindoos (beggars and tract-sellers by day) live with English and Irish women as their wives, and live, as it would seem, not always so miserably as might be imagined.[39]

Popular as Tiger Bay was as a haunt of social investigators, it was eclipsed by the den at Bluegate Fields off the Ratcliff Highway, which entered into popular iconography. J.C. Parkinson described it in familiar terms:

> There is a little colony of Orientals in the centre of Bluegate-fields, and in the centre of this colony is the opium den. ... The livid, cadaverous, corpse-like visage of Yahee, the wild excited glare of the young Lascar who opens the door, the stolid sheep-like ruminations of Lazarus and the other China-men coiled together on the floor, the incoherent anecdotes of the Bengalee squatted on the bed, the fiery gesticulations of the mulatoo and the Manilla-man who are in conversation by the fire, the semi-idiotic jabber of the negroes huddled up behind Yahee, are all due to the same fumes.[40]

Ewing Ritchie inquired further into the effects of opium, expressing little surprise that the oriental experienced none of the mystical pleasures induced in the English mind:

> With the somewhat doubtful confessions of De Quincey and Coleridge in my memory, I tried to get them to acknowledge sudden impulses, poetic inspirations, splendid dreams; but of such things these little fellows had never conceived; the highest eulogism I heard was: 'You have pains – pain in de liver, pain in de head – you smoke – all de pains go'.[41]

Tiger Bay was demolished and the Ratcliff Highway cleared as part of a slum clearance programme in the mid 1870s, but the area continued to hold the same grim fascination for scribbling visitors because like all such waterside spaces it provided refuge for a transient seafaring population and thereby the readiest opportunities for racial intermixing. With the obliteration of the dens, peculiar interest focused on one of the previously identified and most visible participants, the site of the most profound moral danger and desire: the active, orientalised, predatory female. *Wonderful London*, published in 1878, welcomed the abolition of Tiger Bay, where 'swarms of Lascars and Malays herded together to indulge in mad opium orgies', but noted that 'the tigresses remain'.[42] Here a reversal was effected. A savage was not the male who 'tracks and brings down the game to share it with the she', but was the female who 'hunts, while the he creature lurks in ambush to give assistance if need be, or remains home at the den'. And while the Highway was a 'spectacle which no visitor from the country should miss; the whole human family ... is here perambulating the streets, with every shade of colour', tigresses were not always alert to this 'great variety of game', because like 'other carnivora, they are not partial to hunting by daylight'.[43]

This nexus of hybridity, orientalisation, degradation and covert desire marked both an apotheosis of the racialisation of the poor and the onset of a transformation, for from this point the poor assumed a more threatening aspect which could not be adequately theorised using contemporary racial discourse.

Crowds Bred in the Abyss

The predatory prostitute was emblematic of a new and distinctly modern concern that the poor were transgressing the imaginative and spatial boundaries of the metropolis. The prostitute's attraction for urban travellers since the time of Mayhew can only in part be explained by her position within male voyeuristic fantasies; the prostitute also transgressed the gendered boundaries of the metropolis.[44] By asserting an active presence within the public spaces of the city, the prostitute defiantly challenged prevalent norms of female virtue centred on a passive domesticity, and around the body of the prostitute was articulated moral, sexual and medical concern. In the course of the 1870s, anxieties about the transgressive threat of the prostitute were generalized to include the metropolitan poor as a whole:

> The savage class in question comprises the 'roughs' who infest every one of the hundreds of shady slums and blind alleys that, despite metropolitan improvements, still disgrace the great city. We held up our hands in speechless horror and indignation at the time when the scum and dregs of humanity which cling to the bedraggled skirts of Communism committed such frightful ravages in Paris; but it is as certain as that night succeeds day, that we have lurking in our undercurrents a horde of ruffianism fully equal to similar feats of carnage, plunder, and incendiarism, should occasion serve.[45]

Here was signalled something of the transformation in constructions of the poor. Detectable elements of earlier racialised discourses around savagery, dirt and degradation were to be expected, but qualitatively new was the politicisation and spatial reordering of the poor. The modern metropolis, in spite of improvements undertaken as part of a civic mission to rid its streets of the residuum, was found still to be infested by their numbers. Indeed, the suggestion was that their presence had increased to the point at which they could not be contained. No longer savage tribes confined to the racialised spaces of East and South London, the poor were a mob which, guided by the example of the 1871 Paris Commune, threatened in an act of supreme transgression to seize the metropolis as a whole.

This transformation was underpinned by structural change within the metropolis.[46] The social and economic crisis of the 1880s was deeper and more widespread than that of the 1860s. The cyclical depression impacted on a far broader range of occupations; slum clearance schemes and housing reform had done little to solve the chronic problem of working-class housing, let alone the slums; evangelical missions had for the most part been met with indifference and even hostility by the poor; and the spectre appeared of socialist currents in working-class organisation and thought. Incidences of the poor rampaging through the streets of the respectable West End bore witness that the worst fears of mob rule were being realised. All this fostered in the bourgeois consciousness a sense of fragmentation, self-doubt and loss of confidence in inexorable progress at a time of imperial expansion. The attendant 'epistemological crisis ... precipitated changes in the visual image of the city that produced new representations of the self and the Other'.[47]

During the 1880s the metropolitan poor were rediscovered and re-

constituted in ways that defy neat generalisation. The sensational revelations of a new breed of social investigators articulated older discursive
formations with contemporary political and moral concerns. Of these,
Andrew Mearns' *The bitter cry of outcast London* had the greatest impact.[48]
Originally published as a pamphlet of approximately eight thousand words
in 1883, it appeared to have little sociological or literary merit. It had
neither the originality of Mayhew nor the flair of Greenwood; it was
poorly structured, misquoted sources and was based insecurely on an
extremely limited survey of housing in Bermondsey, Ratcliff and Shadwell.
But its unprecedented reception suggests that the pamphlet resonated
powerfully with the growing sense of unease and guilt about the state of
the metropolitan poor.

Mearns highlighted the gulf that was daily widening between the 'lower
classes of the community' and 'all decency and civilization', as a result of
which a 'TERRIBLE FLOOD OF SIN AND MISERY IS GAINING UPON
US'.[49] This population, however, was not racially distinct, but belonged 'as
much as you, to the race for whom Christ died', and, given the appalling
conditions in which they are condemned to exist, they were 'entitled to
credit for not being twenty times more depraved than they are'.[50] If urgent
measures were not taken, then the political consequences would be dire:

> The only check upon communism in this regard is jealousy and not virtue.
> The vilest practices are looked upon with the most matter-of-fact indif-
> ference. The low parts of London are the sink into which the filthy and
> abominable from all parts of the country seem to flow.[51]

And the measures? These from the outset had to be based on a comprehensive collectivism:

> without State interference nothing effectual can be accomplished upon any
> large scale. ... The State must make short work of this iniquitous traffic
> [rack renting], and secure for the poorest the rights of citizenship; the right
> to live in something better than fever dens; the right to live as something
> better than the uncleanest of brute beasts.[52]

This confused and contradictory text best represented the stumbling
attempts to comprehend the nature of a problem that had beset the
Victorian metropolis but which at a time of a crisis of confidence in the
imperial formation assumed an unprecedented political urgency. The flood
of moral depravity evident amongst the lowest sections of the population
had to be stemmed, Mearns contended, by social and political reform lest
the nation as a whole be engulfed by communism.

As the poor demonstrated an increased propensity to transgress spatial
barriers and bring closer the lessons of Paris, so anxiety escalated. H.J.

Goldsmid, travelling among lodging houses, recorded his impressions of discontented dossers:

> We have not been without warnings. When last winter a brutal mob rushed through the streets and looted the shops of the West-end, most people said it was the work of roughs and larrikins whose only object was plunder. They grievously misunderstood the facts. Many – nay most – of the men who took part in the riots of that day came from the low lodging houses, and though the majority were actuated solely by cupidity and greed, there were many a stern, determined man there who believed that in plundering and destroying he was merely executing the righteous wrath of starved, op-pressed, and discontented labour against harsh, bloated, and unsympathetic capital. ... [B]efore very many years have flown we shall be compelled to read in haggard, wolfish faces, robbed of every tender or human expression, to hear in coarse cries of menace, ay, even of lawless triumph, that lesson that has been taught so sharply in other lands than ours – that what might once, not long since, have been reformed, has grown and swelled and gathered force and volume until the torrent can no longer be stemmed, and we are confronted by REVOLUTION.[53]

Events around the 1889 dock strike and the early struggles of new unionism dissipated political anxiety. Fears that an impoverished residuum organised by a socialist-inspired leadership would provoke mob rule were not realised; instead bands of dockers marched in orderly and good-humoured fashion in furtherance of modest demands. The more militant and threatening struggles of gasworkers were defeated by military-style police tactics which enabled employers to bring in large numbers of un-skilled, strike-breaking labourers.[54] But if immediate political fears had receded, the problem remained of incorporating the poor within an interpretive framework for the metropolis as a distinctly modern totality.

The seventeen volumes of Charles Booth's *Life and labour of the people in London*, published between 1889 and 1902, constituted the single most comprehensive and systematic attempt to capture this totality.[55] Fired by a vision of social and moral progress removed from the orthodoxies of contemporary political economy, Booth set out to classify and quantify the metropolitan poor as the first step in formulating ameliorative measures. The focus was on production and distribution, and the multiplicity of social – and to a lesser extent cultural – relations built upon them. As the investigation progressed in a climate of relative political ease, so the diversity and dynamism of the metropolitan experience emerged. Although this challenged convenient polarisations of the poor and respectable so characteristic of previous social inquiry, Booth was unable to break com-pletely with the genre. He and his army of co-workers remained urban travellers inhabiting psychological oppositions between the bourgeois and the low other, carrying with them all the familiar baggage of degeneration, depravity and gender disorder.[56]

The Booth survey was situated uneasily –in some respects it defined the moment – between past racialisations of the poor and modernist impulses to see them as part of the metropolitan totality. The theory of hereditary urban degeneration may have been endowed with a certain authority by the survey,[57] but the theory implied no essential racial separateness; on the contrary, it both generalised and encompassed the poor within the metropolitan, and hence national, whole. While slum dwellers were perceived as degenerate populations whose pathological features were transmitted from one generation to another and who carried contamination with them when forced as a body to migrate, there was little sense in Booth that degeneracy was the product of irreversible hereditary processes.[58] Recommendations for eliminating poverty were moral and socio-economic, not social darwinist. At other times the poor were perceived in terms of a modern experience. Mile End fair was described as a vortex attracting the young, and the East End as a 'rush of human life as fascinating to watch as the current of a river to which human life is so often likened'.[59]

It was only with respect to the wave of Jewish immigration in the 1880s that more familiar racial constructions obtained. Even then there were contradictions. Jews may have possessed characteristic features of a racial other – high cheekbones, thickened lips, darker complexion and unmistakable noses – but they were sober and industrious, private and respectable. 'The Jews', Walkowitz concludes, 'were a peculiar people who eluded and challenged Booth's categories of class and gender Otherness'.[60]

The same ambiguities were evident in much of the considerable literature that addressed the problems posed by this immigration. Thus, while the East End was seen to contain an internal orient larger and more visible than before, there is a subdued sense of moral degradation or political threat. The popular works of Walter Besant went further, actually identifying the *re*generational potential of English culture. In *East London* he observed the 'narrow-chested and pasty-faced Polish Jew', asking one of their scholars if this was the 'race which defied the legions of Titus', or a descendant of 'Joshua's valiant captains'. The scholar answered that 'these are the children of the Ghetto. … Come again in ten years' time. In the free air of Anglo-Saxon rule they will grow; you will not know them again'.[61]

Other writers saw the racialisation of the poor less ambivalently. Arnold White began his publishing career in 1886 with *The problems of a great city*.[62] Here the problems were the 'problems of the race', which had to be resolved through a 'moral revolution' rather than delegation 'to governments or to a clerical caste' lest the 'dark seeds of poisonous and eternal evil' were sown to threaten the empire:

> Distress in London is not the distress of a great city – it is the distress of a great empire. ... The social question in England is shrouded in greater darkness than the social questions of Imperial Germany or Republican France. ... Great as is the sum of poverty and degradation inherited by this generation from that which preceded it, we are making no sensible reductions of this debt to humanity, and are in a fair way to hand down to the next generation greater embarrassment, with more efficient machinery for the manufacture of larger masses of human degradation.[63]

White proposed legislation to sterilise the unfit, ban early marriages and force immigration, which with eugenicist logic he claimed would harmonise with 'the inexorable tendencies of our natural law'. By linking the social crisis caused by the threat of the metropolitan poor to fears in the imperial formation via theories of degeneration, White intensified the racialisation of the poor. He may have been an erratic figure, working in isolation, but he represented an important response to the crisis.

William Booth emerged as part of the same strand of social imperialism; his writings were enormously popular, however, providing a secure financial and ideological basis for the expansion of the Salvation Army. *In darkest England and the way out*, published in 1890, sold 200,000 copies in the first year.[64] The referent was H. Stanley's *In darkest Africa*, in which the explorer described an immense area 'where the rays of sunshine never penetrate, where in the dark, dank air, filled with the steam of the heated morass, human beings dwarfed into pygmies and brutalised into cannibals lurk and live and die'.[65] The parallels between degenerated Africans living in foetid darkness and the metropolitan poor were only too obvious:

> It is a terrible picture, and one that has engraved itself deep on the heart of civilisation. But while brooding over the awful presentation of life as it exists in the vast African forest, it seemed to me only too vivid a picture of many parts of our own land. As there is a darkest Africa is there not also a darkest England? Civilisation, which can breed its own barbarians, does it not also breed its own pygmies?[66]

Within this barbarian population, the racialised female reappeared to occupy a privileged site:

> The lot of a negress in the Equatorial Forest is not, perhaps, a very happy one, but is it so very much worse than that of many a pretty orphan girl in our Christian capital? We talk about the brutalities of the dark ages, and we profess to shudder as we read in books of the shameful exaction of the

rights of feudal superior. And yet here, beneath our very eyes, in our theatres, in our restaurants, and in many other places, unspeakable though it be to name it, the same hideous abuse flourishes unchecked.[67]

The impact of social imperialism was to be felt in the formation of the Edwardian welfare state.[68] But as the century turned, more pressing concerns around continued immigration and the standard of recruits for the Boer War intensified fears that degeneration was consuming the heart of empire.[69] With this more extreme current of racial theory surfaced views that seemed to traverse political boundaries. G. Haw cited with approval Lord Rosebery: 'What is an Empire unless it is pillared on an Imperial race, and what are you doing to allow this Imperial race to be vitiated and poisoned in the dens of crime and horror in which too many of them are reared at this moment?[70]

Epilogue

The complex development of social imperialist and mass-society theories in the twentieth century is beyond the remit of this chapter. In the troubled context of an extended franchise and the failure of social reform to eradicate poverty, the crowd came to represent the hidden presence in modern society of destructive atavistic features – a regressive trend in civilisation which, by signalling the onset of mass irrationality, marked the end of human development. The crowd thus became the dominant site of degeneration, effectively displacing the individual, the family and the 'tribe'; linked to the threat of social chaos and the fall of empire, the crowd was 'a commentary upon modernity itself'.[71] Paradoxically, as Young has noted, these raceless masses, by threatening to erase difference, both asserted and subverted the trope of degeneracy, leading to a more intense and sinister racialisation of the crowd.[72] 'Crowd' and 'abyss', then, lay at the centre of imaginative attempts to appropriate the metropolitan poor at a time of alienation and fragmentation. The abyss was a swamp in which the crowd dwelt, but as a site of existential despair it offered the modern subject an opportunity for renewal.[73]

We have examined the discursive appropriation of the metropolitan poor in the second half of the nineteenth century. In evangelical and journalistic accounts located within the tradition of urban exploration founded by Mayhew, racial coding assumed stridently novel forms, at the heart of which lay the symbolic repertoires of dirt and degeneration. By linking physical appearance to moral and cultural difference the metaphor of dirt gave meaning to and legitimised racial hierarchies; by ascribing innateness the trope of degeneration gave racialisation a sinister and menacing twist.

Degeneration assumed increasing significance as fears of social disorder and imperial decline took hold, and attention turned to internal dangers. Perceived threats in the late 1880s, from the poor and from Jewish immigration, redefined racial boundaries. Social imperialists took up extreme eugenicist stances on the degenerative strains identified within the imperial race, and on the threats posed by the increased presence of the Jewish race. More influential were modernist impulses, the key imaginative sites of which were occupied by the crowd from the abyss.

The shifting and unstable boundaries of racialisation of the poor resulted from attempts to understand the anachronistic presence in the modern metropolis of a population that defied modernity.[74] It was historically coterminous with the emergence of a distinctly modern colonialism characterised by a 'coherently "anthropological" mode of typifying natives'.[75] Race facilitated the imagined interconnectedness of colonial and metropolitan others in the imperial formation as it strove to survey and position them within an objective totality, and hence to assimilate threats to its future. The task to 'find a single, comprehensive principle of explanation which would underpin a rational theodicy of racial privilege and anchor structural inequality within an organic image of the body politic'[76] found urgent application in both domestic and colonial spaces. This process was strategically partial and complex, as a result of which within broad shifts there were continuities, within continuities shifts. None the less, overall the dialectic of capitalist modernisation in asserting the superiority of colonisers over the colonised necessarily constructed inferiority at home; this suggests why the poor were racialised in the first instance and why toward the end of the century, as the forces of modernisation accelerated, racialised boundaries expanded to encompass not only the poor but the masses as a whole.

Notes

1. Warm thanks are due to David Webb for his expert guidance around the outstanding collection on London history held at the Bishopsgate Institute.

2. J. Garwood, *The million peopled city, or One half of the people of London made known to the other half,* Werthleim and Macintosh, 1853, p. 263.

3. J. Hollingshead, *Ragged in London in 1861,* Smith, Elder & Co., 1861, p. 8.

4. J. Greenwood, *In strange company; being the experiences of a roving correspondent,* King, 1874, p. 14.

5. W. Phillips, *The wild tribes of London,* Ward and Lock, 1855, p. 12.

6. J. Hollingshead, *Ragged London,* p. 44.

7. W. Cosens, *London dens and mission work among them; a lecture,* Rivingtons, 1863, p. 7. Note that Prince Albert had died of typhus two years earlier.

8. G. Godwin, *London shadows; a glance at the 'homes' of the thousands,* Routledge, 1854, p. 1.

9. G. Godwin, *Town swamps and social bridges,* Routledge, 1859, reprinted with an

introduction by A.D. King in 1972 by Leicester University Press. Although swamps referred most immediately to the housing conditions of the poor, they were a metaphor for a whole range of related social pathologies including crime, poverty, disease, ignorance and superstition. 'Bridges' were the institutional infrastructures required in an urban society to combat them, particularly adequate schooling and public health. Godwin's manifesto was 'Drain the Swamps and increase the Bridges' (p. 102).

10. Ibid, p. 56.

11. P. Stallybrass and A. White, in *Politics and poetics of transgression*, Methuen, 1986, actually refer only to the city, but as I will attempt to demonstrate, the arguments apply equally to the colonies. See also the useful discussion on the materiality of dirt in the bourgeois imagination in P. Cohen, 'The perversions of inheritance', in P. Cohen and H.S. Bains (eds), *Multiracist Britain*, Macmillan, 1988, pp. 72–3.

12. Stallybrass and White, *Politics and poetics of transgression*, p. 135.

13. A. McClintock, *Imperial leather. Race, gender and sexuality in the colonial contest*, Routledge, 1995, p. 61.

14. Stallybrass and White, *Politics and poetics of transgression*, p. 145.

15. Note that in a curious inversion, collectors of dog-shit described in Mayhew were known as pure finders.

16. D. Lorimer, *Colour, class and the Victorians: English attitudes to the negro in the mid-Victorian period*, Leicester University Press, 1978, pp. 67–8; K. Malik, *The meaning of race: race, history and culture in Western society*, Macmillan, 1996, p. 91.

17. J. Grant, *Lights and shadows of London life*, Saunders and Otley, 1841, p. 164.

18. Phillips, *Wild tribes of London*, p. 10.

19. R. Rowe, *Picked up in the streets, or Struggles for life amongst the London poor*, Allen & Co., 1880, p. 4.

20. D. Rice-Jones, *In the slums. Pages from the notebook of a London Diocesan home missionary*, Nisbet, 1884, pp. 69, 149.

21. See the useful A. R. JanMohamed, 'The economy of the manichean allegory: the function of racial difference in colonialist literature', *Critical Inquiry*, 12, 1985.

22. R. Inden, *Imagining India*, Blackwell, 1992.

23. This is a reworking of David Lloyd's formulation in 'Race under representation', in *Oxford Literary Review*, 13, 1991.

24. Ibid., p. 77.

25. Cited in ibid., pp. 76–7, and in M.J. Hickman, *Religion, class and identity. The state, the Catholic Church and the Education of the Irish in Britain*, Avebury, 1995, p. 49. These are two of very few examples of where the term 'white' was used. 'White' was more generally noted by its absence in racial discourses – an indication of the lack of any felt need to subject it to scrutiny. This is a silence that has recently been broken, albeit in a different context, by T.W. Allen, *The invention of the white race. Racial oppression and social control*, Verso, 1994, and D. Roediger, *Towards the abolition of whiteness. Essays on race, politics and working-class history*, Verso, 1994.

26. The most impressive work on this is to be found in L.P. Curtis, *Apes and angels. The Irishman in Victorian caricature*, Smithsonian Institution Press, 1997, particularly Chapter 4, 'Simianizing the Irish Celt'. This is a revised version of the 1971 edition, having a useful new chapter – 'Historical revisionism and constructions of Paddy and Pat' – in which Curtis, drawing on recent writings from postcolonial theory, effectively challenges critiques of the earlier work.

27. Ibid., p. 121.

28. It was at this time that the term 'nigger' was widely used to describe not only blacks and the Irish, but also Indians (J. Walvin, 'Recurring themes: white images of black life during and after slavery', *Slavery and abolition*, vol. 5, 1984, pp. 118–40.

29. G. Stedman Jones, *Outcast London. A study in the relationship between classes in Victorian society*, Oxford University Press, 1971, p. 15.

30. D. Pick, *Faces of degeneration. A European disorder, c. 1848–1914*, Cambridge University Press, 1989, pp. 38–9; see also Malik, *The meaning of race*, pp. 109–14.

31. Pick, *Faces of degeneration*, p. 7.

32. Ibid., p. 21.

33. Malik, *The meaning of race*, p. 111.

34. R.J.C. Young, *Colonial desire. Hybridity in theory, culture and race*, Routledge (1995).

35. Ibid., p. 19.

36. Phil Cohen has used the notion of an internal orient to describe 'a dark mysterious continent whose dense localisms formed the heart of That Other England, where the Empire was already preparing to strike back', *Demos*, no. 6, 1995, p. 6.

37. J. Salter, *The Asiatics in England. Sketches of sixteen years' work among orientals*, Seeley & Co., 1873, p. ii.

38. Ibid., pp. 21–2.

39. T. Archer, *The pauper, the thief and the convict. Sketches of some of their homes, haunts, and habits*, Groombridge & Sons, 1865, p. 133. James Greenwood was also a regular visitor; see his 'An opium smoke in Tiger Bay', *In strange company*, and 'A visit to Tiger Bay', in *The wilds of London*, Chatto and Windus, 1974.

40. J.C. Parkinson, *Places and people, being studies from life*, Tinsley Bros, 1869, pp. 25–6. This was a collection of articles previously published in Dickens' *All the year round*, *Tinsley's Magazine*, and the *Daily News*.

41. J. Ewing Ritchie, *Days and nights in London; or, Studies in black and grey*, Tinsley, 1880, pp. 178–9.

42. Anon, *Wonderful London. Its lights and shadows of humour and sadness*, Tinsley, 1878, p. 337.

43. Ibid., p. 339.

44. See J. Walkowitz, *City of dreadful delight. Narratives of sexual danger in late-Victorian London*, Virago, 1994; and E. Wilson, *The sphinx in the city. Urban life, the control of disorder, and women*, Virago, 1991.

45. Anon., *Wonderful London*, p. 215.

46. G. Stedman Jones, *Outcast London*, especially Chapter 16.

47. Walkowitz, *City of dreadful delight*, p. 38.

48. A. Mearns, *The bitter cry of outcast London. An inquiry into the condition of the abject poor*, Clarke & Co., 1883, reprinted with an introduction by A.S Wohl by Leicester University Press, 1970. Mearns was a member of the London Congregational Union, but was aided by members of the London City Mission and the East London Tabernacle. The introduction provides a measured assessment of the impact of the pamphlet.

49. Ibid., p. 56. This was the only phrase in the pamphlet to be capitalised.

50. Ibid., p. 60. This was a misquote from one of George Sims' articles that appeared earlier in the year in *Pictorial World*.

51. Ibid., p. 61.

52. Ibid., p. 69.

53. H.J. Goldsmid, *Dottings of a dosser, being revelations of the inner life of low London lodging houses*, Fisher Unwin, 1886.

54. See Stedman Jones, *Outcast London*, and my 'London over the border. A study of West Ham during rapid growth, 1870–1910', unpublished Ph.D thesis, University of Cambridge, 1984.

55. C. Booth, *Life and labour of the people in London*, Macmillan, 1887–1902. For useful critical assessments of Booth, see D. Englander, 'Comparisons and contrasts:

Henry Mayhew and Charles Booth as social investigators', in D. Englander and R. O'Day (eds), *Retrieved riches. Social investigation in Britain, 1880–1914*, Scolar, 1995; Stedman Jones, *Outcast London*; Walkowitz, *City of dreadful delight*.

56. Walkowitz, *City of dreadful delight*, p. 33.

57. Stedman Jones, *Outcast London*, p. 128.

58. The point is well made by Jose Harris that the widespread currency of the language of degeneracy did not always reflect a commitment to the intellectual framework of social darwinism. See J. Harris, 'Between civic virtue and social darwinism: the concept of the residuum', in Englander and O'Day (eds) *Retrieved riches*.

59. Booth, *Life and labour*, vol. 1, p. 64, cited in Walkowitz, *City of dreadful delight*, p. 34.

60. Walkowitz, *City of dreadful delight*, p. 36. For the description of Jews in Booth, see D. Englander, 'Booth's Jews: the presentation of Jews and Judaism' in *Life and Labour of the People in London*', *Victorian Studies*, vol. 32, 1989.

61. W. Besant, *East London*, Chatto and Windus, 1901, p. 199.

62. A. White, *The problems of a great city*, Remington, 1886. A wide traveller with a deep interest in social problems, White had contested Mile End as a Tory candidate in 1886, and was to contest Tyneside in 1892 and 1895. His racism in publications such as *The modern Jew*, *English democracy*, and *Efficiency and empire* became increasingly shrill. He was sent to prison in 1903 for contempt of court, but was liberated by public subscription, and gave evidence to the inquiry which established the 1905 Aliens Act.

63. Ibid., p. 12.

64. W. Booth, *In darkest England and the way out*, Salvation Army, 1890. The book was, in part at least, ghost written by W.E. Stead, editor of the *Pall Mall Gazette*, who had five years previously been responsible for one of the most successful endeavours of sensational journalism. His investigation of juvenile prostitution in the 'Maiden tribute of modern Babylon' had an estimated circulation of one and a half million copies. The whole episode is well discussed in Walkowitz, *City of dreadful delight*.

65. Booth, *In darkest England*, p. 9.

66. Ibid., p. 10.

67. Ibid., p. 13.

68. Stedman Jones, *Outcast London*, p. 312.

69. The metaphor of the heart of empire became popular, particularly in titles of books such as C.F.G. Masterman (ed.), *The heart of empire. Discussions of problems of modern city life in England, with an essay on imperialism*, Fisher Unwin, 1902; G. Haw, *Britain's homes. A study of the empire's heart-disease*, The Clarion Press, 1902; and L. Cope Cornford, *The canker at the heart. Being studies from the life of the poor*, Grant Richards, 1905.

70. G. Haw, *Britain's homes*, p. 53.

71. Pick, *Faces of degeneration*, pp. 4, 223.

72. Young, *Colonial desire*, p. 19.

73. See my 'Sensation of the abyss. The urban poor and modernity', in M. Nava and A. O'Shea (eds), *Modern times. Reflections on a century of English modernity*, Routledge, 1996.

74. For a discussion of the premodern character of casual labour throughout the nineteenth century see my 'Sensation of the abyss'.

75. N. Thomas, *Colonialism's culture: anthropology, travel and government*, Polity Press, 1994, p. 49. The few brief references I have made to this important work rather understate the influence it has had on the development of my thought in this piece.

76. Cohen, 'The perversions of inheritance', p. 18.

6

An Immigration Offence

Patricia Tuitt[1]

Bugdaycay, Vilvarajah, Khan and Sukhvinder walked among an uneven line of travellers – holiday-makers, workers, students, the occasional thespian, singer or scribe – with documents that located them within this free, eclectic traffic. So long as they too could be silent and let their documents speak, their fears could not be detached from their fantasy. For that moment, destiny lay in invention. Whether through entering the hallowed walls of a British university, bargaining their skills or simply resting upon their leisure, they were able to avoid the pitiful retelling of a story that convention had taught its listeners to disbelieve. Nor would they soon confront again their fading trust in those that govern.[2]

It was a moment that would soon pass. If this disguise of freedom, of independence, of means, created a kind of refuge, it was transitory. When extrinsic evidence of nationality, citizenship or origin becomes a 'legitimate' guide to rights of entry and settlement, the time that it takes for official indifference to turn to scrutiny, to curdle into suspicion and crystallise into certainty that something is not quite right with the history related is all too short.[3]

What gave the lie to these stories was never made clear. Perhaps it was no more than the stamp of craft upon the passports, the subconscious revealing its guilt, the vagaries of chance, or the story-teller being too much in thrall to her own history. No matter what, that brief moment was to turn hopes of some kind of refuge into certainty of confinement. From this enclosure an investigation into an immigration offence would begin – an investigation that has given rise to many publications. It is with the hope of offering a very different account of an immigration offence that this narrative is written.[4]

Beginnings

There were no spaces left. Impossible to imagine that any but a very few would find physical safety, even fewer a degree of dignified survival.

Countries in the South had traded their inhabitants to an optimum degree: the West neither needed nor desired such trade. The borders hummed – a physical but intangible presence, the manifestation of a diagnosis of a sickness which many feel will only be contained, never cured.

For many these obstacles were a glorious (and ludicrous) gloss upon their confinement. Weariness and fatigue had combined with physical sickness and malnutrition to ensure that refuge was, at best, no more than a village away – at worst beyond mortal reach. Young and old women, young girls and babies bound together in these roughly pieced-together camps, all routinely herded on to some other place whose superiority, although assumed, was seldom apparent.[5]

The safe places of the West were a dream away for any that dared such indulgence, for even if will and imagination were to put wings on feet that were weak with suffering, there was no assured path out for those whose pain reflected merely the vicissitudes of the world. Their relief must come *in situ*; it would come through slow and bitter negotiation and in the guise of bags of corn. And humanity would live another day because the food had come.[6]

In another time, another place, humanity would be seen in the guise of the 'stranger at the gate.' Juan could see his face dimly reflected in the face of the stranger. His body, although bruised, was whole. There was no gnawing ache at the pit of his stomach, no weakness in his mind, no burden in his arms, and as a man in this culture of men, he could claim a kind of spatial liberation. He had little knowledge, but a strong, almost religious, belief that in some other world – one that was more than an image in his head, was tangible, drawn upon a map – what he did, what he was, was neither shame nor transgression. He would be enfolded and protected.[7]

He was not wanted here but he knew he would be neither kept nor given away. Everything would be done – was done – to prevent his departure. He could not request entry in the ordinary way for he was nothing and no-one in this strange between-world of immigration control. He could not seek recognition or welcome in any place of asylum, for the person he would eventually become did not yet exist. Indeed for now nothing existed save that which could be fashioned. There was no place to go, no means to get there and no one capable of leaving. All was dependent upon first creating an identity that would allow entry into the moral, conscious world of states.[8]

Thoughts turn to alienage and display, an alien world whose material physicality, so often conjured up, is strangely, openly absent. An insubstantial realm constituted through the language of hope and despair, humanity and freedom, or metaphors of war and peace, food and hunger, refugees and economic migrants, stalwarts and parasites. A world of shifting oppositions. One that welcomes the refugee but cannot move to aid her sanctuary. In which the suffering of peoples is supposedly the world's primary concern but in which a fence is placed around every arena of crisis in order to box the sufferers in. And where the heroic effort of those who escape is weighed in coin. A world consciously unregulated – ironically in the name of immigration control. A space between the place of persecution and the site of asylum where an altered ethical and moral order prevails. A constructed realm that compels – almost obsessionally – toward further fabrication. Increasingly it stands apart, without territory, drawn from the imaginings of those whose thoughts of refuge are radically dissimilar. Magnificent in its uncoordinated ugliness and decadence.

Leaving

Today an identity was purchased. With this mythical assembly comes reality. Belief was then but a short step away, constituting much more than a state of mind that could be abandoned upon a bare command, but an 'active process of forgetting'. A process measurable in a number of material discards of that from which an inner identity had been constructed: family, whose absence must needs be explained; friends who became enemies of this present ambition. Home, work, social allegiances discarded in favour of a temporary edifice within which would grow a future that, it was hoped, would, in turn, embrace the past.[9]

And with this (metamorphosis) other things took shape and came into focus, as if hidden behind a structure penetrable only through a special agency. In the space beyond Juan's territory – before just an empty vastness impossible of habitation – there emerged shelters, distant and few, but places wherein the elements could be confounded. The paths to these places, though still steep and incomplete, were penetrable. And faint, but discernible upon the fresh canvas on which this was drawn, stood Juan foregrounded. These possibilities of escape, sanctuary and asylum – now crudely real – were built upon a fragmented myth represented in the little booklet in Juan's hand and the stories in his head.

Before the Law

Before the law these fragments dispersed. Before the wholesome image of the law's rational being, the chaos that was Juan fell away and was silenced. His character was set within the text of the law which for three decades or more had sought to establish normative standards of behaviour for any person who presents herself for entry at a foreign port. In this process the chaotic imaginings of the victim of trauma had been subjected to a higher realm of pseudo-scientific rationality. Inevitably something is left behind, replaced by a canonical text whose authority rests upon the absolute conviction that a person can be known by her desire to circumvent immigration procedures and controls; that such a desire has a pathological cause, constituting not merely a deviation from the norm but an 'offence' with criminal properties.[10]

Largely abstracted from any scientific or psychological knowledge bearing upon the causes and consequences of a refugee's neurosis, a discrepant, contingent world is bypassed. In its place is erected a vast ahistorical, non-contextual epistemology that cannot hope to know the refugee. A violent civilising process is put in train in which the deviant strains of the asylum law context are simply cut away.[11] In the abstract world created by these aesthetic categories, the asylum-seeker assumes a coherent identity. She comes before the authorities with 'clean hands.' She is prompt to seek the protection of the state and to reveal in minutiae the processes of her suffering and salvation. She is characteristically frank and open, and, if necessity compels temporary involvement in deceit, she is quick to own her transgressions and seek the indulgence of the law.

Before the law, to come to a state to seek asylum is to come in a state of nature,[12] for past torture, persecution or inhuman treatment or punishment at the hands of a similar authority is erased and does not inform the actions and motivations of the idealised subject fashioned within the canonical text. The denial of self, of personality, culture, context, time and space characterizes the relative roles of the asylum-seeker and host state officials as they develop in the forced and intimate atmosphere within which an immigration offence is investigated, a relationship in which one stands as the blank page, the other the scribe.

Testimony and Interrogation

The room represented the void Juan had become. There was nothing upon which memory could become fixed and unlocked. Encouraging neither thought nor speech, it stood receptive merely to the retelling of a smooth linear history. There stood the authority that Juan could not speak to and who could not speak to him. Between them stood the one who was the voice of both – one upon whom too much of Juan's hope and safety depended.[13]

As if on cue, memory slips away. Time and space stand hostage to no more than an elusive grasp of reality. Fear becomes all that is real – palpable and all-encompassing. What is conveyed through the myriad verbal and non-verbal modes of communication conforms little to the constructed order that sits so consciously over investigative proceedings. Yet the disciplinarian strand of the 'Father' compels some order over this abstract narrative; a need to rewrite it for the general populace, to smooth its structure, explain away its crazy experimentation with time and its unconscious self-contradiction. To relegate it, not within some subtle place between memory and imagination from which these symptoms of neurosis manifest themselves, but to some deviant realm of lies and deceit – aligning Juan with other 'case histories' of 'offenders' who, veiled behind spurious claims of torture and persecution, seek to advance a claim upon a state that had long denied them.[14]

Some order had been obtained after three decades of conscious resignification of late claims, externally or internally inconsistent testimony, and concealment, so that the motivations, actions and omissions of the victim of trauma, losing their multiplicity of symbolic meanings, become one, at one with the deviant strain of postmodern immigration pirates. The danger of the law looking to one side and recognizing chaos is avoided, and the child's muddled interior is made as whole as her outward limbs.[15]

Conclusion

The application before the High Court had failed. In those few hours, the stillest and quietest of all, gathered a memory that had become once more a promise – remote, suspended, without the concrete shape or substance of this very temporary and remote host.[16]

There was no persecution in this prison. Only at this moment could this be believed, for the time had come to leave it. To leave in the knowledge that the 'detention of refugees during the consideration of their claim cannot be considered, even arguably, to be a breach of the Convention'.[17] A judicial pronouncement is made, but not to Juan, for in the ethical time-span of the courts Juan had already gone. The statement was not present, but contingent, modelled for those who, in future, in an abstract setting, might conceivably wish to learn of the unique immunity of the British prison, for those within could not comprehend the 'innocence of law'[18] in their fate. It was a jurisprudential trope said with all the passion and certainty of an epistemology that confronts a discrepant world by excluding the possibility of inner doubt and creating an outer world of chaos.

So that we doubt Juan from the moment that he, without host, friend or family and with documents that can serve as his lifeline only if they are not true, is placed in detention.[19] And we doubt him each day he is in detention although we do not know when he will be free.[20] We doubt him though many echo his claim, and we believe our silence over the nature of his transgressions in preference to his voice that shouts 'I have been persecuted.'[21]

Notes

1. Law Department, Birkbeck College, University of London.

2. Bugdaycay (1987) AC 514; Vilvarajah (1990) IMM AR 457; Khan (1995) NLJR 216 and Sukhvinder (1992) IMM AR 14 sought asylum in the United Kingdom, and on various grounds were deemed illegal entrants. It is argued that their cases illustrate the rather dangerous application of the concept of illegal entry – now given statutory form by virtue of sections 4 and 5 of the Asylum Act 1996 – to asylum-seekers. Illegal entry can be established by proof of 'any deception by words or conduct as to fact or present intention' (Macdonald and Blake 1997: 102). Establishing deception by one who presents a false passport, even without any accompanying verbal representation, or misrepresents their reasons for seeking leave (for example, by claiming visitor status rather than refugee status) is relatively straightforward, despite the Khawaja decision that denied that persons seeking leave within the UK were placed under a 'duty of candour'(1984) AC 74. It has long been argued that asylum-seekers may misrepresent their intentions without wishing to deceive the authorities. Asylum-seekers are often reluctant to make a claim for asylum in advance of receiving legal advice (Morrison 1998). Fear of authority may also explain a failure to disclose on the part of the asylum-seeker. (For discussion see Dignam 1992: 335–6; Anker 1987: 4).

3. Fear of 'bogus' asylum-seekers has resulted in the intense scrutiny of migrants, particularly those travelling from countries deemed to produce a disproportionate number of asylum-seekers. A number of statutory provisions have been enacted as part of this general 'surveillance' culture. The paragraph alludes in particular to Section 12 of the Asylum and Immigration Appeals Act 1993 that permits the imposition of transit visas, taking account of 'nationality, citizenship or origin.' Carrier's liability legislation, enacted in the UK and in most countries in western Europe, also has the effect of vesting in a small, insufficiently accountable body (airline officials) the power to make assessments concerning the bona fides of those seeking asylum. The Immigration Act 1971, schedule 2, confers powers on immigration officials to 'examine' those seeking entry into the UK with a view to establishing whether they have a ground of entry. This 'examination' includes a right to board carriers and seize relevant documents. (For discussion of the latter point, see Stanley 1992: 126).

4. A finding of illegal entry will, almost certainly lead to the detention of the asylum-seeker pending examination of the substantive merits of his/her claim. The Home Office justifies detention in these circumstances on the grounds that the asylum-seeker/illegal entrant 'would not comply with the terms of temporary admission'(see Amnesty International 1996: 64). Of particular concern is the fact that asylum-seekers are too often detained with criminal offenders (Amnesty International 1996: 105). For one of the most comprehensive reports on the detention of asylum-seekers in the UK, see Dunstan (1994).

5. It is argued here that official discourse on the illegal entry of asylum-seekers is confined to a particular psychological moment in the asylum-seeker's immediate history, when the accumulation of her traumatic experiences manifests itself in a 'slippage' in her story. Such a narrow focus will almost certainly lead to the conclusion that the behaviour exhibited is revealing of something other than the ordinary neurosis of the asylum-seeker. It is argued that a more holistic approach to the question of an 'intent to deceive' should be adopted. Such an approach would locate the beginnings of the asylum-

seeker's 'dilemma' when confronting receiving authorities in the well-documented crisis in the institution of asylum brought about by the increasing incidence of civil unrest. That the refugee problem has proved to be intractable is amply evidenced by the fact that many refugees seek asylum in states producing their own refugees (see Abdullahi 1994: 4).

6. Two important aspects of the refugee law regime are raised here. First, the construction of the refugee as a moving entity within both legal and other sociological discourses has been a significant preoccupation of the present writer. This perception is most obviously reflected in Article 1.A (2) of the Convention Relating to the Status of Refugees, 1951 that defines a refugee, *inter alia*, as one who is 'outside (his) country of nationality' (Tuitt, forthcoming). This perception is challenged by modern refugee-producing phenomena, such as famine, drought and other natural disaster, which tend to immobilize the refugee population. The second issue alluded to in the paragraph is the common position adopted by governments as well as commentators on refugee law that the refugee definition, focusing principally upon 'persecution' as being the legal cause of the refugee's disenfranchisement from her/his state of origin or domicile (see Article 1.A. (2)), excludes those victims of indiscriminate violence (civil wars) and natural disaster. In response to this, aid agencies have been forced sometimes to go beyond the traditional boundaries of their mandate in order to assist the refugee populations, for example UNCHR 1995, chapter 11.

7. Much of this narrative is very loosely anchored around the case of R v Secretary of State for the Home Department *ex parte* Juan Carlos Arias (1997) IMM AR 7. However, considerable poetic licence is taken. Juan, a citizen of Ecuador, was found to have travelled through Miami in search of asylum in the UK. His application was 'certified'(deemed unfounded) under schedule 2 (2) of the Asylum Act 1996 on the basis that the US authorities ought to have considered his substantive application for asylum. The case is particularly interesting because it was argued (ultimately without success) that the US was unsafe for asylum-seekers because their alleged 'practice' of detaining asylum-seekers amounted to persecution of a 'social group' (refugees) contrary to Article 1.A. (2) of the 1951 Convention. The case puts in dispute the conventional line between the transgressors and upholders of immigration laws. It is no coincidence that a male asylum-seeker is the focus here. In recent years there has been much scholarly debate over the position of women within the asylum process. Men, it is argued, have benefited most from the institution of asylum, because of cultural factors – men have a greater ability to travel to seek asylum; Kaplan 1996 at p. 45 speaks of the 'relentless gendering of expatriation as masculine' – and because of the substantive content of the refugee definition. For an excellent analysis of the latter, see Castel (1992). See also Tuitt (1997 and forthcoming).

8. Refugee law, it is said, is 'profoundly state-centered' (Aleinikoff 1992). Once a putative refugee has crossed state borders, she/he is eligible for the unique protection of the law. Whilst the refugee's disenfranchisement from her state of nationality triggers international protection, the refugee has somewhat dubious status under international law in cases where her state of origin or domicile cannot or will not protect her but she has not succeeded in crossing international borders (see Goodwin-Gill 1997). Many refugees succeed in exiting their countries of origin only through the employment of so-called 'immigration racketeers.' John Morrison notes that this often occurs at 'great danger' to the refugee (Goodwin-Gill 1997, chapter 2).

9. The final sentence alludes to the concept of 'family unity' that allows those granted refugee status to bring their dependents to the asylum state. The concept does not derive its authority from the Convention, but through the practices of states.

10. Entering the United Kingdom 'by means which include deception' is now an offence under Section 4 of the Asylum Act 1996. On summary conviction a person is liable to a fine or a maximum prison sentence of six months, or both.

11. In this essay the term 'neurosis' is used in the Lacanian sense to encompass a broad range of nervous disorders. Lacan views these 'disorders' as being the 'normal' state of an individual (see Evans 1996: 123). Employing this understanding, the common psychological condition of refugees, which manifests itself in, for example, lapses of memory and fear and evasion of authority, is a perfectly rational condition, exacerbated in victims of trauma. Dignam attributes the inability of many refugees to give a 'coherent account of their experiences' to this condition: 'gaps in memory, confusion, problems in concentration, shame and anxiety all make it difficult to piece a story together' (Dignam 1992: 335-6).

12. A state in which all history, culture and experience is erased. Rawls (1972) places the members of his hypothetical community in this state in order to posit certain fundamental human rights standards.

13. The increasing recourse to interpreters in refugee inquiries has given rise to some academic debate over their responsibilities in other branches of the law, e.g. the tort of negligence. In Patel (1986) IMM AR 208, J. Webster highlighted the dangers of 'adverse findings' in situations where different cultural practices and understandings are mediated through interpreters.

14. Here the writer evokes the idea of Lacan's 'symbolic Father'. 'The symbolic Father is not a real being but a position, a function – the function is none other than that of imposing law' (Evans 1996: 62). In the Lacanian sense 'the law' is not reducible to the normative system bearing that name, however. The imposition of the 'law' is the imposition of some order, structure or discipline on that which is considered undisciplined, or 'split'.

15. Critical legal scholars have drawn upon the Lacanian concept of the 'mirror stage' process of identification in the analysis of law. The law, perceiving itself as whole, rational and objective, is unable to identify with anything outside its self-image. Thus begins an aggressive process of identification in which the 'objects' of the law are forced to conform to that image in order to gain recognition under the law (Bowie 1991).

16. Once an application for asylum is certified on the basis that the claimant travelled through a third, safe country, an appeal against the certification is no longer exercisable within the UK by virtue of section 3(2) of the Asylum Act 1996. It follows that an appeal can only be exercised from the refugee's state of origin or a third state. The practice of limiting the right to an in-country appeal – a feature of UK asylum laws except for a three-year period between the enactment of the Immigration and Asylum Appeals Act 1993 (section 8) and the 1996 Act – results, according to Douzinas and Warrington, in the constant suspension of justice: 'the time for justice is never fully present, but always still to come in a promised but deferred future ... in the refugee's case the deferral ensures that the law will not come face to face with the other'(Douzinas and Warrington 1994: 229). In these circumstances, Juan's only recourse was an action for judicial review. His action was based upon two substantive grounds: that the claim for asylum was wrongly certified since he had not 'entered' Miami and therefore, had no opportunity to bring a claim for asylum before the US authorities. On the basis of this argument the UK ought to have considered the substantive merits of his asylum claim. Juan also argued that the UK authorities would be in breach of their obligations under the Geneva Convention if they returned him to the US authorities whom, it was alleged, operated a 'policy' of detaining refugees which amounted to 'persecution' (imprisonment) on the grounds of social group membership, arguing that refugees

constituted a social group for the purposes of Article 1.A. (2) of the Geneva Convention Relating to the Status of Refugees, 1951.

17. Per J. Collins in R v Secretary of State for the Home Department *ex parte* Juan Carlos Arias (1997), p. 389.

18. The term is Fitzpatrick's (1987).

19. 'The two most commonly cited 'reasons' for detention were that the applicant arrived without documentation or with forged documents and the applicant has no relatives in the UK' (Dunstan 1994: 25).

20. The Home Office does not keep statistics on the average length of time asylum-seekers are detained. Dunstan suggests that the average period is over five months. Some asylum-seekers in his study were detained for more than ten months (Dunstan 1994: 17).

21. The failure of the Home Office to give adequate reasons for detaining asylum-seekers has been widely criticised. Dunstan argues that this omission constitutes 'a significant impediment to any legal challenge' (Dunstan 1994: 17).

Bibliography

Abdullahi, A. (1992) 'The Refugee Crisis in Africa as a Crisis of the Institution of State' in *International Journal of Refugee Law*.

Aleinikoff, A. (1992) 'State Centred Refugee Law: From Resettlement to Containment' in *Michigan Journal of International Law*.

Amnesty International (1996) *Cell Culture: The Detention and Imprisonment of Asylum-Seekers in the UK*, London: Amnesty International.

Anker, D. (1987) 'Discretionary Asylum: A Protection Remedy for Refugees Under the Act of 1980', in *Virginia Journal of International Law*, vol. 28, no. 1.

Asylum and Immigration Appeals Act, 1993 (UK).

Asylum Act, 1996 (UK).

Bowie, M. (1991) *Lacan*, London: Fontana (Fontana Modern Masters series).

Bugdaycay v Secretary of State for the Home Department (1987) IMM AR 250.

Castel, J. (1992) 'Rape, Sexual Assault and the Meaning of Persecution', in *International Journal of Refugee Law*.

Convention Relating to the Status of Refugees, 28 June 1951, 189 UNTS 150.

Dignam, Q. (1992) 'The Burden and the Proof: Torture and Testimony in the Determination of Refugee Status in Australia, in *International Journal of Refugee Law*.

Douzinas, C. and Warrington, R. (1994) *Justice (Mis) Carried: The Ethics and Aesthetics of the Law*, Hemel Hempstead: Harvester Wheatsheaf.

Dunstan, R. (1994) *Prisoners Without a Voice: Asylum Seekers Detained in the UK*, London: Amnesty International.

Evans, D. (1996) *An Introductory Dictionary of Lacanian Psychoanalysis*, London: Routledge.

Fitzpatrick, P. (1987) 'Racism and the Innocence of law', in P. Fitzpatrick and A. Hunt (eds), *Critical Legal Studies*, Oxford: Basil Blackwell.

Kaplan, C. (1996) *Questions of Travel: Postmodern Discourses of Displacement*, Duke University Press.

Macdonald, I. and N. Blake (1997) *Immigration Law and Practice. Fourth Edition Supplement*, London: Butterworths.

Morrison, J. (1998) *The Cost of Survival: Stowaways and the Trafficking of Refugees to Britain*, London: British Refugee Council.

R v Secretary of State for the Home Department *ex parte* Khan (1995) NLJR 216.

R v Secretary of State for the Home Department *ex parte* Juan Carlos Arias (1997) IMM AR 385.

Rawls, J. (1972) *A Theory of Justice*, Cambridge, Mass.: Harvard University Press.

Sokha (Sukhvinder) v Secretary of State for the Home Department (1992) IMM AR 14.

Stanley, A. (1992) 'The Legal Status of International Zones: The British Experience with Particular Reference to Asylum-Seekers' in *Immigration and Nationality Law and Practice*.

Tuitt, P. (1997) 'Human Rights and Refugees', in *International Journal of Human Rights*.

— (forthcoming) 'Rethinking the Refugee Concept', in F. Nicholson and P. Twomey (eds), *Refugee Rights and Realities*, Cambridge: Cambridge University Press.

UNHCR (1995) *The State of the World's Refugees*, Oxford: Oxford University Press.

Vilvarajah and Another v Secretary of State for the Home Department (1990) IMM AR 457.

7

As If Being a Refugee Isn't Hard Enough: the Policy of Exclusion

Alice Bloch

This chapter examines the social and economic position of refugees. Drawing on data from a survey in the London Borough of Newham, I will look at citizenship rights, English language skills, labour market participation, the migration process and social networks, all factors that affect the settlement of refugees.

Background: Refugee Migration and Policy Responses

Refugee migration to Britain is not a new phenomenon. People have sought refuge in Britain for hundreds of years. But the policy responses to it have become increasingly restrictive during the course of the twentieth century.

Until the end of the nineteenth century, refugee migration to Britain was largely unrestricted, because asylum served both an economic and a political function (Schuster and Solomos 1999). Emigration to the colonies and the United States meant that Britain was, for the most part, a country of net emigration (Coleman 1995). Refugees helped to meet the labour shortfall brought about by emigration and the increasing demand for labour due to the industrial revolution and the resultant economic booms. However, increased Jewish migration from Eastern Europe in the 1880s, coupled with economic recession, resulted in the first piece of immigration legislation, the 1905 Aliens Act (Cohen 1994).

The twentieth century has seen numerous pieces of legislation designed to curtail immigration into Britain (Miles and Clearly 1993; Solomos 1993). This legislation was initially concerned to restrict migration from the Commonwealth rather than refugees; the Commonwealth Immigrants Act 1962 was the first major restriction.

By this time, a clear distinction had emerged in official thinking between refugees and immigrants. Immigrants were black and came from former colonies and the Commonwealth (regardless of their motives for leaving), while refugees were white and came from Communist regimes (regardless of their motives for leaving) (Schuster and Solomos 1999: 57–8).

In 1968, the Commonwealth Immigration Act was passed by Parliament in just three days amid fears of large numbers of East African Asians exercising their right as UK passport holders to migrate to Britain from Kenya after the end of colonial rule. The 1971 Commonwealth Immigration Act restricted the entrance to Britain of non-patrials, including UK passport holders. The Act narrowed the definition of British citizenship, and this reduced the flow of labour migration to Britain. Layton-Henry argues that the legislation 'devalued British citizenship by creating two classes of citizens: one subject to immigration controls and the other not' (Layton-Henry 1992: 53). The 1981 British Nationality Act came into force in 1983 and was criticised for reinforcing racial discrimination (Layton-Henry 1984). The effect of the Act was to exclude British citizens, mostly of Asian origin, from living in Britain. The legislation in the 1960s, 1970s and early 1980s meant that migration to Britain became increasingly restricted to refugees and asylum-seekers, and those seeking entry on the basis of family reunion.

Government policy towards refugees and asylum-seekers during the course of the twentieth century has varied. However, it is only with the increase in refugees and asylum-seekers from Asia, Africa and Latin America in the 1970s, coinciding with a decline in the economy, that immigration rules and new legislative measures were put in place to reduce the number of asylum-seekers entering Britain. Visa requirements were made compulsory for nationals of refugee-producing countries such as Sri Lanka in 1985, Turkey in 1989 and Uganda in 1991. The Immigration (Carriers Liability) Act 1987 imposed fines on airlines and shipping companies who allowed people to travel to the UK without the correct documentation (Cohen 1994). However, these measures did not stop asylum-seekers from entering Britain and, in response, the government introduced the Asylum Act 1993, whose provisions included the need to appeal against decisions within 48 hours, compulsory finger-printing and the removal of rights to public-sector housing. In reality, however, the Act exacted harsh new measures on asylum-seekers and was designed to reduce the number of refugees and to discourage new arrivals (MacDonald 1993: 158).

In 1996, the government introduced the Asylum and Immigration Act, which included a clause relating to employment. The Act specified that any employer wishing to employ someone who does not have the appropriate documentation will be subject to a fine. This may affect the willingness of employers to take on people whose country of origin is not the UK, because it entails the additional task of checking documents (Carter 1996). Morris (1997) argues that the legislation has reduced opportunities for poor migrant populations.

> internal policing will tend to focus suspicion on the 'visibly different' minorities and have the effect of eroding their legitimate rights, affecting both employment opportunities and access to services ... the requirement of employers to police the legality of their workers ... common elsewhere in Europe and known to discriminate against legally present minorities, has been introduced in Britain by the 1996 Asylum and Immigration Act. (Morris 1997: 255)

Alongside changes in immigration legislation, which have made it increasingly difficult to enter Britain as an asylum-seeker, changes in domestic social policy have affected their position within Britain. It is necessary to be clear about the distinction between refugees and asylum-seekers, because their situations differ quite markedly. A refugee is someone whose status has been officially recognised by the host or receiving country. There are two types: 'quota' refugees and 'spontaneous' refugees. Quota or programme refugees are those who are taken in a group under an organised programme, such as the Vietnamese; quota refugees are accepted as refugees on arrival in Britain. Spontaneous refugees arrive of their own accord and apply for asylum on arrival (Joly 1992). An asylum-seeker is a person who is seeking asylum on the basis of his or her claim to be a refugee. People waiting for the Home Office to consider their case are known as asylum-seekers. This is regardless of whether or not their claims are valid or will eventually be accepted as legitimate.

Asylum-seekers who are not recognised as refugees are not always expelled. In some cases they are given exceptional leave to remain on humanitarian grounds. An asylum-seeker granted exceptional leave can stay for one year, subject to renewal then and again after three years. Non-governmental organisations argue that 'humanitarian status is being used as a means of enabling refugees to be settled without the rights and in worse conditions than if they were granted refugee status' (Joly 1992: 18). For instance, people with exceptional leave to remain lack security of settlement, because their cases are periodically reviewed and the Home Office can withdraw the right. Asylum-seekers and people with exceptional leave to remain are not entitled to statutory student grants until they have been resident in Britain for three years. Asylum-seekers are not entitled to apply for family reunion, while those with exceptional leave to remain can apply only after they have maintained their status for four years.

Between 1985 and 1995, around 23,000 people were granted full refugee status, and around 70,000 were given exceptional leave to remain (Joly 1997). Many more asylum-seekers, however, had their claims rejected, which Black (1993) argues is more to do with the decision-making procedures than the legitimacy of any particular application.

Much attention has been paid to asylum-seekers, in terms of policy and by the mass media, with campaigns against 'bogus' claims and fears of 'tidal waves' and 'swamping'. Most recently, such reportage was devoted to the Roma arriving in Dover. But in reality asylum-seekers amount to only a small proportion of the UK population. The ratio of asylum-seekers to UK residents in 1995 was 1:3,431; in the Netherlands it was 1:509, in Germany 1:633 and in France 1:2,876 (Joly 1997).

The Research and Main Characteristics of the Sample

Research was carried out among three refugee communities – Somalis, Tamils from Sri Lanka and Zaireans – in the London Borough of Newham. The three communities were selected for the study on the basis of size, length of residence and historic links with Britain. Somalis and Tamils form the two largest refugee groups in Newham, while Zaireans are the largest group of recent arrivals to settle in the borough (Bloch 1996). Migration patterns and historic links with the host society are known to have an impact on the settlement of refugees.

Somalis have been resident in London's East End, mostly as seafarers, since the end of the nineteenth century; larger numbers started to arrive as asylum-seekers in the late 1980s. Somalia has colonial links with Britain. The northern part of Somalia was a British colony which gained independence in 1960, while the south was an Italian colony. Tamils from Sri Lanka started to arrive in Britain in large numbers in the mid-1980s. Sri Lanka is an ex-British colony and there were large south Asian communities already settled in Britain when Tamil refugees started to arrive. Refugees from Zaire began to arrive in 1989. Zaire had no colonial links with Britain and there was less of an established network of voluntary organisations to provide help and advice to new arrivals.

One hundred and eighty face-to-face interviews were carried out: sixty with members of each of the three communities. Respondents were identified by negotiating access through a number of different organisations working with refugees in Newham. Quotas were set for age, sex and length of residence in the UK to ensure that the survey included different experiences which were known, theoretically, to affect refugee settlement.

In the final sample, 53 per cent of respondents were male and 47 per cent female. Sixty-two per cent of the sample were under 35 years old, while 38 per cent were 35 or over. Forty-eight per cent arrived in the UK before 1992, 52 per cent in 1992 or later. In terms of housing, 7 per cent of refugees were owner-occupiers, compared with 50 per cent of Newham's population (information from 1991 Census).

Citizenship and Settlement

Immigration status and the associated citizenship rights are known to have an effect on the settlement of refugees. Cohen (1994) addresses the notion of different types of migrant when he identifies three categories of people within European states: citizens, denizens and helots. While people with full convention refugee status (those recognised in accordance with the 1951 Geneva Convention) are considered citizens because they have full citizenship rights, asylum-seekers fall into the category of helots, who have very few rights. Anything less than full citizenship will impede settlement, because the host society does not see the migrant as part of the society, and for the migrant there is always an element of insecurity attached to their position in the society (Weiner 1996).

Robinson (1986) set up a typology of the stages of settlement and noted that one of the prerequisites of settlement is the absence of any legal restrictions while Loescher highlights the links between status and settlement, arguing that 'In many cases, the desire to integrate depends crucially on whether immigrants feel secure about their resident status' (Loescher 1993: 172).

Debates around citizenship stress a number of features that concern the position of asylum-seekers not only in the UK but also in most Western European countries. These include issues of nationality (Meeham 1993), immigration controls (Mitchell and Russell 1994) and social citizenship, which is operationalised through welfare entitlements (Crompton and Brown 1994). The link between immigration control and welfare entitlement is not new: 'the preoccupation of British immigration controls has been to prevent poor racial minorities from obtaining any right of citizenship which might entail an expenditure of public funds' (Dean 1996: 83).

In the last decade, a number of changes to social security have impacted harshly on people from minority ethnic communities by curtailing rights to welfare (Bloch 1997). Most recently, the Social Security (persons from abroad) Miscellaneous Amendment Regulations, which were contained in the 1996 Asylum and Immigration Act, mean that asylum-seekers who apply in-country rather than at the port of entry and those appealing against a Home Office decision on their case are no longer entitled to income support, housing benefit or council tax benefit. This removal of social security is particularly worrying, because asylum-seekers are not allowed to apply for a work permit until they have been resident in Britain

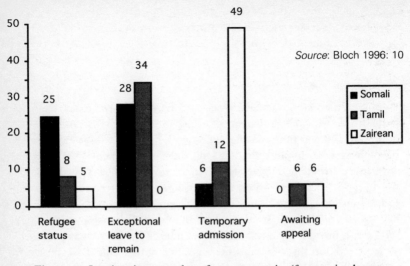

Figure 7.1 Immigration status by refugee community (frequencies; base number: 179)

for six months, after which the process of obtaining one might be slow. A Home Office survey of refugees and asylum-seekers found that 86 per cent of applicants for a work permit had to wait for between six months and a year for a decision to be made, while 14 per cent had to wait longer (Carey-Wood *et al.* 1995), which leaves many without access to money.

In this way, an individual's immigration status is crucial to the whole process of settlement. It regulates access to the social and economic institutions of the host society as well as affecting the psychological position of the individual migrant. In total, 20 per cent of respondents had refugee status, 35 per cent had exceptional leave to remain, 39 per cent were on temporary admission and 7 per cent were appealing against a Home Office decision.

Figure 7.1 shows that status varied by community. People from Somalia were more likely than were others to have refugee status. Of the 25 Somalis with refugee status, around half had refugee status with family reunion. Nearly all respondents from Zaire were asylum-seekers on temporary admission, while Tamils from Sri Lanka were most likely to have exceptional leave to remain.

There is a relationship between the year of arrival in the UK and immigration status. Four-fifths of those with either refugee status or exceptional leave to remain arrived in the UK in 1992 or before. Conversely, of the 37 per cent of respondents with temporary admission, two-thirds had arrived in the UK after 1992. However, as many as one-third arrived in 1992 or earlier and were still waiting to have their asylum applications processed by the Home Office. The delays leave asylum-seekers in a state of limbo, with limited rights, while they wait for their cases to be assessed.

It is not surprising, therefore, that when respondents were asked whether there were any factors which affected the ability of refugees from their community to settle in Britain, immigration status was mentioned most often (41 per cent). Zaireans were more likely than others to mention immigration status as the factor affecting settlement of members of their own community, which is understandable given how many are on temporary admission. One Zairean woman said, 'If you are not accepted as a refugee or resident, you are not able to do whatever you would like so long as your application is under consideration'. A Somali man said, 'I have been granted exceptional leave to remain, which is for a one-year term. Therefore it is difficult for me to settle in Britain.'

In addition to immigration status, there are other factors which affect the capacity and willingness of refugees to settle. The next section will examine migration theories and explore their relevance to the situation of refugees.

Migration

The circumstances of migration and migrants' attitudes towards it are known to have an impact on refugee settlement. Although the differences between refugees and economic migrants is subject to much debate, Loescher (1993) argues that if you are pushed from your homeland you are a refugee and if you are pulled to a receiving country by potential economic opportunities you are a migrant.

Push–pull theories have been criticised for their parsimony. Kunz (1973) offers a kinetic model, which makes a distinction between anticipatory refugee movements and acute refugee movements. Anticipatory refugees, Kunz argues, prepare to leave their homeland and migrate before the situation prevents their departure, and as a result they are often confused with economic migrants. Acute refugee movements, in contrast, arise from sudden political changes or military activity. Refugees who flee under these conditions do not have time to prepare their flight and so the push factor is the most important determinant of acute refugee migration. However, Kunz's distinction can blur the main factor differentiating refugees from economic migrants, which is the involuntary nature of all refugee decisions (Kunz 1981).

Unlike voluntary migrants, who often follow a pattern of chain migration based on social networks, kinship ties and colonial links, such as the migration of South Asians to Britain (Robinson 1980; Shaw 1988), forced

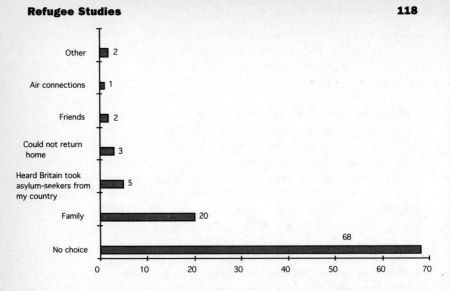

Figure 7.2 Reason why Britain was the country of asylum (percentages;
base number: 177)

migrants may find themselves in countries where they have no prior links. Networks, often in the form of ethnic enclaves, are known to assist new arrivals in their transition from the old to the new country (Robinson 1993; Marcuse 1996) but many refugees have little or no choice over their asylum destination, and so find themselves in countries where they have no prior links or networks.

In Newham, as Figure 7.2 shows, more than two-thirds of asylum-seekers came to Britain because they had no choice. In some instances, an agent arranged their flight and organised tickets and documents.

Figure 7.2 shows that there was an element of chain migration, as one in five came to Britain owing to family ties. Somalis and Tamils were more likely than Zaireans to come to Britain because of family connections. Indeed, one in four Somalis were in Britain on the basis of family reunion. Chain migration among Tamils and Somalis can be explained by the fact that both these communities have a longer history of migration to Britain and a colonial link, which was not the case for Zaireans.

Once within Britain, however, chain migration was influential in determining where people lived. Two in five of all respondents moved to Newham having already lived somewhere else in Britain. The pattern of secondary migration, within the host country, has been found among Vietnamese, who were dispersed on arrival in Britain and then moved to areas with larger proportions of people from the same ethnic group (Stalker

Table 7.1 Main reason for living in Newham, by refugee community (frequencies; base number: 176)

	Somalia	Sri Lanka	Zaire	Total (%)
Family	20	20	9	28
Friends	13	13	16	24
Placed in Newham on arrival	5	2	25	18
Other refugees from community in Newham	5	8	2	9
No deposits on rented housing	5	–	3	5
Housed in Newham by another local authority	8	1	–	5
Cheaper housing	–	6	–	3
Community places of worship	–	6	–	3
Availability of rented housing	1	–	2	2
Community food	–	3	–	2
Good services for refugees in Newham	–	–	1	1
Other	–	–	2	1
Total	57	59	60	100

1994). Table 7.1 shows the main reason for living in Newham, by community, and demonstrates the importance of social networks.

The differences between the three communities were very marked. People from Zaire were most likely to live in Newham because that was where they were placed on arrival, while Somalis and Tamils came to Newham owing to family ties. Among the Somali community, placement in Newham by another local authority was also an important reason for coming to live in the borough.

Community ties were strongest among Tamils from Sri Lanka. Virtually all Tamil respondents gave their main reason for living in Newham as either kinship or friendship ties or other factors relating to the community, such as the presence of others, the availability of places to worship and community food. This helps to explain why there is a concentration of Tamils in particular wards in the borough (Bloch 1994).

Attitudes about the migration destination and identification with the homeland are known to affect refugee settlement. Respondents were asked if they would have preferred a different asylum destination, had they been given a choice; 44 per cent said that they would. There were differences between the three communities: 63 per cent of Zaireans would have preferred a different asylum destination, followed by Tamils (48 per cent), then Somalis (22 per cent). The differences between the three communities were linked to social networks, colonial ties, language, perceptions about

Table 7.2 Preferred asylum destination, by country of origin (frequencies; base
number: 79)

	Somalia	Sri Lanka	Zaire	Total
Canada	3	6	12	21
Anywhere that takes asylum-seekers and is safe	–	5	11	16
USA	4	–	8	12
Australia	1	3	5	9
Other European countries	7	–	–	7
France	–	–	7	7
Any French-speaking country	–	–	7	7
Germany	–	5	1	6
Belgium	–	–	6	5
Singapore	–	5	–	5
India	–	5	–	5
Norway	–	2	–	2
Switzerland	–	–	2	2
North America	1	–	1	1
Italy	–	1	–	1
Japan	–	1	1	1
Asian countries	–	1	–	1
Total	16	33	60	109

asylum policy and immigration status. Those who had family connections
were much more positive about coming to Britain in the first place. Among
them, only one in five said that they would have preferred a different
destination. By contrast, nearly three in five of those who had no choice
would have preferred to go elsewhere.

The destinations that would have been preferred provide some insight
into the factors that were important to refugees, such as language skills
and colonial ties. Table 7.2 shows the range of different asylum destinations
that respondents said that they would have preferred had they had a choice.
In some instances, respondents gave more than one destination so the total
adds up to more than the base number.

The preferred destinations of Zaireans included ex-colonial countries
(France and Belgium) as well countries where French is one of the official
languages, such as Canada and Switzerland. This reinforces the importance
of historic links and language in relation to asylum-seekers' preferences,
although in reality this is hypothetical, as many in this group were without
choice. Respondents who would have preferred a different asylum destination were asked why that was the case. Although networks, both social and
historic, were important to refugees, of much greater significance were

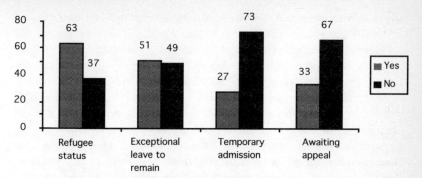

Figure 7.3 Whether the respondent sees Britain as their home, by immigration status (percentages; base number: 177)

structural factors, especially the immigration policies and attitudes towards refugees of potential receiving countries. The overwhelming concern was to be in a country which had a more open immigration policy and which understood the position of refugees better than Britain. Language was also a factor which concerned refugees from Zaire. A few mentioned their historic ties with Belgium and France due to colonisation.

In spite of these attitudes towards Britain as the asylum destination and factors affecting settlement, 43 per cent of respondents said that they saw Britain as home. Tamil respondents were more likely to see Britain as home than were Somalis and Zaireans. Immigration status was a crucial factor in determining perceptions of Britain as home, as Figure 7.3 shows.

When respondents were asked if, given the right circumstances, they would like to return to their county of origin, 71 per cent said that they would. Nineteen per cent said that given the right circumstances they might go home and 10 per cent said that they did not want to return home. Once again immigration status was influential. People with refugee status were less likely to say that they would definitely like to return home than were those with exceptional leave to remain or temporary admission. Nearly everyone who wanted to return home said that it was dependent on peace and democracy in their homeland. Among the 10 per cent of respondents who did not want to return to their homeland, the main reasons were the length of time already spent in Britain and having children who would feel out of place in the homeland having spent time in Britain.

Settlement: Participation in the Labour Market

Work has been identified as a key factor affecting refugee settlement (Finnan 1981; Valtonen 1994). 'Though successful employment need not necessarily lead to social integration, its importance as a first step towards successful integration cannot be denied. Employment as a key to the settlement of refugees is increasingly stressed (Srinivasan 1994:13). Employment is important for a number of reasons. Material well-being and the opportunity to live according to society's standard is a basic element of citizenship (Oomen 1997). In addition, employment allows refugees to make social contact with members of the host society; policies that prevent participation in the labour market also exclude potential citizens. In a study of Vietnamese refugees in Finland, Valtonen (1994) found that integration was the norm except among those who were unemployed, who were in danger of not integrating. Clearly for some asylum-seekers, even if there was a desire to settle in Britain, structural factors relating to policy impede the process.

Nationally, refugees remain the most underemployed group in Britain; estimates from the Refugee Council (1992) place the levels of unemployment among refugees in London at about 70 per cent. Research carried out by the Home Office found that only 27 per cent of refugees were employed at the time of the survey and that 56 per cent had never had a paid job in the UK (Carey-Wood *et al.* 1995). In Newham 14 per cent of respondents were employed or self-employed at the time of the survey.

According to Ginsburg (1992), the labour market demonstrates the most basic operation of racial inequality, and refugees are even more disadvantaged than people from other minority ethnic communities in terms of both levels of pay and levels of unemployment (Bloch 1996).

Work carried out by Stein (1979) among Vietnamese refugees in the United States found that most changes in occupation occur within the early years in the new society. Some factors are ameliorated over time, but if changes do not occur quickly then motivation declines and refugees tend just to accept their situation and lack motivation to change it. Structural factors in the form of work-permit restrictions may have a long-term impact because the longer an individual is unemployed, the more likely it is that they will stay that way (LETEC 1995).

Language skills as a key to settlement, indeed as the first stage in the settlement process, have been highlighted in previous studies (see Robinson 1986; Bun and Kiong 1993). Moreover, language has been identified as a key factor affecting labour-market participation and therefore refugee settlement (Wooden 1991; Thomas 1992).

In Newham, most people could speak, read and write some English, although on arrival in the UK Somalis and Tamils were much more likely to be fluent than were Zaireans. Around a quarter of Somalis and Tamils were fluent on arrival, compared with only one respondent from Zaire, reflecting the different colonial histories between the countries.

The general pattern, with the exception of Somali women, was a positive correlation between length of residence in the UK and English language skills. The most marked improvement was among Zaireans, while Somali women had the most difficulty communicating in English. In total, 21 per cent of respondents spoke no English, of whom 81 per cent were women. Of those women who did not speak English, two-thirds were Somali and most were also lone parents. Being a lone parent can make participation in language classes more difficult owing to a lack of child-care provision. Research carried out among South-East Asians in the United States also highlighted the disadvantage experienced by some women. 'Refugee women ... arrive in the United States with lower levels of English language proficiency than men. ... Yet refugee women's lower initial level of English proficiency is compounded by less access to training classes and by relative social isolation through staying at home (Bach and Carroll-Seguin 1986: 388). The isolation of some Somali women may be increased by cultural and religious constraints, which, in some instances, also make it difficult for Somali women to participate in ESOL classes and in social and cultural activities (Duke 1996a). Host society language skills are very important both socially and economically. Without them, it is virtually impossible for refugees to make contacts with members of that society either socially or through employment.

Most refugees said that they found it difficult to meet members of the host society, and a lack of language skills compounded the difficulty. Although 93 per cent of respondents had made friends since living in the UK, most said that their new friends were mainly from their own community. Although English languages skills made it easier for refugees to meet members of the host society, as many as 39 per cent, despite speaking either simple sentences or fluent English, still found it difficult, indicating separation from the wider society.

Labour market participation was affected by English language proficiency. Of the 36 per cent of respondents who were working at the time of the survey or had worked in Britain in the past, only three did not speak English at all. The other main factor which affected labour market participation was immigration status. Those who had refugee status or exceptional leave to remain were much more likely to be employed than were those with temporary admission (asylum-seekers). The proportions working were 22 per cent of refugees, 23 per cent of those with exceptional leave to remain and 5 per cent of asylum-seekers.

There has been a dramatic change in the activities of refugees in Britain. Figure 7.4 shows the increase in the numbers unemployed and the decrease in the numbers working or studying.

The shift in activity from employment in the country of origin to

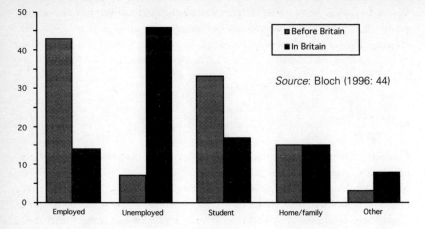

Figure 7.4 Main activity before coming to Britain and main activity in Britain (percentages; base number, before: 180; base number, in Britain: 178)

unemployment in Britain is all the more striking when it is put in the context of the high levels of skills, qualifications, education and experience that many refugees have on arrival in Britain – teachers, mechanical engineers, broadcasters, business people, and so on.

Before coming to Britain, 22 per cent of respondents had attended university and 75 per cent had some qualification. Clearly refugees are an educated group with an impressive range of qualifications. However, only 23 per cent of those qualified said that their qualifications were recognised in Britain, and only 11 per cent had tried to get them recognised, with a success rate of just one person. The propensity for overseas qualifications to be devalued or unrecognised means that refugees are unable to fulfil their potential in the UK labour market.

Among those who were working, the sorts of jobs they had were, for the most part, unskilled and low-paid, with poor terms and conditions. Security work, cleaning, shop and cashier work were the norm, and most worked unsocial hours including regular weekend and night work. This reflects Sivanandan's (1990) thesis that illegal immigrants and asylum-seekers, because they have no rights, find themselves forced to accept poor wages and conditions which no other workers would accept.

The employment aspirations of refugees were very low, with most looking at a much lower level than their skills and experience would predict. Graduates were looking for shop work and postgraduates for clerical or office jobs.

Research carried out by Al-Rasheed (1992) with refugees from Iraq found that attitudes towards settlement can result in an orientation towards people from the same community rather than the host society, and this affects labour-market participation.

This prohibits people from having access to local information networks regarding job opportunities. Lack of social relations with the host society also entails lack of knowledge about how occupations are organised here, potential gaps in the market which might be exploited, and a general feel about how businesses work in this country (Al-Rasheed 1992: 543).

Certainly this pattern was found among refugees in Newham, who were heavily dependent on friends for finding employment. A quarter of those who had worked in Britain had found work through a friend, and less than one in ten had successfully used the Job Centre. Those looking for paid work were also quite dependent on informal contacts, especially the most recent arrivals.

The Voluntary Sector

Many refugees arrive without previous contacts in the host society, and much of the resettlement work is carried out by the voluntary sector in the absence of formal programmes (Stein 1981; Balloch 1993; Joly 1996). In Newham, nearly nine out of ten respondents had heard of, and of those, eight had been in direct contact with, one or more local voluntary organisations. Contact with the voluntary sector was inversely correlated with English language skills. However, more than half of those who spoke English fluently had still had such contact. Voluntary organisations were contacted most frequently for immigration advice (82 per cent) and welfare rights (81 per cent). However, they were also used as a mechanism for meeting people and participating in social activities (35 per cent).

One of the functions of voluntary organisations is the provision of community-specific social and cultural activities (Duke 1996a). According to Thomas (1992), the more groups that exist to meet the cultural, social and religious needs of migrants, the more separate the community is from the wider society. Nearly two-thirds of refugees in Newham had participated in community activities. Figure 7.5 shows the level of participation by community and gender.

Among Somali women with children, only one attended a group, and she lived with her spouse. All the others were lone parents, and none of them attended groups with other members of their community. This group remains more isolated not only from the host society but also from each other.

Bun and Kiong (1993) argued that attendance at religious groups was

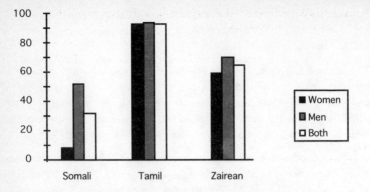

Figure 7.5 Attendance at a social, religious, cultural or political group, by sex and country of origin (percentages; base number: 111)

the strongest indicator of community separation. In this study, religious groups were attended more often than were other types, although there were differences by community, as Table 7.3 shows. (Some people attended more than one type of group, so the totals add up to more than 100 per cent.)

Members of the Tamil community were much more involved in cultural activities, such as Tamil New Year celebrations, than were others. Comparative research in Denmark and Britain found that the Tamil support community in Britain had a large impact on the settlement experience (Preis 1996). Moreover, Preis argues that the traditional narratives of Sri Lanka affect life in exile among this group, and the desire to maintain tradition is all the more important owing to the experience of colonialism, and then exile, as part of a minority group.

With the exception of one Somali respondent, all those involved in political activity were from the Zairean community. Zaireans are more likely than Tamils and Somalis to be making their case for asylum on the basis of political persecution, which could affect participation in political activity. Moreover, they are a newer community, and this might also affect their attachment to the political situation in the homeland, which will in turn affect their attitudes and propensity to get on with their lives in Britain (Kunz 1981).

The politicisation of the Zairean community reflects earlier research among Chileans, which found that during their early years of settlement, most political activity was concerned with overthrowing the dictatorship.

Initially the sole objective was the immediate or rapid overthrow of the dictatorship, with the perspective of returning home in the near future. As

Table 7.3 Attendance at social, religious, cultural or political groups, by country of origin (frequencies; base number: 110)

	Somali	Sri Lankan	Zairean	Total (%)
Religious	4	48	21	66
Cultural	8	21	0	26
Social	3	0	15	16
Political	1	0	21	20
Total number	16	55	39	110

the period of exile lengthened ... the Chileans abroad became involved in more diverse social, cultural and sports activities and many loosened their direct connections with political parties. ... A few of the associations then began to address issues pertaining to life in the host society (Joly 1996: 173).

It is too early to ascertain what the pattern of ethnic association will be among Zaireans, but if it follows the same course as that of the Chileans, the emphasis will shift to settlement in the host society or return migration, should the situation allow it, rather than political activity in the host society.

Tamils are most involved in community activity, and in relation to the settlement of people from minority communities, living in an ethnic enclave is seen as a first and necessary stage in the process of adjustment to the host society (Thomas 1992). '"Enclaves" is a term often given to areas of spatial concentration, which are walled in socially if not physically, but which have positive consequences for their residents, as opposed to ghettos which are entirely negative' (Marcuse 1996: 38). Self-segregation into enclaves is not necessarily a barrier to settlement, so long as those living in the enclave have equal access to the structures of the host society, including employment (Weiner 1996). In Newham, Tamils were more likely to be working than were others, and were generally more content to be and to stay in Britain. It is difficult to ascertain the direction of the correlation but there is a clear relationship between community involvement and other indicators of settlement.

Conclusion

Refugees remain isolated both socially and economically from the host society. There are many reasons for this isolation. Some are the characteristics of refugees themselves, such as attitudes towards migration and English language skills, while immigration status and employment derive from structural aspects of the society.

If refugees are going to be able to use their skills and experience in order to get on with their lives and to contribute to the host society, then structural changes to enable this need to be made by the government. Clearly, refugees are not in Britain by choice, and attitudes towards this group of migrants should be reassessed. Being a refugee, with the associated upheaval and pre-migration experiences, is hard enough without policy in the host society diminishing opportunities for involvement.

References

Al-Rasheed, M. (1992) 'The Iraqi community in London', in *New Community*, vol. 18 (4), pp. 537–50.

Bach, R.L. and R. Carroll-Seguin (1986) 'Labour force participation, household composition and sponsorship among Southeast Asian refugees', in *International Migration Review*, vol. 20 (2), pp. 381–404.

Balloch, S. (1993) *Refugees in the Inner City: A study of refugees and service provision in the London Borough of Lewisham*, London: Centre for Inner City Studies, Goldsmiths College, University of London.

Black, R. (1993) 'Refugees and asylum-seekers in Western Europe: new challenges', in R. Black and V. Robinson (eds), *Geography and Refugees: Patterns and processes of change*, London: Belhaven.

Bloch, A. (1994) *Refugees and Migrants in Newham: Access to services*, London: London Borough of Newham.

— (1996) *Beating the Barriers: The employment and training needs of refugees in Newham*, London: London Borough of Newham.

— (1997) 'Ethnic inequality and social security policy', in A. Walker and C. Walker (eds), *Britain Divided: The growth of social exclusion in the 1980s and 1990s*, London: Child Poverty Action Group.

Bun, C.K. and T.C. Kiong (1993) 'Rethinking assimilation and ethnicity: The Chinese in Thailand', in *International Migration Review*, vol. 27 (1) pp. 140–68.

Carey-Wood, J., K. Duke, V. Karn and T. Marshall (1995) *The Settlement of Refugees in Britain*, London: HMSO, Home Office Research Study 141.

Carter, M. (1996) *Poverty and Prejudice*, London: Commission for Racial Equality and the Refugee Council.

Cohen, R. (1994) *Frontiers of Identity: The British and the others*, London: Longman.

Coleman, D.A. (1995) 'International Migration: Demographic and socio-economic consequences in the United Kingdom and Europe' in *International Migration Review*, vol. 29 (1), pp. 155–99.

Crompton, R. and P. Brown (1994) 'Introduction', in P. Brown and R. Crompton (eds), *A New Europe: Economic restructuring and social exclusion*, London: UCL Press.

Dean, H. (1996) *Welfare, Law and Citizenship*, Hemel Hempstead: Harvester Wheatsheaf.

Duke, K. (1996a) 'The resettlement experiences of refugees in the UK: Main findings from an interview study', in *New Community*, vol. 22 (3), pp. 461–78.

— (1996b) 'Refugee community groups in the UK: The role of the community group in the resettlement process', paper presented to the British Sociological Association

Annual Conference, 'Worlds of the Future: Ethnicity, nationalism and globalisation', University of Reading, April.

Finnan, C.R. (1981) 'Occupational assimilation of refugees', in *International Migration Review*, vol.15 (1), pp. 292–309.

Ginsburg, H. (1992) *Divisions of Welfare: A critical introduction to comparative social policy*, London: Sage.

Joly, D. (1992) *Refugees: Asylum in Europe*, London: Minority Rights Publications.

— (1996) *Haven or Hell? Asylum policies and refugees in Europe*, London: Macmillan.

— with L. Kelly and C. Nettleton (1997) *Refugees in Europe: The hostile new agenda*, London: Minority Rights Group.

Kim, K.C. and W.M. Hurhn (1993) 'Beyond assimilation and pluralism: Syncretic socio-cultural adaptation of Korean immigrants in the United States', in *Ethnic and Racial Studies*, vol. 16 (4), pp. 696–713.

Kunz, E.F. (1973) 'The refugee in flight: Kinetic models and forms of displacement', in *International Migration Review*, vol. 7 (2), pp. 125–46.

— (1981) 'Exile and Resettlement: Refugee theory', in *International Migration Review*, vol. 15 (1), pp. 42–51.

Layton-Henry, Z. (1984) *The Politics of Race in Contemporary Britain*, London: Allen and Unwin.

— (1992) *The Politics of Immigration*, Oxford: Blackwell.

Loescher, G. (1993) *Beyond Charity: International co-operation and the global refugee crisis*, New York: Oxford University Press.

LETEC (1995) *Economic Assessment*, London: London East Training and Enterprise Council.

Macdonald, I. (1993) 'Current law and practice in the UK', in V. Robinson (ed.) *The International Refugee Crisis: British and Canadian responses*, Macmillan, London.

Marcuse, P. (1996) 'Of walls and immigrant enclaves', in N. Carmon (ed.), *Immigration and Integration in Post-Industrial Societies: Theoretical analysis and policy-related research*, London: Macmillan.

Meehan, E. (1993) *Citizenship and the European Community*, London: Sage.

Miles, R. and P. Clearly (1993) 'Migration to Britain: Racism, state regulation and employment', in V. Robinson (ed.), *The International Refugee Crisis: British and Canadian responses*, London: Macmillan.

Mitchell, M. and D. Russell (1994) 'Race and citizenship in "Fortress Europe"', in P. Brown and R. Crompton (eds), *A New Europe: Economic restructuring and social exclusion*, London: UCL Press.

Morris, L. (1997) 'A cluster of contradictions: The politics of migration in the European Union', in *Sociology*, vol. 31 (2), pp. 241–59.

Oommen, T.K. (1997) *Citizenship, Nationality and Ethnicity*, Cambridge: Polity Press.

Preis, A.B.S. (1996) 'The vagaries of refugee resettlement: Power, knowledge and narrativity', in *Anthropology in Action*, Vol. 3 (1), pp. 4–8.

Refugee Council (1992) 'Careers guidance – where and when it's needed', in *Exile*, no. 64, London.

Robinson, V. (1986) *Transients, Settlers and Refugees: Asians in Britain*, Oxford: Clarendon Press.

— (1993) 'Marching into the middle classes? The long-term resettlement of East African Asians in the UK', in *Journal of Refugee Studies*, vol. 6 (3), pp. 230–47.

Schuster, L. and J. Solomos (1999) 'The politics of refugee and asylum policies: Historical patterns and contemporary reality' in A. Bloch and C. Levy, *Refugees, Social Policy and Citizenship in Britain and Europe*, Basingstoke: Macmillan.

Shaw, A. (1988) *A Pakistani Community in Britain*, London: Blackwell.

Sivanandan, A. (1990) *Communities of Resistance: Writings on black struggles for socialism*, London: Verso.

Solomos, J. (1993) *Race and Racism in Britain*, Basingstoke: Macmillan, second edition.

Srinivasan, S. (1994) 'An overview of research into refugee groups in Britain during the 1990s', paper presented at the fourth International Research and Advisory Panel Conference, Oxford, January.

Stalker, P. (1994) *The Work of Strangers: A survey of international labour*, Geneva: International Labour Office.

Stein, B.N. (1979) 'Occupational adjustment of refugees: The Vietnamese in the United States', in *International Migration Review*, vol. 13 (1), pp. 25–45.

— (1981) 'The refugee experience: Defining the parameters of a field study' in *International Migration Review*, vol. 15 (1), pp. 320–30.

Thomas, D. (1992) 'The social integration of immigrants in Canada', in S. Globerman (ed.), *The Immigrant Dilemma*, Vancouver: The Frasier Institute.

Valtonen, K. (1994) 'The adaptation of Vietnamese refugees in Finland' in *Journal of Refugee Studies*, vol. 7 (1), pp. 63–78.

Weiner, M. (1996) 'Determinants of immigrant integration: an international comparative analysis', in N. Carmon (ed.), *Immigration and Integration in Post-Industrial Societies: Theoretical analysis and policy-related research*, London: Macmillan.

Wooden, M. (1991) 'The experience of refugees in the Australian labour market' in *International Migration Review*, vol. 25 (3), pp. 514–34.

8

'Rights and Wrongs': Youth, Community and Narratives of Racial Violence

Les Back & Michael Keith

Introduction[1]

> Avoid the Isle of Dogs if you want a quiet life. It is one thing after another. On Wednesday 21 January [1998] fourteen-year-old Paul Sammut was walking along West Ferry Road when he was viciously attacked for no apparent reason by a twenty-strong gang of Asian youths. (*The Islander*, April 1998)

> At the end of the day the majority of the people are not racist, all they want is fairness. (White community activist, Isle of Dogs)

The Isle of Dogs – and east London more generally - has provided a key location for disquiet about male youth styles, be they mods, rockers or skinheads (P. Cohen 1972). The origin of the name Isle of Dogs is not known. One account has it that Henry VIII kept his hunting dogs on the inside of this meander of the Thames, another that it takes its name from wild dogs left to roam the Island after their medieval masters were killed in a freak accident. The ghosts of these dogs are said still to haunt the district. With the emergence of London as the heart of Empire, the Island became the centre of imperial trade through the excavation of West India Dock (Porter 1994). The dock workers and communities formed on the banks of the river were thus irrevocably connected to imperial hinterlands (Linebaugh 1991; Rediker 1987). What is interesting about the Isle of Dogs is that it has both maritime global associations and an intense sense of local patriotism.

Chris Husbands (1983) has argued that the racism prevalent in these neighbourhoods was the product of an archaic, pre-modern, irrational streak in the communities of the East End. His work takes in a catalogue of incidents of local racism, from popular anti-Semitism which helped pioneer the Aliens Act of 1905 (Britain's first immigration control), through the Mosleyite agitations of the inter-war years, and the dockers' support of Enoch Powell's 'rivers of blood' speech in 1968, to the harassment of the Bangladeshi community during the 1980s. Husbands argued that a generationally transmitted culture of racism provided the underlying link between these phenomena, fostered through the persistence of an ethnically homogeneous working-class community, centred originally in Hoxton and Bethnal Green and subsequently diffused to other areas of white flight. He describes the community as exhibiting:

> a culture with profoundly economistic expectations and orientations, which has a very limited and confused perception of social structure and a corresponding readiness to apportion blame in inappropriate directions. Its political sophistication has been similarly limited, it was long resistant to sustained mobilisation by the left, and even its more recent left-wing voting has had a narrowly pragmatic and poorly articulated ideological basis. A continual readiness to engage in right-wing racial exclusionism, despite the more recent tendency to left-voting, suggests the ongoing existence of the 'rootless volatility' that Stedman Jones (1976: 343) saw as a feature of nineteenth-century working-class politics in the East End' (Husbands 1983: 56).

But the racism of white workers was not the product of a pre-modern lack of enlightenment. If anything, East End racism was the product of its population being 'over-civilised' (Cohen 1996). From the 1880s onwards the mass of East Enders were transformed, slowly and unevenly, from dangerous revolutionaries or denizens of the underworld into cheerful patriotic cockneys. This was achieved through the combined and cumulative influence of the labour movement, the church, state education, better housing and sanitation, and strategies of self-improvement provided by settlements, clubs and missions. Even the music hall played its part. The emergence of a conservative, inward-looking, but above all respectable culture of labourism in the East End is held to epitomise a wider process in the remaking of the English working class in and through the late Victorian culture of imperialism (Stedman Jones 1989).

The victory of the British National Party (BNP) candidate, Derek Beackon, in the local council bye-election in 1993 was seen by some as an expression of the intrinsically racist culture of east London. This implies a version of ecological logic that locates racism in particular places (Keith 1995). The result is a kind of spatial determinism that echoes early American urban sociology, which was itself the product of a particular transatlantic conversation (Kurtz 1984; Kent 1981). Wirth and Park took their inspiration from early social explorers such as Charles Booth and Henry Mayhew, both of whom conducted investigations into urban poverty in London during the nineteenth century (Mayhew 1968; Booth 1902–3). This way of understanding urban life was repatriated through the publication of the classic study *Family and Kinship in East London* (Young and

Wilmott 1957), which drew inspiration from the urban sociology practised in Chicago. The point that we want to argue here is that these ways of framing the social life of cities result in a kind of ecological fallacy. Instead, we want to look at the manifestations of urban life and territories of belonging as *iterative* and *emergent*. The essential point we argue is that 'community' is as much a narrative product as an organic achievement. We are working between the representation of space ('the conceived') and the spaces of representation ('the lived') drawn from the work of Henri Lefebvre in *The Production of Space* (Lefebvre 1991). We have tried to avoid slipping into the kind of intrinsic determinism which, like the myth of the nomadic howling dogs, haunt much of the public debate about violence and racism on the island. It is precisely this sensibility about how to theorise urban life that has informed our methodology (Cohen, Keith and Back 1996).

The category 'youth' has constituted perhaps the prime anxiety in post-war moral panics in Britain (S. Cohen 1972; Brake 1985). In particular, the intersection between youth, race and gender has been the focus of a variety of public forms of disquiet that produced a line of youthful urban villains. Anxieties about lawless masculinities (Campbell 1993) and 'yob culture' among a 'new underclass' (Murray 1994) certainly contain echoes of earlier debates on crime, violence and public safety in the inner city (Hall *et al.* 1978; Smith 1986); similarly we can see the residue of popular fears of a black crime wave (Jefferson 1988) that was orchestrated throughout the 1980s by the new right agenda. White male working-class youth are now also the object of public alarm focused on the theme of 'rampant racism'. In both cases the burden of explanation is no longer carried by the issue of immigration, but by the destabilisation of 'settled' identities and/or boundaries due to rapid socio-economic change (Keith 1993).

In contrast to the new pathologisation of African–Caribbean and white working-class cultures, the Asian community is often held up as a model minority espousing 'traditional family values', stiffening the backbone of the nation, provided they throw off the yoke of Islamic fundamentalism (Modood *et al.* 1994). Nevertheless, we have also heard in recent years reports of popular Islamic movements of Asian youth that invoke the British orientalist imagination (Said 1978) through the currents of Islamo-phobia. A secular version of the moral panic about Asian youth coalesces around fears of Asian criminality and gang formation (Centre for Bangla-deshi Research 1993). It is this question of 'Asian gangs' that has resonated particularly within our research, especially in relation to the question of how ideas about 'dangerous youth' are generated.

Previous studies of racial violence and public safety have tended to assume that these stereotypes are primarily constructed by moral panics which originate in some 'non-place realm', produced by political discourses or the mass media, which then syphon down to the streets where they are taken up and amplified by local networks of gossip and rumour (Smith 1986). Alternatively, it is argued that racialised images of deviance attempt to sum up, and make common sense of, local experiences of crime or race (Kinsey *et al.* 1986). Both these approaches miss the significance of specific networks of gossip and rumour – communal and institutional – which provide the web of communication through which moral panics are defined by distinctly local processes of amplification and simplification. It is with this kind of approach that we want to discuss young people's notions of safety and racial danger and the significance of the attack on Paul Sammut and its aftermath.

Boundaries and Homelands: the Habitus of Safety and Racial Danger

During 1996–97 extensive research was conducted with young people on their views of safety and racial danger in a local school.[2] We designed a multi-media methodology in order to open up a space of representation for young people to record their landscapes of familiarity and risk. The exercises involved the use of photography, audio diaries, video walkabouts, art work and mapping. One of the themes that emerged from the work with young white islanders was a pervasive sense of threat from 'Asian gangs'. In large part this threat was mapped at the northern boundary of the Isle of Dogs, in a belt from Limehouse, through Poplar, to Lower Lea Crossing. This border zone was made explicit in a mapping exercise conducted with the young people in school. We asked them to plot on a map particular associations, including 'no-go areas' and places where they hung out with their friends. Using Geographical Information Software (GIS) we generated composite representations of their mappings. Figure 8.1 shows the GIS map of the places white children did not go to or saw as 'no-go areas.' The concentration around Poplar, Westferry and Blackwall is immediately apparent.

The meaning of this boundary was rarely made explicit in the follow up interviews. Comments like 'I just don't like it' or 'I dunno, I just don't go there' were common. This type of response was due in part to the pervasive sense that such issues could not be articulated openly in the context of school. The young whites in particular were conscious of the prohibitions on 'race talk' imposed by the school. However, something else was going on in these responses that suggested how landscapes of risk and safety were embodied, operating through practical meanings, or what Bourdieu has referred to as 'practical consciousness' (Bourdieu 1977, 1991,

1992). The habitus of safety and danger often worked through implicit means that echoed broader class, cultural and communicative practices (Bernstein 1971, 1977). This made it necessary to unpack how the implicit boundaries related to the territories of whiteness and difference.

Accordingly, Figure 8.1 represents implicit meanings that are unspeakable but assumed within the mapping of a 'dangerous border'. This boundary is significant in at least three senses. First, it marks a boundary in the built environment. A band of offices and commercial land crosses West India Docks and almost seals off the Island from the rest of Tower Hamlets. Second, this zone has the qualities of a transitional ethnoscape (Appadurai 1990). The quality of the housing stock is low, particularly in Will Crooks Estate and Robin Hood Gardens. Within the circuits of gossip it was said that the ethnic demography of the housing tenure has changed from white dominance to a more mixed area, including a significant number of Bengali families. Third, within the moral panics around youth gang violence, Tower Hamlets College is perceived to be a place where Bengali students constitute the majority. Poplar High Street and the park on its northern borders are seen by police, local residents, council workers and local newspapers as the battlefield for fights between Bengali gangs. Hence one of the rumours which circulated within the institutional gossip network and within the youth public sphere was that gangs from neighbouring areas (the Brick Lane Massive and the Canon Street Posse) had been involved in a serious fight on Poplar High Street. Other gang panics have focused on Bengali boys in the college from Stepney, Shadwell and even Camden. Tower Hamlets College is consequently often positioned as 'outside' the local community in the sense that it is a 'Bengali college' in a white 'homeland'.

In the course of this research the Isle of Dogs was defined as a 'safe place' for whites. The places that were identified as 'no-go places' on the Island tended to be on the river front, converted docks, open wasteland and parks (see Figure 8.1). When we asked the young white people to mark the places where they met with friends, a strong concentration and commitment was shown to the island (see Figure 8.2). This showed that white friendship networks in the youthful public sphere were consigned to staying local. While the island was viewed by whites as safe, it was also viewed as being prone to the incursion of 'outsiders'. In discussing youth violence with young whites, a distinction was often made between black and white youth on one side and Bengalis on the other. This, as we shall see, was very much alive in the local circuits of rumour and gossip.

The distinctions, divisions and alliances within the youth community are made plain in the following account by a young white woman:

Like even black and whites fight and things like that, but you don't hear of
many white people fighting with weapons and things like that, that is the
thing. They couldn't just fight with their fists or anything, they have to have
their knives and things like that and that is the worst bit. Like my Dad said
years ago, there wouldn't be weapons, that it would be like getting in a ring
and that, and my Dad says they should put them all in a ring and let them
just beat each other up, using nothing, but these days they have to use
weapons all the time [...] It just the Asians ... the boys act 'flash', sit in
their cars as if they own the place.

Here, young male Bengalis constitute the local folk demon, who use
weapons, fight unfairly and act 'flash.' It is interesting that the Bengali
young men are accused of mirroring the exact forms of masculine embodi-
ment associated with white working-class male culture (Robson 1998).

During a filmed video walkabout on the island two white boys spoke
about their exclusion from the neighbouring district of Whitechapel in
precisely these terms:

TONY: They're all racist down there; they are, they stare at you 'cos they
think it's theirs, their town.

JOHN: You see them bowling along (he starts to rock shoulders, strutting
holding his head upright and looking around mimicking 'the bowl' walk).

TONY: I guarantee you'd find a blade [knife] on every single one of them.

In a sense some young Bengalis have assimilated all too well the public
dance of working-class masculinity. Yet these forms of masculine em-
bodiment (acting 'flash' or 'the bowl') are a dangerous violation because
they are viewed as either offering a challenge to 'normal' (coded white)
territories, or as establishing sovereign exclusive zones into which whites
cannot venture.

The island's youth clubs occupied a particular status in this landscape
of safety and racial danger. These places were 'bolt holes' that operated as
part of a micro-public sphere between home and the streets. The clubs were
associated with particular racialised patterns. During the period of the
research there were five main youth clubs on the Isle of Dogs. Their location
is shown in Figure 8.3, and their associated users are summarised on p. 137.[3]
The importance of these codings are more than symbolic projection; in each
case there has been a local struggle over issues of use and predominance.
A Bengali youth worker told us of an experience he had in 1993 at the One
O'Clock Club in Millwall Park. He wanted to set up a youth club and attract
Bengali boys to use it:

We had the local white youth coming in saying, 'Oh, the Pakis are getting
the preferential treatment now'. One night a group of white kids came in

Youth Club	Racialised Coding
Alpha Grove	Mixed with Bengali boys' groups Monday–Wednesday
Cubitt Town	Predominantly white, predominantly male
Harbinger School	All Bengali older boys 16–25, predominantly male
Docklands Settlement	Predominantly white, gender mixed
St Andrews	Mixed club: white and African–Caribbean, also significant numbers of Bengali boys and girls.

the club on the rampage through the club with baseball bats smashing things and breaking up the session. The police came and they were very arrogant and they just told us to get out of the club. We said, 'Well this is our club'. All they told us to do was to take the Bengali kids and get out.

It is quite clear that youth provision is the arena in which some of these questions of ownership are acted out. This worker was following a strategy of creating youth clubs for particular users, then integrating them after they had been established and had attracted previously excluded groups. We will return to this issue later, but interestingly the youth club that Paul Sammut attended was the St Andrews Centre, reputed to be the most culturally mixed club.

In summary, the white young people defined the island as a safe space for them generally. While, 'Asian gangs' were identified as a dangerous threat, they were either located outside the island, in the borderland of Poplar and Bow, or seen as a temporary incursion into their local space. Additionally, we want to emphasise that the attack on Paul Sammut occurred in a place that was viewed as a safe homeland for whites. This incident disrupted the maps of racial safety and danger operated institutionally by the police and local authority officials. It also challenged the popular landscapes of safety and risk for adults and young people. What is also telling is that the sequence of events leading up to the attack started in a place reputed for interracial harmony.

Violence, Fairness and Symmetry in Racist Discourse

In the attack, Paul Sammut suffered a deep cut to the head, and his index finger was cut to the bone. This incident brought the key concerns of the project into focus in ways that were not captured in the school ethnography. The attack revealed the complex manner in which notions of entitlement, exclusion, safety and danger are articulated in the response to violent conflict. Equally, the incident itself gives shape to the urban tales that define and narrate the meanings of locality on the Isle of Dogs. We have recorded the variety of ways the attack has been described and narrated within the adult civic sphere and in the alternative public spheres controlled by young people.

As Alessandro Portelli has pointed out, 'an experienced event is finite … confined to one sphere of experience; a remembered event is infinite, because it is only a key to everything that happened before and after it' (Portelli 1991: 2). But the infinite possibilities in retelling do not result in arbitrariness, or abandoning the possibility of establishing a verifiable plot. Rather, these versions mobilise cultural and political ideas about legitimacy, entitlement, belonging and identity. A close examination of the way events are recounted 'allow[s] us to recognise the interests of the tellers, and the dreams and desires beneath them' (Portelli 1991:2).

Throughout the incident the ethnic/racial nature of Paul Sammut's identity has been uniformly coded as white. There were, however, some rumours within the political culture that his family was Turkish Cypriot in origin, but in fact it later emerged that his mother is white English and his father Maltese. The racialisation of this incident concealed this diversity.

We want to sketch out the sequence of events leading to the attack on Paul Sammut and the reaction locally in its aftermath. Finally, we will examine what this incident tells us about the ways in which the ideas of fairness, community and entitlement are mapped on to these events.

The plot The sequence of events begins in a place in which equality of access is widely believed to exist. The young people in our wider sample confirm this in their walkabouts and interview accounts from the school-based ethnography. The key sites around which these events unfolded are represented in Figure 8.3. The incident begins with the displacement of a group of users from the Harbinger School Youth Club and a conflict between a young black boy and a Bengali boy in St Andrew's Youth Club.

The chronology of these events:

- Monday 20 January 1998 – A group of Bengali boys is banned from Harbinger Youth Club after a violent confrontation between a Bengali youth worker and the group.
- Tuesday 21 January 1998 – The banned group attends St Andrews. The youth worker there is unaware of what happened the previous evening. There is a scuffle and a dispute between one of the Bengali boys and one of the black boys. A local youth worker described the event:

They were watching the television or something and one of them, the Asian boys, and one of the other guys I think they had something in school, I think it went back from ages, because there seemed to be some kind of friction between them. ... Because they knew each other and there was some kind of scuffle broke out between two of them and the next minute there are half a dozen of them trying to converge with one another and then we broke it up.

- The Bengali boys leave the club. Thirty minutes later there is a report of an attack on West Ferry Road. Paul Sammut, 14, walking home with two female friends aged 14, is attacked by a group of Bengali boys, probably eight–twelve in number. He is slapped up against a wall and beaten with belts. The girls are threatened but not attacked. One of the attackers slashes down with a heavy-bladed knife; Sammut puts his hand up to his head and the knife cuts through his index finger and into his head. Later he needs 20 stitches in his skull and microsurgery to re-attach his partially severed finger.

- Some of the Bengali boys run into a nearby Islamic Community Centre. The two girls go off for help. The police arrive on the scene. Paul Sammut's father arrives. There is an altercation with the police.

I was losing my temper saying 'what's happened? Who's done it?' Four or five of them [policeman] grabbed me, they've got my hands round my neck, they threw me in a police car while Paul's still on the floor. But what did they expect me to do? To me he looked like he was dying. I just couldn't handle it, I thought his face was cut to pieces. (Paul Sammut senior, *East London Advertiser*, 29 January 1998, p. 2).

- A crowd of three hundred local people gathers on West Ferry Road and the police seal off the area. The police empty the Islamic Community Centre without questioning or arresting anyone. The crowd is angered and tensions run high.

- Wednesday 22 January 1998 – The local youth worker canvasses the community and decides to hold a meeting in St Andrew's Youth Club. Some of the parents – not including Paul's mother, Gillian Sammut – produce a crude leaflet advertising the event. 'Although the leaflet was free of any racially motivated messages, the mere fact that this method was used meant that from the anticipated small audience it now became likely that the numbers would be ten-fold' (local community worker).

- Thursday 23 January 1998 – Approximately 270–300 people turn up at St Andrew's for the meeting. The youth club is too small for such a number. A local councillor hastily arranges for the use of Calder's Wharf, a place where 'Rights for Whites' meeting have been held, and a bastion of the local white community.

- February/March 1998 – Police offer a £3,000 reward for anyone giving information leading to the arrest of the perpetrators. Because of a story in the *Islander* newspaper, and fears that the BNP would make political capital from the incident, the police brought forward the charging process by prioritising the DNA testing necessary to link eight Bengali boys with the attack.

- Friday 3 April 1998 – A feature on BBC Radio 4's *Today* programme links the case with the electoral chances of the BNP in Millwall. 'Race has long been the fitfully slumbering dragon of East End politics. The attack on young Paul appears to have awoken it. The police say he is the victim of a racially motivated assault. The incident is being used by the racist extreme right-wing British National Party to get votes for the London council elections in May.' (Andrew Hoskin) The programme quotes Paul Sammut senior saying that he thinks the BNP will win.

- Early April 1998 – The BNP produces a video aimed at the east London electorate; BNP flyposters appear on the Isle of Dogs. The video featured local BNP candidates talking explicitly about the Paul Sammut incident as an example of the 'unfairness' of police and local government responses to Asian racism.

- 1 May 1998 – Six Bengali boys are charged by the police for the attack. The weapon is recovered with traces of Paul Sammut's blood on it. Traces of blood are also found on the clothing of some of the arrested boys.

- 5 May 1998 – A further two boys charged. The charges are affray (for the original fight at St Andrew's Youth Club), conspiring to cause grievous bodily harm (six out of the eight), and violent disorder.

- 7 May 1998 – In the election the three BNP candidates in Millwall poll 637 (Gordon Thomas Callow), 606 (Steven Richard Harrington) and 665 (David Hill), but are nowhere near their electoral showing in 1993.[4]

- August 20 1998 – *East London Advertiser* reports that charges against the eight boys have been dropped owing to insufficient evidence.

In the aftermath of the attack these events became a focus for a whole spectrum of fears. In the political culture there was a widespread fear that the reaction to the attack would bolster the BNP's chances in the local elections. Among white parents, concern was voiced about the safety of their children. For Bengali families and community activists there was a sense of foreboding about possible reprisal attacks. For young people involved in the incident as victims, bystanders or perpetrators there was a fear of recognition that might lead to retribution. The incident also became the context in which declarative statements of legitimate belonging and entitlement were articulated. It revealed divisions within the Isle of Dogs community that otherwise remained latent or implicit. The response of the police and their treatment of Paul Sammut's father came to represent the official attitude of the local police and the state to the local white community. We want to identify and reflect on a series of these themes.

Symbolic and Racialised Framings

In the aftermath of this incident all sort of rumours circulated locally around neighbourhood and friendship networks, in the political culture and among local authority workers and people in the youth service. The resulting moral panic is best understood in terms of the circuits of rumour and gossip that laid claim to the meaning, sequence and substance of the events both leading up to the attack and the reactions in its aftermath. One rumour circulating among the young people and their parents was that the knife used in the attack was spirited away to Bangladesh, in order to frustrate prosecution. Another claim was that the Bengali boys went into the Islamic Community Centre first to mobilise support before attacking Paul Sammut. The point we want to stress here is that these accounts are authorised in different ways.

Some of these narratives are *presence-authorised*, in that the speaker invokes first-hand proximity to give legitimacy to the account: 'I was there. I saw it with my own eyes.' This does not necessarily mean that the account is free of current or widely held versions of the events or particular discourses. Here the teller might invoke other specific authorities (parent, friends, politicians) to give the account further legitimacy. Alternatively accounts may be *performance authorised*, that is, dependent on the retelling of rumours in common circulation. The legitimacy of the account is derived from the narrative content of the rumours and the way it is brought to life in the telling of the tale. Such accounts are reproduced through the ritual codes of gossip or rumour and the social arenas in which these performances take place, whether it be for neighbours, friends, housing officers, youth workers or researchers. In what follows we want to map these events within an emergent symbolic geography of racialised and gendered space.

Who's who? Racialised splits, triangulation and conflict The claims made about the number of people involved in the attack varied considerably. A local community worker commented:

> I think it was maybe twelve or whatever people actually involved in the attack on Paul, but I heard stories that went from twelve to twenty to fifty, which is crazy. You have got to think people who are saying around fifty

people ran out of a mosque or whatever, then they are doing that for a particular reason, to agitate, and that is not good really, just exaggerating numbers *to create a kind of fear zone*. [emphasis added]

Some of the key features of the transformation of this district into a 'fear zone' rely on quite clearly racialised divisions.

Paul Sammut's identity had been uniformly coded as white. A feature of this has been that the conflict is understood as a result of a racial bifurcation between Bengali youth and white/black youth. This is significant because it has been utilised both within the community and by members of the British National Party. It is interesting that even within organised racist politics there is some account of shifting patterns of racialised inclusion and exclusion. An activist within the BNP commented in a research interview that 'in some ways the blacks are getting a much harder time than the whites because they are sick and tired of being attacked by Asians'. The assimilation of 'black people' within these ideas makes it easier to disavow accusations of racism while still defining Asians as the problem.

For the islanders, black residents have become defined as contingent insiders within an 'islander first' local hybrid identity. This is exemplified in a passage from Phil Cohen's notes from an Isle of Dogs Action for Equality Group meeting held in Calder's Wharf in March 1993, the same building in which the public meeting was held after the attack.

A prominent white community activist addresses the meeting. 'Everyone here is an immigrant, there are no true-blooded Englishmen, there were Huguenots, Irish, Jews. But they became English first. But the Bangladeshis don't try and fit in. They put Bangladeshi not English down as their nationality. Now they are in the West, they should try and behave like Westerners, not Easterners ...' Someone shouts out. A woman calls out: 'Now they're in England they should follow our rules, like we would have to do in Bangladesh.' He agrees. 'It's gone too far. Enough is enough. There is no more room for them. We are being driven under. We are becoming extinct. At this rate we'll all end up on Canvey Island. Our hands are tied. We want the rights of the locals put first. But they ignore us. They call us racists when we protest about being discriminated against.' Someone shouts out, 'we're cockneys. Enoch Powell was right.' Someone in the crowd makes a reference to Tebbit. 'No-one is allowed to stick up for their country any more. The Union Jack, pride in being English has been made a dirty word. But the Bangladeshis – they're the main problem round here. They are getting more than their fair share of housing and education.' Loud applause.

While reference to Powell and Tebbit for some might inhibit the possible extension of the islander-first identity to local black youth, it does not necessarily preclude such an extension. In fact, we think that precisely such an extension has happened in the Paul Sammut case. So in this sense Islander nativism is self-consciously hybrid while at the same time problematising the Bengali presence. There may well be two distinct types of Islander nativism here: an openly racially exclusive and explicitly white identity discussed previously (Cohen 1996); and another, less explicitly coded in racialised terms. The latter may even flaunt its hybridised qualities while defining another group – the Bengalis – as outsiders. However, this second version of nativism is defined through a) the assimilation of difference and b) the emergence of an islander-first identity. In the meeting that occurred after the attack it was precisely this second version of localism that was being articulated.

Double standards? Accusations of preferential treatment and 'political correctness' In the aftermath of the attack there was much talk about multiculturalism on the Isle of Dogs, particularly in relation to youth clubs. The St Andrew's Centre was highly praised for doing 'multicultural work' while other clubs were vilified for providing only separatist provision. A local youth worker talked about this:

> So it is these kinds of things that plays up in the area because people begin to think well, is it multicultural, or is it separatist work in an area where we are supposed to be working multiculturally? So you get some people who are ignorant of the facts and they can be spoonfed all kinds of racist stuff and incidents like [this] feed fuel to the fire. Some people who are not racist, who are just confused, and they just can't understand why the goalposts keep getting moved – in the middle of that, people get hurt.

When we put it to him that this could be a coded way of attacking the Bengali presence in the area he replied:

> Yes, I think from talking to several people, there are two or three types of views that come to the fore. Some people claim there is too much separatist-type work going on and it is claiming it is not fair because if we live in a multicultural society then work should be geared towards multiculturalism. Some people just blatantly are against Bengali people, and other people will say they are just confused and they don't know; they are totally confused because every time you talk to them there is a different answer. So, yes. I think there's some people who tend to think – well, multiculturalism is a way of trying to code what they really think, but I think generally the majority of people I come in contact with would be quite happy for provisions to be across the board, where everyone could tap into them. I do

genuinely think that. I don't think there are so many hard-nosed people round here; I mean there are some, of course there are some.

The discourse about separatism and multiculturalism elides the fact that there is a history of struggle over access to these facilities. Initially, there is the phenomenon of exclusion by whites, in which Bengali kids felt such provision was not for them. As a response to this, we have the phenomenon of Bengali entryism, where particular clubs became safe havens for (predominantly) young Bengali men. The whole discussion about multiculturalism versus separatism dehistoricises the struggle for access to the island's youth clubs. Ultimately a triangle of racial divisions emerges in which white and black young people are presented as being unfairly discriminated against in favour of the Asians. This was made explicit in the meeting that occurred in the aftermath of the attack. One of the people in the meeting said, in relation to the perpetrators of the attack, 'If it was a white or African–Caribbean youngster they would have been arrested and in the cells by now.'

One of the consistent claims in response to this incident is that the police and the local state operate double standards. This needs to be examined closely because this is often legitimated through observed experience as well as through second-hand narrative sources. A community worker commented:

> You see it is awkward because a lot of people said when the police arrived at the time there was a controversy because when the police arrived they didn't go into the Mosque because they felt they didn't want to inflame things. But all that does from a bystander's point of view is once again they think this is double standards. I mean why wouldn't you go into a mosque – would you go into another building?

The bystander's account is presence-authorised, and becomes an authoritative position from which to argue that the police operate 'double standards'. Through this narrative mode, the incidents and the context are separated from the past. All that is seen is the inaction of the police with no sense of the histories which might have informed that hesitation, such as the legacy of insensitivity in policing Bengali communities and the history of racial attacks against that community. By erasing the past a new space of locality is created. This both wipes clean the slate of history and provides the mechanism through which a moral panic about 'Asian gang violence' is created. A proportion of the white community forms the view that, in the words of one member of the meeting at Calder's Wharf, 'The police are protecting the Pakis.'

More broadly, the sense of an anti-white 'double standard' is generalised to the whole local authority. Local authority support for community centres and religious needs is taken as evidence of the unequal allocation of resources for specialist provision. So the Islamic Community Centre on West Ferry Road becomes both an emblem of unfairly allocated resources and the incursion of unwanted cultural difference. The rumour that Paul Sammut's attackers had gone into the Islamic Community Centre to raise support for the attack implicates in the violence the very existence of the Centre and those who gave it permission to be there. As one prominent member of the white community said at the meeting:

> Special provision had been assigned in recent times to specific cultural groups in preference to members of the indigenous population. This has gone too far now, and we've see the confidence of a group of Asian boys to launch such a vicious attack using the mosque as a safe haven.

It is at this point that these local concerns converge with the agenda of the extreme right. The BNP has mounted a concerted campaign to highlight instances of racial attack where young whites are the victims (see Figure 8.4). This strand in racist expression is by no means new, in fact it is reminiscent of right-wing propaganda of the 1970s focusing on black youth violence. Local white community narratives of 'Asian violence' and fascist propaganda share the claim that young white boys are now the main victims of racial violence.

Safe havens and prayer rooms: the symbolism of the Islamic Community Centre   The symbolic location of the Islamic Community Centre is defined in a variety of ways in the accounts of this event. The people associated with the Centre disassociated themselves from the attack, sympathised openly with the family and co-operated fully with the police. Some see the Centre as the launch-pad for violence, the exemplar of separatist provision and alien incursion on island soil. For others it is a safe haven, a place of moral propriety and religious observance. The Centre is also a former public house. While it is a place where prayers take place, it is not a mosque in the strict sense of the word. But there is confusion here, because in Islamic tradition there is not such a strict division between the secular and the religious as there is in the tradition of European Christianity. Although an equivalence tends to be drawn between churches and mosques as sacred places – particularly in terms of issues surrounding planning permission – this can be misleading. A mosque is not like a church because it is not sanctified ground, and therefore by nature it is a more multi-purpose space. There is, therefore, no clear equivalence between a church and a mosque. Almost any room or place where Bengali people come together to pray regularly can come to be known colloquially as a 'mosque'. Confusion and heated debate have often resulted in high-profile rows over such things as the difference between a prayer room and a mosque.

The controversy over the status of the Centre has been manifest at all levels and in all agencies involved in the incident. A policeman commented: 'They claim it's a community centre but I know it's a mosque because I've seen them praying in there.' At stake in this argument about the status of the Centre are the underlying terms of belonging and entitlement. In a sense the police articulate a liberal form of petty racism. This revolves around the operation of a system of equivalence. It is liberal in that it is about establishing equivalence between the rights of the Bengalis and the whites locally, but it is also about the assertion of an equivalence of wrongs. So in this logic, the 'mosque' has to be protected from the 'natural resentment' of the 'indigenous people', while the indigenous people need to be protected from vengeful cycles of retaliation from Asian youth. Implicit within this system of equivalence is a normative model of those who count as indigenous and those who are the outsiders. Put simply, the white islander group is given the status of indigenous citizens and legitimate locals, while the 'mosque' is designated an incursion of cultural and religious difference, and Asian gangs defined as dangerous urban interlopers.

This symbolic geography is not necessarily fixed, and people's commitment to these ideas can change over time. There are some people who have shifted on this point because it is clearly contentious; the police, for example, have stopped referring to the Centre as a mosque. However, the power of this symbolism is considerable. There have been murmurs within the political culture that action should be taken to ensure that the Centre doesn't get planning permission to become a mosque. Some people in the Labour Party suggested that preventing this was a way of pre-empting the racist Right. The logic here is that if planning permission was given, the BNP would be able to use the presence of the mosque to invoke local white fears.

Mosques often figures in racist iconography as an emblem of unwanted difference and the import of 'foreign religions' that have no place on Christian soil. Figure 8.5 shows an advertisement for a racist poster carried in a series of BNP and racial nationalist publications. The poster represents a mosque overwhelming the background of an 'archetypal' British street. In the foreground is a Christian church and a street-corner pub called the Union Jack Tavern. The caption reads: 'It could be your town, your neighbourhood, your street ... Next!' The sign of the Islamic crescent and the sounds of the call to prayer are represented as looming over the terraced streets of English cities. Perhaps what is so threatening about the Islamic Community Centre on West Ferry Road is that these separations are collapsed, making it a hybrid of incommensurable difference: an ex-public house, an East End home, a mosque, an Islamic community resource, a 'safe haven' for young Bengalis.

The status of the Islamic Community Centre is further complicated by the fact that some people in the Bengali community refer to the Centre as a mosque. The local newspaper, *The Islander*, picked up on this for its own ends:

> The *Islander*'s understanding is that the so-called Islamic Cultural Centre have planning permission which exclude the use as a mosque, and indeed there is external evidence that it is a mosque. It caused some surprise, therefore, when Mr Sammut received a letter from the centre, very properly extending sympathy to young Paul and the family and condemning the attack and the resort to violence, which referred to the centre as a mosque.

The point is that a 'mosque' means different things to different people, and its symbolism is intimately connected to struggles over entitlement, legitimacy and belonging.[5]

The BNP – inside and outside The reaction to this incident was made sense of in terms of 'inside' and 'outside' interests. As we have already shown, East End racism is often understood as the product of the intrinsic nature of the area. Alternatively, the success of the BNP in 1993 has been explained in terms of political opportunism in which this extreme right-wing political group exploited the discontent of the islanders for their own advancement (Cohen 1996). But viewing the success of the far-right or the currency of popular racism as 'intrinsic' or 'extrinsic' misses the complexity in the relationship between this particular place and racist politics. The news of the attack on Paul Sammut was certainly appropriated by the far right, but the BNP was also invoked at different times from the 'inside'. The Sammut family has been positioned in a complicated way throughout this incident. The family has resisted going public, although they have been offered money for their story by several national tabloid newspapers. One version had it that decent white East Enders protected the family from insidious outside interests. However, the threat of turning to the BNP for support has also been invoked from the 'inside'. At one public meeting a man stood up and said: 'Unless something is done about this [the attack], my vote will switch from Labour to a more controversial party.'

Despite the efforts of the BNP, there was no electoral swing towards the right in the May 1998 elections. The video they produced and circulated locally was quite sophisticated in its mode of address because it combines local reference, including a discussion of the Paul Sammut incident, alongside national themes. Yet the BNP were in the main unsuccessful in using this incident to make racist politics more electorally attractive. In fact, the BNP vote dropped to a little over a quarter of what it had been in 1994. In the run-up to the election, the local Labour Party was extremely concerned that local discontent would lead to a repeat of 1993. This panic was in large part a reaction to a rash of BNP flyposters that appeared on the island in late April 1998. We sought out the posters, numbering 75–100, almost certainly put up during a single afternoon of BNP canvassing. Figure 8.6 shows an abandoned pub – the Dorset Arms on Manchester Road, a frequent target for commercial fly posting. BNP 'Rights for Whites' posters were plastered over a range of billboard advertisements for pop bands. The iconic juxtaposition of a BNP poster over a promo for a black American R&B group resonated beyond mere coincidence. It seemed that white islanders had in large part heeded Destiny's Child's appeal and rejected electoral far-right politics. But how might the relationship between the BNP agenda and the local white community be re-thought, beyond viewing it as either the result of local/intrinsic racism or instrumental/outside political opportunism?

As we have already shown, there is a clear divergence between the sensibilities of white islanders and anything that might approach racial nationalism. However, the connection between local politics of race and the BNP might be better thought of in terms of the point at which local themes coalesce with the ultra-nationalist political agenda and vice-versa. This is not a matter of reducing these two different political/ discursive forms to the same entity, but rather that they enter into a relationship of narrative harmony. In this sense the mutual appeal to 'fairness' and the assertion of anti-white 'double standards' and 'political correctness' provide the point at which a common chord is struck between otherwise distinct social and political phenomena. Therefore it is perhaps more accurate to see the relationship between local patriotism and racist politics as a matter of the collation of parallel narratives. We now want to turn to examine critically what is at stake in the narratives of fairness and white victimhood.

Fair's Fair? Symmetry and Asymmetry in Narratives of Fairness

The American political philosopher Amy Gutmann has argued that a colour-blind notion of fairness can be combined with colour-conscious social policies in a morally defensible way. 'The colour-conscious policies that this political morality defends are based on a colour-blind principle of fairness. ... I have argued against advocates of colour-blind policies, that fairness in our society demands colour-consciousness' (Gutmann 1996: 177). She argues that colour-conscious policies can be defended because they aim to redress the unfairness inherent in racism. Whites may be encouraged to accept the fairness of positive action policies as forms of corrective asymmety that aim to redress this legacy. But it is striking in the context of London that white talk about 'fairness' and 'unfairness' in matters of race is implicated in concealing racial injustice, or inhibiting wider discussion of issues of racial inequality of the type that Gutmann proposes. This seemingly paradoxical situation produces a form of talk in which the appeal for fair treatment for whites goes hand in hand with an implicit denial of the legitimacy of claims by ethnic minority communities about experiences of racism and urban injustice.

Roger Hewitt has highlighted the significance of narratives of unfairness in his recent work in Greenwich, South East London (Hewitt 1996, 1997). In the Isle of Dogs, we found accounts that were strikingly similar to Hewitt's findings. The claims of unfair treatment in white narratives worked through an assertion that housing officers, policemen or local politicians do not behave even-handedly with regard to white and non-white communities. These contentions commonly include statements like: 'There's one law for them and another one for us'; 'Asians get housed while white families are forced to move away'; or 'If a white attacks a Bengali, politicians scream racism, but if a Bengali attacks a white, the police turn a blind eye.' The suggestion that whites are treated unfairly is underpinned by an implicit appeal to the ideal that everyone should be treated equally, which on the surface seems a viable and unproblematic ideal. It appears to propose that all, regardless of background, should get equivalent rights – economic, housing, citizenship – and that wrongful behaviour should be treated with equal condemnation. But such appeals are far from universal. Rather, they are bound into a context in which the debate about racism and racial inequality is frozen in the present, so that histories of racism and disadvantage experienced by ethnic minorities are rendered inadmissible. While affirming symmetry and fairness at one level, this discourse actually confirms racial asymmetry and inequality at another level. As one white islander commented, 'There are far more attacks on white people by Asians here than the other way around. Now the police deny that publicly [and] the politicians will deny that publicly.' Claims like this pre-empt any challenge. Statistical police evidence of racism against minorities, which, as we shall see, gives a very different picture, can be dismissed as biased – 'the police turn a blind eye when the victim is white'. The appeal to symmetry – that violence against whites should count – results in the erasure of ethnic minority experiences of racial injustice or manifest racism.

The pervasive notion amongst white islanders is that they are treated 'unfairly' and have become 'second-class status' citizens. But others in

Asymmetry	Symmetry
Structure of Racialised Urban Inequality	*Rhetorics of Citizenship*
Racial inequality, violence and attack, housing discrimination, residential segregation and overcrowding.	'English fairness,' the city as a meeting place and an open public sphere. Equality before the law.
Positive Action to combat disadvantage	*Rights and Legal Framework*
Corrective attempts to establish parity in housing provision, police, education/ shifting of policing strategies for Bengali community, provision of specialist community organisations/ youth clubs.	Assertion of equal rights to housing and 'fair policing.' Open access to leisure resources and public life.
White Accusations of Unfairness	*Assertion of 'Equal Rights for Whites'*
'Second class citizens,' preferential treatment leading to white disadvantage, lack of even-handed treatment by the police.	

Tower Hamlets claim that the island is better provided for, in terms of local services, than anywhere else in the borough. Overcrowding is far less prevalent on the island than in other parts of East London. Open space and leisure facilities are better here than elsewhere. The way in which the discourse of unfairness pre-empts these comparisons is crucial to understanding its power. This is where arguments that depend on the idea that working-class racism is due to deprivation fall down (Phizacklea & Miles 1979). On the one hand, there are real class inequalities within the region, made more stark by the gentrification of the local economy and the insertion of highly paid service and financial sectors. At the same time there are privileges enjoyed by white workers which the shroud of 'unfairness talk' conceals.

The manner in which time and space mediate and re-inscribe the visibility and invisibility of these symmetries and asymmetries provides the dynamic at the heart of localised moral panics. It is perhaps telling here that in the local debate about the Paul Sammut case there has been little discussion of the history of racist violence against Bengali young people in the area. Some of the concerns about Bengali boys hanging about together are separated from the context in which these patterns of sociability were established. In the period when gratuitous attacks on Bengalis took place, young men were advised by their families not to go out alone. It is important to place these accusations within the context of the recorded racial incidents in this part of Tower Hamlets when compared to the borough as a whole. Between January and March 1998, 59 incidents by 67 perpetrators were reported in the borough as a whole. Half of those incidents (34) took place on the Isle of Dogs. Not all of the perpetrators were known, but of those incidents where the victim identified the perpetrator, sixteen were white (ten male and six female), four were Bangladeshi (all male) and five were Somali (all male). In eight incidents perpetrators were unknown.[6]

We might then think about how notions of racial/ethnic symmetry and asymmetry work both through inclusion and erasure. This might be best thought of at three spatial and temporal levels. The 'Rights for Whites' call for fairness has both a synchronic quality that erases or elides the past *and* is defined through a local particularity that masquerades as a universal value. The white appeals to even-handed treatment and symmetry denies or erases the diachronic racial asymmetries that have existed and continue to exist; all the talk about 'unfairness' in this context is quite difficult to argue against. This is partly because the discourse acknowledges, even draws legitimacy from, the forms of positive action enacted by the local state against racial inequality. It focuses on a *corrective asymmetry* while concealing the underlying inequality to which these policies relate. The 'rights for whites' mantra denies the racism and differential treatment enshrined in the racialised structure of urban inequality. These ways of constructing the issue of 'fairness' become a powerful means to argue for inequality and white privilege.

Perhaps one way to engage with the discourse of 'unfairness' is to try and make explicit the connections between the levels outlined above. However, this form of 'fair talk' is pervasive and manifest within the local community, the police and the political sphere. As one police officer said to us: 'I've been looking into this stuff about racial attacks and it's not all one-sided. It's much more fifty-fifty.' This effectively effaces the memory of racism and violence, which has all too often had devastating consequences for the Bengali community of east London.

Conclusion

We have argued that the old languages of 'fairness', 'equality' and 'rights' have been assimilated within the terrain of the local political culture producing far from commensurate effects on the population as a whole. We want to emphasise that these apparently 'universal principles' take on a particular meaning when situated in both time and space. Kenan Malik has argued recently that, 'Equality can have no meaning in the plural. Equality cannot be relative, with different meanings to different social, cultural and sexual groups. If so it ceases to be equality at all ... Equality requires a common yardstick, or measure of judgement, not a plurality of meanings' (Malik 1998: 127). But this misses an important point. To invoke a notion of universalism in this way is to do it outside of space, time and context. Rather we want to argue that there is a need for a radical contextualisation of precisely the 'plurality of meanings' that such notions of 'equality' and 'fairness' embody. The meanings of fairness are achieved in and through time and place. We are proposing that political interventions need to acknowledge and account for these inflections within talk about fairness and appeals for equal rights.

Establishing the 'rights and wrongs' of incidents of violence means confronting a possible tension between 'rights' as an entitlement or a legal and moral claim and correct types of action or probity. For a section of the white islander community, Bengalis simply did not have an equal right to belonging and local entitlement. More than this, the lack of equivalent rights in the local body politic may explain why the undeniable violence suffered by Bengalis was so easily forgotten or erased from public narratives. Jordan, a 15-year-old black boy and friend of Paul Sammut, told us:

> Well, maybe the adults are more racist than what the kids are. Fair enough, I ain't surprised when there was a fuss, but if that was a Bengali person there wouldn't be all these people kicking up a fuss. I know the whites wouldn't and I know the blacks wouldn't – they wouldn't be saying that is out of order, 'get people off the island', or do this or do that.

For Jordan, accountability for wrong-doing is based on those particular individuals who have violated codes of public propriety. He explained that the lack of violent escalation or retribution in the aftermath of the attack was due to the shared understanding among young people that this was about particular people and not whole social groups. This, he claimed, stood in stark contrast to the way adults viewed the situation.

> They think it is the end of the world. They just think that the Bengalis go on like that, but they don't just go on like that, that is a fact. I bet more black and white people have killed more people than what the Bengalis have. Don't get me wrong, I am not glad about what happened to Paul. I am not saying I don't want nothing done about it, but I don't want everybody to gang up on the Bengalis. [I want] for them boys to be sorted out because they did it, the boys that did it, they should get sorted, not the whole community. Because one set of Bengalis done that, they expect all the rest to be like that ... They must be racists obviously.

Perhaps there are some clues in Jordan's 'good sense' concerning how to begin to talk openly about youth violence of this kind. He points us towards the importance of separating deeds from categories of being. He appeals for violence to be specified, for the boys who were guilty to be 'sorted.' This avoids conflating these actions with a category of person – the Bengalis. It was precisely this elision that came to dominate the way the Paul Sammut attack was debated publicly. Following Jordan's prescription, deeds define the crime, rather than racial categories delimiting types of criminal. As Nietzsche commented famously, 'there is no "being" behind doing, acting, becoming; "the doer" is merely a fiction imposed on the doing – the doing itself is everything' (Nietzsche 1996: 29). Perhaps real dialogue needs to be first premised on concentrating on the 'acts' themselves. This means uncovering the crude charade at the centre of moral panics, whether they be about 'Asian gang violence' or the existence on the Isle of Dogs of a homogeneous 'racist culture'.

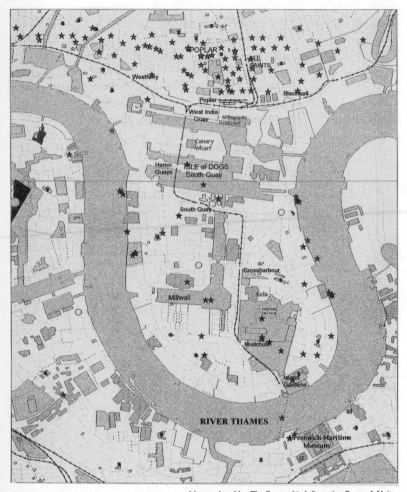

★ White Children 'No Go' Areas

Map produced by The Geographic Information Research Unit,
School of Surveying, University of East London.

Bartholomews map data courtesy of the Midas Service,
University of Manchester and CHEST.
Copyright Bartholomews 1998.

FIGURE 8.1 Places that white children do not visit

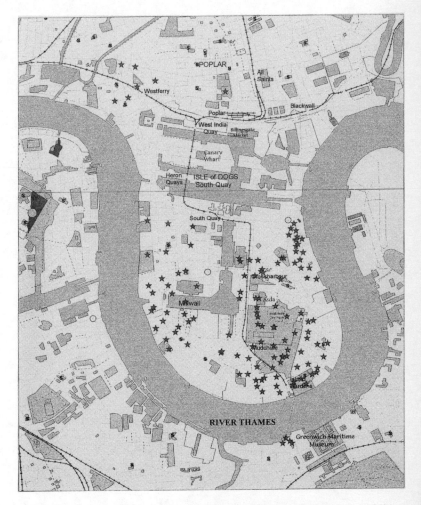

Map produced by The Geographic Information Research Unit,
School of Surveying, University of East London.

★ White friends

Bartholomews map data courtesy of the Midas Service,
University of Manchester and CHEST.
Copyright Bartholomews 1998.

FIGURE 8.2 Places where white children meet with friends

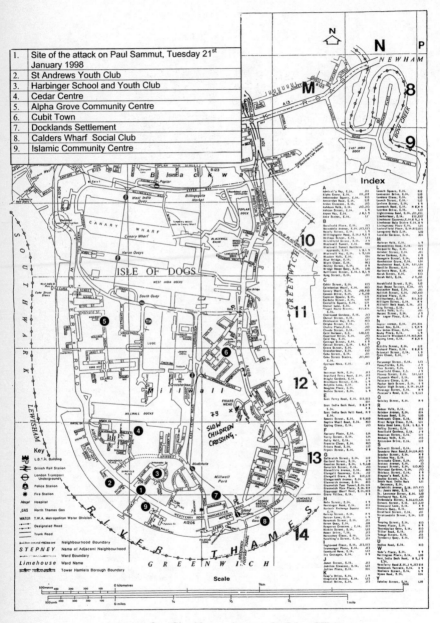

1.	Site of the attack on Paul Sammut, Tuesday 21ˢᵗ January 1998
2.	St Andrews Youth Club
3.	Harbinger School and Youth Club
4.	Cedar Centre
5.	Alpha Grove Community Centre
6.	Cubit Town
7.	Docklands Settlement
8.	Calders Wharf Social Club
9.	Islamic Community Centre

FIGURE 8.3 Significant sites on the Isle of Dogs

STOP THE RACE ATTACKS!

A White boy lies in a coma close to death on a life support machine because politicians have forced an unworkable multi-racialism upon us with all the violence that entails.

Little Daniel Moore, aged 12, was attacked by a gang of 20 racist Asians armed with bricks, bottles and lumps of wood. He had been playing football with two friends when the 20 older youths chased the three, screaming: "You pieces of white trash." Poor Daniel couldn't get away and stood no chance as the 20 battered him near to death. *It wouldn't be acceptable if whites had attacked an Asian boy and this attack is not acceptable either.* While the media took up the story, there was no linking of this attack to others showing *a definite trend of attacks against whites.* Only four months before this, an eight-year-old in Halifax was racially attacked by three older Asians who beat him, set him on fire and ran off laughing. At the same time in London, 15 white boys playing football, aged 14-16, were attacked by 20 older Asians armed with knives, bottles and axes. More

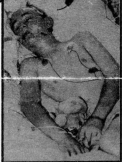

Asians joined in to ensure that the boys could not escape, and horrific injuries were inflicted. There is a near conspiracy of silence in the media about these and other attacks. LAST YEAR NO FEWER THAN FOUR WHITES WERE MURDERED BECAUSE OF THE COLOUR OF THEIR SKIN: Christopher Farrell, Andrew Steventon, Mark Sharp and Danny Westmacott. But the media only talk about the murder of black Stephen Lawrence. Don't white victims count? Is the BNP the only group speaking up for white people and against the violence? Yes! But you'll not be reading that in the controlled media!

The BNP says: stop the racial attacks — ALL OF THEM!

BNP Information Line:- 0374 454893   Web site:- http://www.webcom.com/bnp

Please tick a box, fill in and send to the address below.

Please send me more information about the BNP — I enclose 50p to cover costs. ❑
I want to join the BNP and enclose £20.00 (£10 for OAPs, students and unwaged). ❑
NAME...
ADDRESS..
....

Printed & published by the British National Party P.O. Box 117, Welling, Kent DA16 3DW

FIGURE 8.4 British National Party leaflet circulating in East London, 1998

FIGURE 8.5 'Mosque symbolism': Islamic community centre, West Ferry Road, and a far-right anti-Mosque poster

FIGURE 8.6 British National Party posters, Manchester Road, Isle of Dogs,
April 1998

Notes

1. This chapter is based on work carried out in the Economic and Social Research Council-funded project: 'Finding The Way Home: young people, community safety and racial danger' (R000236301). The chapter is authored by Les Back and Michael Keith, with inputs from Phil Cohen, but it is also the product of a research team that included Tim Lucas, Tahmina Maula, Sarah Newlands and Landé Pratt. We would like to thank the ESRC for their support. We would also like to thank Ben Gidley and Garry Robson. Lastly, a special thank you to Richard McKeever for his critical comments on earlier drafts of this paper.

2. The fieldwork was conducted on the Isle of Dogs by Tim Lucas and Tahmina Maula. We would like to thank them and acknowledge their contribution.

3. This situation has changed since the research period; some of these clubs have been closed or changed their user groups.

4. In the 1993 bye-election, the BNP candidate Derek Beackon, was elected with 1,480 votes, against the Labour candidate's 1,473. In 1994 all three seats in Millwall ward were won by the Labour party with votes of between 3,446 and 3,547. Derek Beackon came fourth, polling 2,041 votes, with two other BNP candidates coming in fifth and sixth.

5. The controversies over the status of Islamic places of worship are all the more disingenuous given that Christianity is being used to foster racial segregation locally. It is precisely through religion that much of the racial segregation in education is being maintained. Church schools which principally admit Catholic or Church of England students have become the chief way in which white parents secure their children places in schools that are almost exclusively white.

6. Data taken from Tower Hamlets Directorate of Housing Services – Racial Harassment Support Unit (1998).

Bibliography:

Appadurai, A. (1990) 'Disjuncture and difference in the global cultural economy', in *Public Culture*, 2, 2: 1–24.

Bernstein, B. (1971) *Class, codes and control*, vol. 1, St Albans: Paladin.

— (1977) 'Social class, language and socialisation', in J. Karabel and A.H. Halsey (eds), *Power and ideology in education*, New York: Oxford University Press.

Booth, C. (1902–3) *Life and labour of the people in London* (seventeen volumes), London: Macmillan.

Bourdieu, P. (1977) *Outline of a theory of practice*, Cambridge: Cambridge University Press.

— (1991) *Language and symbolic power*, Cambridge, Mass: Harvard University Press.

— (1992) *The logic of practice*, Cambridge: Polity.

Brake, M. (1985) *Comparative youth culture: the sociology of youth culture and youth subcultures in America, Britain and Canada*, London: Routledge and Kegan Paul.

Campbell, B. (1993) *Goliath: Britain's dangerous places*, London: Lawrence and Wishart.

Centre for Bangladeshi Research (1993) *Young Bengalis and the criminal justice system*, London: Queen Mary and Westfield, University of London.

Cohen, P. (1972) *Subcultural conflict and working-class community*, Working paper in Cultural Studies 2, Birmingham: University of Birmingham.

— (1996) 'All white on the night', in M. Rustin (ed.) *Rising East*, London: Lawrence and Wishart.

— , M. Keith and L. Back (1996) *Finding the way home: issues of theory and method*, CNER/CUCR Working papers, London: Centre for New Ethnicities Research and Centre for Urban and Community Research

Cohen, S. (1972) *Folk Devils and Moral Panics*, London: MacGibbon & Kee.

Gutmann, A. (1996) 'Responding to racial injustice', in K. A. Appiah and A. Gutmann, *Color Conscious: The Political Morality of Race*, Princeton: Princeton University Press.

Hall, S., C. Critcher, T. Jefferson and B. Roberts (1978) *Policing the crisis*, London: Macmillan.

Hewitt, R. (1996) *Routes of Racism: the social basis of racist action*, London: Trentham Books.

— (1997) *Routes of racism: the manual*, London: Greenwich Council's Central Race equality Unit and Greenwich Education Service.

Husbands, C. T. (1983) *Racial Exclusion and the city: the urban support of the National Front*, London and Boston: Allen and Unwin.

Jefferson, T. (1988) 'Race, crime and policing,' in *International Journal of the Sociology of Law* 16, 4: 521–39.

Keith, M. (1993) *Race, riots and policing: lore and disorder in a multi-racist society*, London: UCL Press.

— (1995) 'Making the street visible: placing racial violence in context', in *New Community* 21 (4): 551–65.

Kent, R. A. (1981) *A history of British empirical sociology*, Aldershot: Gower.

Kinsey, R. *et al.* (1986) *Losing the fight against crime*, Oxford: Blackwell.

Kurtz, L. (1984) *Evaluating Chicago sociology*, Chicago: University of Chicago Press.

Lefebvre, H. (1991) *The Production of Space*, Cambridge, Mass: Blackwell.

Linebaugh, P. (1991) *The London Hanged: crime and civil society in the eighteenth century*, Harmondsworth: Penguin

Malik, K. (1998) 'Race, Pluralism and the Meaning of Difference', in *New Formations* 33 (Spring): 125–36.

Mayhew, H. (1968) *London labour and London poor* (vols 1–3), New York: Dover Publications.

Modood, T. *et al.* (1994) *Changing ethnic identities*, London: Policy Studies Institute.

Murray, C. (1994) *The Underclass: the crisis deepens*, London: Inner London Education Authority Health and Welfare Unit.

Nietzsche, F. (1996) *On the genealogy of morals*, Oxford: Oxford University Press.

Phizacklea, A. and R. Miles (1979) 'Working-class racist beliefs in the inner city', in R. Miles and A. Phizacklea, *Racism and political action in Britain*, London: Routledge and Kegan Paul.

Portelli, A. (1991) *The death of Luigi Trastulli and other stories: form and meaning in oral history*, Albany: State University Press.

Porter, R. (1994) *London: a social history*, London: Hamish Hamilton.

Rediker, M. (1987) *Between the devil and the deep blue sea: merchant seamen, pirates, and the Anglo-American maritime world*, Cambridge: Cambridge University Press.

Robson, G. (1998) '"No one likes us we don't care": Millwallism, class, community and identity', Ph.D thesis, Goldsmiths College, University of London.

Said, E. W. (1978) *Orientalism*, London: Penguin.

Smith. S. J. (1986) *Crime, space and society*, Cambridge: Cambridge University Press.

Stedman Jones, G. (1976) *Outcast London: a study in the relationship between classes in Victorian society*, Harmondsworth: Penguin.

— (1989) 'The "cockney" and the nation 1780–1988', in D. Feldman and G. Stedman Jones (eds), *Metropolis London: histories and representations since 1800*, London and New York: Routledge.

Tower Hamlets Directorate of Housing Services, Racial Harassment Support Unit (1998) *Tower Hamlets Racial Harassment Quarterly Reports January–March 1998*, London: Tower Hamlets Council.

Ware, V. (1996) 'Island racism: gender, place, and white power' in *Feminist Review*, 54: 65–86.

Young, M. and P. Wilmott (1957) *Family and kinship in East London*, London: Penguin.

9

It's Just Not Cricket! Ethnicity, Division and Imagining the other in English Cricket

Ian McDonald and Sharda Ugra

Ask people to describe 'Englishness' and there is a chance that they will mention cricket on the village green. It will perhaps form part of a cluster of images evoking an unchanging, organic pastoral society, where conflicts are dealt with peacefully through well-mannered point-making and where hierarchy is embraced. No image seems to encapsulate this idea of Englishness better than cricket on the village green. Whether there is something peculiarly English about cricket, or whether cricket, with its formal dress, rural grounds and rituals represents Englishness is less clear, and perhaps less important, than the entwining of cricket and Englishness in the popular imagination. It does not matter that the assumptions underpinning English cricket's *Englishness* are wrong. Since when have myths depended on hard historical facts? Cricket's origins, in contrast to the myth peddled by many of the game's commentators, are in the messy, unprincipled world of commerce, politics, patronage and an urban society (Marqusee 1998: 43–71). However (following the famous saying of the American sociologist W.I Thomas), if men define situations as real they are real in their consequences, and the consequence for the cricket culture in England is that it is emblematic of a particular construction of Englishness as rural, hierarchical and knowing how to behave. The BBC Test Match cricket commentator Christopher Martin-Jenkins summed it up well: 'Cricket is a game which must always be less than its true self if it is taken out of England and out of the weather of our English summer … In every village a cricket field is as much a part of the landscape as the old church (quoted in Roy 1998).

This is also a landscape that is culturally white. It is overwhelmingly white people, or rather white men, who are playing cricket on the village green, because, as Robert Henderson attempted to argue in the pages of *Wisden Cricket Monthly*, only white men are 'unequivocally English' (Henderson 1995). Most people would accept that this is now a dated, stereotypical, racist view of Englishness. English culture is now more plural, dynamic, urban and multicultural (though not necessarily less racist). Importantly, the position of black and Asian people within this culture is not defined by their absence.

Similarly, within cricket culture, as with other major sports in England, such as football, boxing and athletics, non-white players have made their presence felt. Indeed, while cricket is struggling to gain and keep the attention of young white people, the game's popularity is thriving within Britain's mainly urban Asian communities. However, to a much greater extent than these other sports, cricket in the black and Asian communities exists outside the official structures of the game, while mainstream cricket continues to be associated with a mythical bygone era of white imperial England. The fact that Henderson was able to get his article published in *Wisden Cricket Monthly* reveals that the culture of Englishness as whiteness still has credibility within the cricket establishment. And as this chapter will illustrate, this culture appears to hold a position of dominance at the recreational end of the cricket spectrum.

This chapter presents some of the findings from a study into the different cricket cultures in east London and Essex (McDonald and Ugra 1998). This study was conducted during the 1997 cricket season and was based on observations of matches and interviews with players, club officials, umpires and schoolchildren. The study identified two distinct but un-equally related cultures of cricket: black and Asian cricket, played in urban settings in public parks in a spirit of competitiveness; and white cricket, played in rural areas on private grounds as a social occasion based on the rituals of English cricket. These cultures are not equal because the white clubs have the power to effect the continued exclusion of black and Asian clubs from the official leagues. Therefore, despite an overwhelming desire by most black and Asian players to play in the official Sunday leagues, cricket in the region has become segregated along lines of ethnicity.

This chapter will draw on the material gathered from the player interviews. Forty-five players were interviewed: of these, eighteen were white, seventeen were Asian and ten were black. The white players were interviewed at cricket matches played in rural Essex, while the black and Asian players were interviewed at matches in urban east London. Whatever changes may affect cricket at the élite level, the myth of English cricket on the village green still holds a protected position in the structure of the game. This chapter will illustrate the ways in which this culture of English cricket in an era of multiculturalism gives rise to racial exclusion and at times racial abuse – a clear case of old ethnicities and new racism. Further, by relying heavily on the voices of the respondents in the study, this chapter will also show how unequal relations between the different cricket communities are shaped by their interlocking interactions based on actor's perceptions and expectations of each other. As C.H Cooley, another famous American sociologist, stated, 'the imaginations we have of one another' are 'the solid facts of society'.

The players were asked: 'Do people from different cultures play/approach cricket differently?' Without any prompting, the majority of white respondents linked cricket to Englishness. Indeed, it was a very specific notion of Englishness – rural, traditional, civilised – which they linked to a specific kind of cricket – 'genteel', non-aggressive village cricket. Interestingly, many of the respondents playing for village teams in Essex lived and worked in London. They travelled to the countryside at weekends to play cricket, thus choosing to tap into their notion of what they considered 'true English cricket'. One respondent lived in Colchester but played for a village team because:

It's always been a great ambition of mine to actually play village cricket. I think the ethos of village cricket – not that sort of romantic ethos – the ethos of actually playing for a small ... for a community. I actually feel cricket reflects that village community as well, it's part of that tradition of a village.

Another provided a picturesque view of his idea of English cricket:

You come down here [to his team's ground during a cricket festival] and you say ... 'That is something which is quintessentially English'. We have the festival at the end of August and you've just got that autumnal feel about it. You come down here at eight o'clock in the morning. It's slightly dewy, a bit of gossamer about and it is glorious, it really is. And to see then the whole game actually starting, the life that is breathed into [the place] ... the marquees round in colour. It's wonderful, it's absolutely wonderful. The only problem is that you can always look out over the council dustbins, we should be looking the other way with the castle behind. That's how cricket should be ... it should have a castle ... or a church spire in the background ... and trees.

In addition to having an understanding of the specific context of English cricket, many white players also contrasted the traditional style of play associated with this cricket with that played in the black and Asian communities. Here are two examples of different responses: 'My first impression would be that an Afro-Caribbean player would be a lot more flamboyant than either an English or a white player.' 'Asian cricketers bat in a very wristy and stylish way and they are generally shorter in stature and play nice wristy shots off the backfoot.' While the majority of white respondents who referred to a distinct black style of play did so in descriptive terms, a small minority were more pejorative in their expressions. For example:

> We had one side we played against a couple of years ago and they had one coloured chap and he was a ferocious little bowler. He really got fired up. For some reason he didn't get on in the club and he was a bit too arrogant and full of himself.

Explanations for the distinct styles of cricket varied according to ethnicity. Some of the white players attributed the more 'flamboyant' style of 'West Indian' cricket to the innate biological traits of black people, for example: 'We had two chaps called the —— brothers who were fantastic sportsmen, I mean obviously, when you've got the coloured people, they're running. They are incredible runners, incredible athletes.'

Many black and Asian players also had clear views about different cultures and approaches to the game. The majority of black and Asian respondents were critical of what they termed 'English cricket' or 'white cricket', the most common criticism being that it was conservative in its approach and not competitive enough. The following remarks, both from Asian players, were typical of the comments made: 'English cricket is too boring and too slow. They kill the game off. We would rather lose the game chasing runs than go for a draw. That's the difference.' 'We [Asians] classify a full toss [as a ball that] should be hit out of the ground, but the English classify it as the most dangerous ball to be facing.' A major point of difference between the white players and the black and Asian players was on the matter of what was most important in playing cricket. Standards of play, competitiveness and aggression, highlighted by the majority of black and Asian respondents, appeared to be secondary to the majority of white respondents. Given that the level of the cricket for both groups was identical (they both played Sunday friendlies), the difference in outlook was significant. The white players tended to state that their cricket was of a social nature ('competitive but friendly'), wherein, as was frequently pointed out to the researchers, winning was 'not the be-all and end-all'. For one, cricket was 'A day out. We all work during the week and come the weekend we want to play cricket for the social side of the game ... it's the social banter during the game, it's the drink after.' Although many of the games were designated as 'friendlies', they were still played in a serious and competitive spirit. However, while winning was the aim of the game, many respondents felt it should not be pursued at all costs. Indeed, upholding the game's traditional rituals and social etiquette was considered more important than being competitive.

The attitudes of black and Asian respondents was very different. One black respondent, who came to this country at the age of 18, described cricket in England as 'soft':

> When I came up here I felt it was very soft cricket, it was not aggressive cricket, or hard cricket. It was more gentle cricket up here. When I say hard cricket I mean you have guys coming in at 90 miles an hour trying to do damage to you and you've got to be good enough to stay there and bat. In this country you don't get that. You get gentle cricket … here it is more social.

Cricket as a competitive sporting experience rather than a social occasion was emphasised by this 23-year-old Asian respondent:

> If the game isn't competitive how are you going to enjoy it? With them [white clubs] we play time games in which you can end up going for a draw and we would never do that. We say win or lose. Because we like to go home saying 'oh we won the game …' even if you lose it doesn't matter, but if it's not competitive, what is the use of sport? It has to be competitive.

Several black and Asian players commented that the importance placed on etiquette in the culture of English cricket was alien to their approach. A 35-year-old black respondent spoke of subtle disapproval by white clubs in this regard:

> The way we play cricket is totally different to them. I mean culturally we are very different to them … we play cricket and we enjoy our cricket. We shout, we laugh and they can't put up with it. They expect you to sit down and say [clapping hands] 'oh, good shot chap' and all that … I mean it's just not in us.

Where differences have been recognised by white, black and Asian players alike, the relationship between black and Asian cricket is an interesting one. Due to the common factors that have kept these clubs out of mainstream cricket, there is greater interaction between the two groups, cultural differences notwithstanding. The captain of an Asian team said his team had 'no problems' when playing in black sides because 'they are also in the same boat as us – wanting competitive cricket'. Another Asian respondent said:

> The atmosphere there [during matches] is more relaxed with them [black teams]. It's good competitive cricket with them. The West Indians know that these guys are a good bunch of cricketers; we have got to give them a tough match … We have a match on the basis of abilities of cricket rather than verbally abusing one another.

The two interpretations of cricket, as a competitive sporting experience and as a social occasion, for most of the time occupy parallel cricketing cultures in Essex and east London. Although, formally, they are playing the same game with the same rules, the combination of distinct environmental settings and attitudes to playing mean that, effectively, two separate codes of cricket characterise the two cricketing communities.

The majority of white respondents were unaware of the extent of black and Asian cricket in the Essex region. When informed about them, they tended to view black and Asian clubs and leagues as 'separatist entities'. For example, the responses from two different white respondents below was common: 'It's a sort of voluntary apartheid policy in action'; 'Isn't that then producing segregation? ... I think if you start Asian-only clubs and that sort of thing you open yourself up to racist problems anyway – if you are only allowed to play if you are Asian, you are segregating to start with.' All of the white players emphasised that black and Asian players would not be discouraged from joining their clubs. However, the welcome that white players were confident of extending to black and Asian players was often conditional. 'Fitting in' was deemed necessary:

> Yes, people do have to fit in, but people only have to be decent, reasonable, polite ... humorous helps, able to give and take micky-taking, that's all they have to be and they're welcomed ... it's a perfectly reasonable system, I think. It's not a conscious system, nobody invented it that way. But if someone comes in and he is too loud, too aggressive, too rude, too sullen, too quiet, too pompous, too earthy, too anything, then they aren't accepted.

Most black and Asian players contested the claim made by some of the white players that they were creating a form of 'voluntary cricket apartheid'. They stated that the black and Asian leagues were formed only after black and Asian clubs found it difficult to break into mainstream cricket. One black respondent said: 'What's the alternative? We can't get into the white leagues so we have to form our own leagues.'

Many black and Asian respondents spoke of their 'disillusion' with the white cricket clubs, while some articulated their participation in black and Asian clubs as a form 'resistance' to the 'English' values of official cricket culture. A section of the Muslim Asian cricket community viewed the development of separate cricket as a positive force. The explicit rationale for the Gujarati Muslim community cricket league is maintenance of community identity. The league has a clear policy of restricting the number of players from outside the community to three per team. In a defence of the league's regulations, an administrator-player stated that the restrictions in his community league were similar to those operating in the official leagues with respect to overseas players. 'Our main reason not to have more than two outsiders is to keep fair competition within the teams and within the community.' Another Asian respondent said that the restrictions were essential to the ethos of the league, which was community-centred, rather than cricket-centred. One of the respondents involved in creating the league, which has grown from six to twenty-four teams over three years, argued that cricket had helped to foster community identity:

> We believe there is nothing whatsoever [for us] after work ... being Muslim, I'm very much afraid our kids will get into lots of other habits which we don't want ... We've been very successful in this league. All our youngsters are occupied on a Sunday ... and people who come from back home they recognise each other by surname or face. We have that sort of culture ... the youngsters now recognise the elder people ... the reason why I chose cricket was because cricket is a kind of sport which is in Asian blood.

Another respondent, involved in the same league, asserted that:

> We opened this league to get our community together because there was a fracture going on for some years. We don't have any community integration. All our young boys are getting into drugs and discos. We, being Muslims, we thought how can we keep them together. Because what had happened here is that nobody knew each other, everybody was alien ... because this is a British form of society, each one for himself. And we thought that by keeping this league, this second generation will keep itself together.

A perception prevalent amongst many of the black and Asian players was that a culture of exclusion exists in Essex cricket. This is thought to work at club level, when dealing with black and Asian clubs asking for fixtures, and at league level, through the imposition of certain criteria for entry into the mainstream leagues. A common perception within Asian clubs is that they are not welcomed by many of the established clubs because they tend not to participate in the culture of the post-match drink. One respondent recalled an experience in trying to secure a fixture for his predominantly Asian team:

> We have had sides that do not want to play us ... a club in Essex discovered we were mainly an Asian team and withdrew the invitation to play because they said they needed the bar takings. ... I always say to them: 'We've got a lot of vegetarians in our side, can you please put on egg and tuna', and that sort of thing, so immediately he said: 'Well, is it a Paki side?' I said: 'It is an Asian side, mainly', so he said: 'We don't really want to play because they don't drink'.

Below are two further examples of resistance encountered by Asians trying to arrange fixtures with white clubs:

I would telephone and say we are looking for an away game because we don't have a home ground. Afterwards, when they were trying to write down our name, they would say 'Name of the team?' and I would say, 'Punjab XI', and they would say, 'Actually we have an away fixture for ourselves at the moment'. Once that happened and once they would go: 'OK, we have a fixture just for Bank Holiday Monday, if you want to come down'. This might have happened three or four times … So I instantly changed the name to Strikers XI and I started getting some fixtures and started playing white teams. But when we turn up, the face expressions we would get were like 'What's happening here?' I don't know whether that is an image of our culture or what.

If the fixture secretary [of a white club] knows that there is even an accent there they're not going to give you a fixture. As soon as they know it's an Asian side they will find an excuse, saying 'We are too strong' [or] 'We haven't got a date free' – even though I find out later on that they have dates.

The exclusion of 'teetotal' Asian teams because of their reluctance to participate in the post-match drink cannot explain why black teams are not part of the cricketing mainstream, although, as the following respondent reports, this reason has been used. A black respondent, whose team had shared a ground with a white team, said his side had lost their ground because the businessman they rented it from said his side did not spend enough in the bar:

My team is predominantly black. To me we do spend. Sometimes the match finish and people don't leave there until minutes to midnight and we don't just sit. We buy and yet they are not satisfied. To me it is just something to get us out. Not only black clubs but Asian clubs, because after we start to establish ourselves on their grounds they get uncomfortable.

Another black respondent stated that the relationship between black and Asian clubs was healthy because of a mutual cultural understanding:

In some of our clubs we have guys who we give permission to go and pray during the course of the match. It's happening among us. Before the match the two captains spoke and one will say: 'Well, I have a Muslim in my team and such a such time he'll need to do certain things' and it's understood among everybody. Whereas a white team – they swear, they say: 'Oh shit!' They don't understand the diversity in the different ethnic minorities and their religions. They don't respect it.

Interestingly, there was one Asian respondent who shared the view held by many white players that the problem lay with black or Asian culture. This respondent, who played for a Sunday club in Essex and a Saturday club in Kent, felt that the Asian clubs needed to be more accommodating to the culture of the white clubs:

> One of the biggest problems I've found with Asians, in particular with Muslims, is the fact that they fail to understand that concept [the post-match social drink] and they are not willing to participate as part of that club. The club is not just about cricket, it is about socialising and keeping that contact with other clubs. And they fail to understand that and they are quite happy to go home after the game. Which, number one, kills the team spirit and, number two, can leave a distinctive hole in the relationships between clubs.

Expressing a world-view that has often been characteristic of first-generation immigrants to a host country, this respondent went on to argue that:

> It's hard work for me to retain fixtures with English sides. I have to spend my own money. I have to stay there [at the 'English' clubs] even if I don't want to have a drink. I have to smile and socialise. ... It's the same as the working environment: you have to somehow try to ... with all the prejudices, you have got to try to fit in.

However, an indication that perhaps his 'hard work' had less to do with an intrinsic belief in the rituals and traditions of white clubs, and more to do with the pragmatics of gaining and maintaining access to good quality cricket facilities, is suggested by his comments below:

> The advantage of playing against English sides is that we come across good facilities – I would rather play Sunday cricket on a good ground with a country side. If these clubs are not welcoming us I have to do as much as is possible in my capacity to retain these games ... in the English sides, they have the money, the grounds, the facilities, they could drop you any day.

It is apparent from the responses of black and Asian players that they tend to make their own cultural identifications with cricket; these are not merely different, but often in opposition to the popular associations of cricket with Englishness. There is also a strong assertion of the distinctiveness of black and Asian cricket, based on a belief in its merits and virtues *vis-à-vis* English or 'white' cricket. Furthermore, black and Asian respondents articulated both an ambition and a right to be accepted, not only as skilled individual cricketers but as whole teams representing a particular way of playing cricket. For example, an Asian respondent summed up one kind of response as follows: "'Your best players come and play with us; you can come into our first teams but no, you can't play in our league because ..." whatever the reason might be.'

According to the black and Asian respondents, it is the failure on the part of the mainstream to accept black and Asian teams as equals that is the core of the problem they face in ethnic minority cricket. The main reason for their teams' exclusion from leagues – cited by many black and Asian respondents – was their failure to meet certain standards: for example, having their own ground complete with bar and pavilion. Black and Asian teams lack the facilities enjoyed by clubs playing official league cricket, and very few own their own ground or club house. The imposition of non-playing standards, say some black and Asian players, is in itself restrictive. An Asian respondent spoke of the difficulties such regulations cause:

> When we go to play English clubs, especially old established clubs, they tend to have better facilities and better grounds. When we play Asian and West Indian teams, usually their facilities are very poor. ... The biggest hurdle a [black or Asian] team faces is where they have got a team, they can get the boys and they've got people willing to come and join, but unfortunately they don't have a home ground. For Essex leagues you can't join any league unless you have got a home ground and you can offer very good facilities.

A black respondent echoed the concern about poor facilities available to black and Asian teams without their own ground:

> When I came to this country twenty years ago, the park pitch was properly prepared. But now when you go and play, any park cricket, you get cracks, holes all over the place, the wicket is not prepared. And who is playing on it? Black people are playing on it.

According to another Asian respondent, even if a club fulfilled the conditions for membership to Essex leagues, admission – fulfilment of the ambition to 'get ourselves recognised' – was not guaranteed: 'When we first applied for the league they [the authorities] used to give us all silly excuses: "You don't have a sight screen", "Oh, there isn't a bar facility", "Oh, there isn't any shower in the changing room", ... make silly excuses, so they could stop you.' An Asian respondent who ran his own team expressed the difficulties faced by the newer Asian clubs:

> We wouldn't be able to join the top league [in Essex] in spite of the strength of our club. What they look for is facilities; basically they keep out clubs they don't want. It's an old boys network. ... There is a Sunday league, organised recently by some of these old white clubs and they did not let my

club in. I applied for it and they said no – you have to have this, that and the other. Basically it was just to keep me out. We've got our bar, we've got a good ground. It's not our own, we play in Fairlop in Barkingside. The thing is we are a club, twelve years old, going from strength to strength but we are not going to be like the ———— and the ———— because these clubs have been established for a hundred years, so they are going to have a lot of money behind them. What we have is talent.

Another Asian respondent said his young club was struggling to find a place to play.

This [he gestures toward the ground where the match is on. It has no sight screen. There is litter on and around it and the club house and changing rooms are a long walk away. The players therefore change behind trees on the perimeter of the field] is what we could afford really. We just phone around councils, clubs, yellow pages. You name it ... I was like a detective trying to find a ground really. Some teams even refuse to play us because they say pitches are not of a standard. Like there's a white team in ————. We played at their ground last year. It was a really good, well-kept pitch. We had teas, the bar, traditional sort of things and they didn't want to come here because it was not up to scratch for them. Too rough really. They didn't want to injure their good heads.

According to one Asian respondent, the conditions set out for admission to leagues were responsible for the formation of black and Asian leagues. His club was one of two Asian clubs playing in a lower Essex league and was trying to gain admission into a higher league, but, he argued:

They have a fear maybe that the Asians will rule the league or maybe they have the fear of losing again to an Asian club. Therefore a lot of clubs like us who can't get into higher leagues have to take an option and join either a West Indian league or an Asian league. The cricket is more or less the same but you can't get recognition from it because the Asian leagues and the West Indian leagues are not recognised. ... We are in a way sick of fighting the system.

All respondents were asked whether they had ever been racially abused, whether they had felt subject to racial discrimination during a match, and how cricket fared on issues of 'race'. Replies ranged from those who said they had not been racially abused to those who stated that racial prejudice was always a feature in their interaction with white teams. Most of the white players, while prepared to accept in principle that racism may be an issue in cricket, stressed that it was not a serious problem. A majority of players were particularly careful to point out that while they received the usual share of 'sledging' (a form of dangerous body-line bowling) during a game, they had never been racially abused. However, most respondents' definition of racism was very specific – for example, to do with racial attacks and verbal abuse. There were references to the 'gentlemanly' nature of cricket and a firm belief that cricket was in fact better off than other sports, especially football. One black respondent said:

> You don't get that [racial abuse]. I don't know whether that is because our cricket is good but I must admit that when you play with a white team, as I said, it's gentle cricket. But you won't find nastiness. You won't find that. Or it won't be shown ... I don't think it's like football. I think cricket is a gentleman's game. You won't find racist remarks and things like that. I've never come across it. Perhaps there is, but I have never come across it.

And yet, as the respondents reflected on their experiences, most could recall incidents that had, at the very least, a racial dimension. The racial incidents that were recounted were seen as inevitable, and therefore unremarkable. There was, for instance, a sense amongst black and Asian players that they had to be much better than their white counterparts in order to be considered for selection in predominantly white teams. For example, this young Asian respondent said that although he had never experienced any racism in cricket so far, it was something that he inevitably had to face:

> A lot of teachers have told us as well that every Asian player will get racism as they grow and you have to learn to deal with it ... everyone experiences a bit of racism throughout their career. Colour does matter when you grow up and when you want to become professional and get into sides. Out of an Asian and a white person, you have the same ability, the white person will get the chance probably ... this is in everything, in jobs and so on.

For most black and Asian respondents, their interpretation of racism was specific to racial abuse during a match and took no account of either institutional or cultural racism. One Asian respondent, who talked of cricket as 'a medium to bring various nationalities together' and as a 'catalyst for good relations', recalled an incident later in the interview:

> Our boys were talking and chatting a lot, and the other team [a white team] was losing a lot of wickets and they couldn't do anything about losing wickets but they was saying: 'Why you people talk a lot on the ground?', things like that. But I mean that's only remarks which you can ignore. We just ignore it.

However, several players reported racial abuse on the field. One Asian team captain said: 'One of my batsmen, normally he's scoring about a hundred runs every match and that day, for example, he wasn't getting his foot movements and everything going off edges. And the guy turned around and said: "What kind of fucking Paki shot is that?"' Another Asian respondent, who ran one of the few predominantly Asian clubs playing in the lower Essex leagues, stated that racial abuse was common, but that complaints against this abuse were ignored:

> There is a lot of racialism ... abuses on the field ... there is a lot of that for every Asian player. Lot of abuses, racially provoking players, making them lose their temper so they can get out, all silly things. If you complain, they totally ignore it. Nothing is done and if the white clubs make a complaint against you, always straightaway, they jump on you and take an action, some sort of action.

Another Asian respondent, who played for one of the two predominantly Asian clubs in an Essex league, also complained of a lack of support from league officials in disputes. He recalled an instance when his club was banned after an incident in which players from his team and players in the opposing team, who were predominantly white, swore at each other, which led to some jostling:

> What they said afterwards is that we pushed the umpire; he was an old man. We didn't do that. And they called the league meeting and because we were Asians – that's my personal experience – they said no, we pushed the umpire and you are out of the league for one year. They listened to their English captain who said that we had pushed the umpire, which wasn't true, and we stayed out of the league for one year. They didn't believe us. In the committee there were all English ... there was no sort of Asian person there. So whatever their side said ... happened, they believed them. They didn't believe us.

What is significant here is not whether the Asian players were in the right or in the wrong, but the perception they had that the league officials had not listened to their testimonies.

Some respondents reported that racial tensions need not consist of overt racial abuse. Here it was more a matter of the hostile feeling that, as black and Asian players, they received during some matches. A black respondent commented on the tension that was often present in matches between all black and all white teams:

> I have observed many times they [white teams] say 'You lot know how to play the game. You gonna hit the ball all over the place. You lot should be in a standard of your own. You are not supposed to play with us, we don't play cricket all the time.' And that makes you think they don't really want

to play with us. I personally feel that they are not comfortable being among black and Asian people ... they just use psychology by saying these things for you not to say ... 'He's a racist' or 'she's a racist'. But you can feel the tenseness when you are playing, for example, with a white team, especially in the dressing room. Most of the time the dressing rooms are closed, so you can feel the tenseness. They [the white teams] are very smart, you know. They attack you, but in such a way where you cannot complain. Very subtle and they use a lot of psychology. If they see you pick up on something they pass it off – 'Oh mate, I'm only joking'. But it does exist. Let me get down to the nitty-gritty ... they don't even want to mix with us.

The widespread feeling amongst black and Asian players that they may be accepted as cricketers, but not as people in their own right, was corroborated by this white respondent, who had played in teams with black and Asian players:

> Several boys have come through my schools set up here [in East London] and are now playing for ——, who have become a much more multi-racial club in the last couple of seasons. But it has been hard and I can understand any kid feeling outside of the club's main circle ... they are tolerated because they are good cricketers, but perhaps not socially.

A rural club that regularly had white players in the side, but no black or Asian players, felt, nevertheless, that non-white players would be accepted – eventually: 'If our foreign chap next year turned out to be coloured you may well find initially the reaction would be, 'Oh, we've got somebody of coloured background'. One or two people might be a bit funny about it but I'm sure you get used to it.' The same player was then asked about whether he had witnessed any racial intimidation on a cricket field and he replied:

> I can never pretend that I've never seen it happen. I've probably been involved once or twice myself. I don't think anybody could sit here and [not] say ... if somebody can bat or if he's been a particularly good bowler, you think, well, 'Get that little bastard out' – that sort of thing. There's been a little of that but you get rivalry of that sort regardless of colour. If someone is particularly good it's through jealousy or whatever. You feel more begrudged against them and you feel you must get them out, whatever way you do it.

There was a tendency on the part of most white respondents to locate the problem of racism only where there is a black and Asian presence.

> I imagine in London, there could be a problem. It all depends on where you are. Certainly, in a lot of places, there is an awful big black population or

Asian population. I'm sure some people take offence to that. I personally don't because it really doesn't bother me, the colour of your skin.

Conversely, in areas where there is a negligible presence of black and Asian people, there is a feeling expressed by some of the white respondents that racism is not an issue. This opinion was articulated by the chairman of an Essex league:

> I think that any issue of cricket and race relations is a non-issue here because there are simply no available players with an ethnic background to play and you very rarely come across them at all. It isn't that we consciously don't encourage any ethnic minorities ... we'd be delighted to have a West Indian fast bowler or something like that.

While black and Asian players were able to identify different forms of racism and exclusion, the majority of respondents also emphasised the civilising influence of cricket, often counterposing it to football. The same traditions and values of the game were also drawn on by the white respondents, but in order to deny the existence of racism in cricket. Where racism had become an issue, the assumption of most white players was that it was precipitated by the presence of significant numbers of black and Asian players, not as a matter of white attitudes.

To understand the nature of any sporting activity, it is necessary to place it in its specific cultural setting. One should not assume that just because two groups of people are playing the same sport, they attach the same meanings and values to it. For example, a match between two teams in a Sunday morning pub-league and a Cup Final at Wembley are both called football, but are a world apart in terms of their cultural significance. Of course, this is apparent in any sport. What is significant about the different approaches to cricket highlighted above is that the divide occurs within the same level or at similar standards of play. Hence our assertion that there exist two distinct cultures of cricket. It is clear that these two cultures of cricket are defined by ethnicity. Black and Asian cricket is urban, located in public grounds, and its players display a determination to win, often backed by vocal support. Cricket in the white communities at this particular level is rural, located in private grounds, and its players, though attempting their best, understand that 'playing the game' in the correct manner is most important. The table on page 178 summarises these differences.

It is not merely that the two approaches co-exist, but that they exist in a dynamic relation to one another. Black and Asian cricketers assert a competitive attitude as a means of denigrating the importance of etiquette,

Traditional 'English' recreational cricket	New non-English recreational cricket
Affiliated to official leagues	Unaffiliated
Rural	Urban
Private grounds	Public spaces
Social occasions	Result-oriented competitive events
Playing by the book	Playing to win
Multi-team clubs	Single team clubs
Age group 30–50 plus	Age group late teens–30 (Asian), 25–50 (Black)

which they see as the predominant value in 'English' cricket. White cricketers, meanwhile, uphold the tradition of the post-match drink as an indispensable element of recreational English cricket, which is then used as a means of excluding black and Asian clubs, who are seen as unable or unwilling to engage with this tradition. Given this mirroring of the two cultures, it should not be surprising that playing incidents (such as 'excessive' appealing to the umpire) and administrative processes (such as non-admittance into official leagues) become racialised. It is also not surprising that these incidents are invariably not perceived within the white community either as racial or as an assertion of power. From the white community's perspective, it is simply a case of upholding tradition, rules and procedures that have been in place for some time. In a changing, multicultural environment, however, these same rules, values and procedures can become barriers to newcomers. Allegations of separatism are then made against any newcomers operating outside these barriers, because, after all, the established clubs are merely applying the same rules and values to all – rules and values, moreover, which have stood the test of time. Feelings of alienation can develop, leading to a process of cultural and institutional estrangement.

It can be argued that our characterisation of 'English' cricket presents a false picture of the totality of cricket in England. That for example, at most levels of the game a strong competitive spirit is the norm, and that gentle recreational cricket played out on the village greens occupies a minor position in the sport. This misses the point. The culture of Englishness may occupy a minor position within the overall structure of the game, but that position is situated at the point – the local Sunday leagues – at which newer black and Asian clubs are seeking to gain entry. Thus while the culture of 'English' cricket, church spires and village greens may not be explicitly racist, it can, as this chapter shows, lead to a culture of racial exclusion, racial stereotyping, and to racial abuse of black and Asian players. As one Asian respondent said on being asked why the white clubs seemed afraid to allow black and Asian clubs compete in the official leagues: 'I think the fear is that we will change the tone of the game.'

References

Henderson, R. (1995) 'Is it in the blood?', in *Wisden Cricket Monthly*, July 1995, pp. 9–10.

Marqusee, M. (1998) *Anyone but England: Cricket, race and class*, London: Two Heads Publishing.

McDonald, I. and S. Ugra (1998) 'Anyone for Cricket? Equal opportunities and changing cricket cultures in Essex and East London', London: University of East London.

Roy, A. (1998) 'Beyond the Boundary', in *India Today International*, 17 August, New Delhi, pp. 24h–24j.

10

Old Whine, New Vassals: Are Diaspora and Hybridity Postmodern Inventions?[1]

Jayne O. Ifekwunigwe

> The recent bag of re-poetics (recuperate, rewrite, transport, transform, and so forth) proffers the opportunity to confront many of the assumptions and confusions of identity I feel compelled to 'reconfigure'. The site of this poetics for me, and many other multi-racial and multi-cultural writers, is the hyphen, that marked (or unmarked) space that both binds and divides ... a crucial location for working out the ambivalences of hybridity. ... In order to actualize this hybridity ... the hybrid writer must necessarily develop instruments of disturbance, dislocation and displacement. (Wah 1996: 60)

In the past six years or so, Wah's literary summons has been answered by a virtual flourishing of North American (Canada and the United States) texts in the forms of websites, fiction, poetry, autobiographies, biographies, and academic texts by 'mixed-race' writers who are overwhelmingly middle-class and either academics or students.[2] On the other hand, there have been relatively few books in England during this period by 'mixed-race' writers about 'mixed-race' identity politics.[3] These countries' different historical legacies *vis-à-vis* immigrant and indigenous communities might explain this discrepancy: 'While the United States is a country of immigrants where ethnic diversity is constitutive of the society, British society has aspired and continues to aspire to monoculturalism: the people of the empire have no claim on British territory' (LaForest 1996: 116). In a more profound way than in the United States and Canada, the rigidity of the class structure in Britain also limits the extent to which 'hybrid' writers are recognised, published, marketed and received (Sabu 1998). However, Friedman would argue that on both sides of the Atlantic a 'hybrid' identity is not accessible to the poor: 'The urban poor, ethnically mixed ghetto is an arena that does not immediately cater to the construction of explicitly new hybrid identities. In periods of global stability and/or expansion, the problems of survival are more closely related to territory and to creating secure life spaces' (Friedman 1997: 84).

My fundamental contention is that as socio-cultural and political critiques, fluid contemporary *métis(se)*[4] narratives of gendered identities engage with, challenge and yet have been muffled by two competing racialised, essentialised and oppositional dominant discourses in England. The first is the territorialised discourse of 'English' nationalism, based on indigeneity and mythical purity. That is, 'Englishness' is synonymous with 'whiteness':

> something to do with an elusive but powerful sense of one's own Englishness and what that means in terms of belonging. The notion of the collective unconscious, after all, suggests the unity of those who partake of the racial memory at the same time as it defines the 'other'. The 'other' is everybody else. (Maja-Pearce 1990: 132).

The second is the deterritorialised discourse of the English African diaspora which is predicated on (mis)placement and the one-drop rule: that is, all Africans have been dispersed and one known African ancestor designates a person as 'black'. For example, Paul Gilroy's configuration of the 'Black Atlantic' is based on compulsory blackness and displacement:

> The black Atlantic, my own provisional attempt to figure a deterritorialised multiplex and anti-national basis for the affinity or 'identity of passions' between diverse black populations, took shape in making sense of sentiments like these which are not always congruent with the contemporary forms assumed by black political culture. (Gilroy 1996: 18)

On the other hand, Avtar Brah's formulation of 'diaspora space' speaks to an 'entanglement of genealogies of dispersion with those of 'staying put''' (Brah 1996: 181). Although Brah's model recognises the forged dialectical relationship between settlers and indigenous communities, her conceptualisation is still both racialised and binary rather than fluid. 'Migrants and their descendants' (black) have been dispersed. The 'English' (white) are 'natives' (Brah 1996: 181). As a result, like Gilroy, Brah has not created conceptual space for *métis(se)* individuals for whom by virtue of both English and diasporic parentage, 'home' is de/territorialised (Pieterse 1995). As such, 'home' represents an ambivalent bi-racialised sense of both territorialised place – England – and de-territorialised diasporic longings. Their family histories are braided from the gendered, bi-racialised and sexualised residues of imperial domination and colonised submission (Young 1995; Lavie *et al.* 1996; Fanon 1967).

I want to illustrate the ways in which, as we hobble towards the new millennium, *métis(se)* declarations delimit and transgress bi-racialised discourses and point the way towards a profound realignment of thinking about 'race', ethnicity and 'English' identity. This chapter engages with notions of biological and cultural hybridities as articulated in nineteenth- and twentieth-century discourses on 'race' and identities. I have divided the chapter into three sections. First, I trace the origins of the term hybridity back to its problematic beginnings in nineteenth-century 'race' science, and especially evolutionary anthropology. Second, I critique contemporary cultural theorising on hybridities which reframes 'race' as difference(s). Third, the testimonies of contemporary *métisse* women provide necessary context and content for my discussions of continuities between theories predicated on so-called biological 'race' science and 'postmodernist' cultural explanations. These autobiographical examples illustrate that the older construct of hybridity as a biological 'grafting' of so-called different 'races' is continuous with its contemporary redefinition as cultural heterogeneity, fragmentation and diaspora(s).

'Hybreed': Biological Hybridities and Cultures

In eighteenth- and nineteenth-century Britain and North America, the false presumption held by evolutionary theorists that 'races' existed as discrete, bounded, biological and ultimately 'pure' entities grew into the dominant imperial white European/American mythology, which attempted to proscribe any interbreeding across 'racial' borders:

> If races are conceptualized as pure (with concomitant qualities of character, including the capacity to hold sway over other races), then miscegenation threatens that purity. Given the actual history of interbreeding in the imperial history of the past centuries, it is not surprising that various means have been found to deal with this threat to whiteness. ... These measures focused on blackness as a means of limiting access to the white category, which only the utterly white could inhabit. (Dyer 1997: 25)

This science fiction of 'race' and social hierarchies fuelled eighteenth- and nineteenth-century anthropological conceptions of human diversity in general and intergroup mating in particular (Young 1995; Stocking 1982). Nineteenth-century 'race' science in general and evolutionary anthropology in particular maintained that discrete 'races' existed, which could be differentially ranked on the basis of heredity, physical characteristics and intelligence (Rich 1986; Rogers 1952). The biological distinction between varieties and species was the intellectual precursor to the major scientific debate of the nineteenth century over whether human 'races' were of one species, monogenesis, or separate species, polygenesis:

In eighteenth-century anthropology a distinction was made between species on the one hand and varieties on the other. Species were regarded as immutable prototypes, perfectly designed for their role in the divine economy of nature. Varieties, by contrast, were merely those members of a single species who – because of such conditioning factors as climate and geography – had changed their appearance in one way or another. (Gossett 1965: 35)

Influenced by evolutionist Herbert Spencer, Darwin silenced advocates of polygenesis (Hannaford 1996; Goodwin 1994). However, as human history has proven time and time again, designated same-species status does not guarantee access to the fruits of citizenship – humanity, equality and justice (Malik 1996; Goldberg 1993).

Prior to Darwin's important intervention, American and European scientists such as Prichard, Lawrence, White, Cuvier and Saint-Hilaire waged war over the unity or diversity of the human species (Hannaford 1996; Stocking 1992). In particular, Linnaeus suggested that successful reproduction of fertile offspring was proof positive in support of monogenesis (Gould 1994). Interestingly enough, however, for my purposes, it was the American physician and natural historian Morton who introduced the concept of biological hybridity to the separate origins position:

Among human races, he admitted that mulattoes were fertile, but his own research into crosses between whites and Negroes indicated that mulatto women bear children only with great difficulty. If these women mated only with other mulattoes, Morton argued, the descendents of this union would be even less fertile and the progeny would eventually die out. From his conviction that half-breeds cannot propagate themselves indefinitely, Morton was led to the conclusion that whites and Negroes are not varieties of a single race but entirely different species. (Gossett 1965: 59)

One of Morton's most vocal opponents was Bachman, who maintained that it was virtually impossible for 'hybrids' to be 'relatively sterile', as Morton claimed. Moreover, Bachman insisted that not only were 'mulattoes' as fertile as so called 'pure races', but that he could provide evidence of successful intermarriage and procreation among 'mulattoes' across five generations. Finally, he adamantly opposed the idea put forward by Morton and his colleague Agassiz that there was a 'natural/moral repugnance' between so-called 'races' which functions as a social prophylactic (Stanton 1960). Whether classified as 'pure' or 'hybrid', according black African people same-species status was not equivalent to allowing them equal status, and Bachman still justified ownership of slaves on the grounds that 'We have been irresistibly brought to the conviction that in intellectual power the African is an inferior variety of our species' (Bachman 1850: 291–2).

Two additional key players in the game of origins were Nott and Gliddon (1854), who were also students of Morton. In their eight-hundred-page volume, *Types of Mankind*, they asserted that individuals without at least one white ancestor were 'uncivilized' and lacked the alleged superior mental capacity of their 'pure' white European/American counterparts. Similarly, French anthropologist Paul Broca asserted:

> The union of the Negro with a white woman is frequently sterile while that of a white man with a Negress is perfectly fecund. This might tend to establish between the two races a species of hybridity analogous to that existing between goats and sheep which we termed unilateral hybridity. (Broca 1864: 28)

Accomplished by the insemination of the black female by the allegedly potent white male, this act of 'racial enhancement' justified sexual violence against enslaved black African women in the antebellum American South, pre-emancipation Brazil, and the Caribbean (De-costa-Willis 1992; Hill-Collins 1990). In *Sex and Racism in America*, African American sociologist Calvin Hernton refers to this (ir)rationalised sexual act as 'the sexualization of racism':

> The sexualization of racism in the United States is a unique phenomenon in the history of mankind; it is an anomaly of the first order. In fact, there is a sexual involvement, at once real and vicarious, connecting white and black people in America that spans the history of this country from the era of slavery to the present, an involvement so immaculate and yet so perverse, so ethereal and yet so concrete, that all race relations tend to be, however subtle, *sex* relations. (Hernton 1965: 7)

The inextricable link between sex and 'race' was never stronger than in the plantation southern United States, wherein 'the one-drop rule' was instituted in order to keep the offspring of white male plantation owners born to enslaved black African women under their control for sexual and economic exploitation (Davis 1991; Omi and Winant 1986). The 'one-drop rule' of social hypodescent dictates that one known African ancestor made a person 'black' (Rogers 1944; Spickard 1989). Hence, the (il)logic of this system ensured that 'mixed-race' children of white male slaveowners became black slave labourers:

> A slave was a slave because he was black. Slaves by definition could not be white. The fact that slavery was getting whiter, that in reality many slaves were more white than black, was a fact with which the proslavery argument could not cope. Either it could ignore the problem, which it did explictly, or it could brusquely dismiss it by applying the one-drop rule to persons in slavery, which it did implictly. (Williamson 1995: 73)

Across the United States, by 1915, the one-drop rule had become firmly entrenched in the collective American conscience (Zack 1993). Legal repercussions of this structural mechanism for the maintenance of the white/black power imbalance manifest themselves in virtually every social institution: marriage, housing, property ownership, inheritance, voting rights and privileges, education, and health (Paredes 1997; Degler 1971; Jordan 1974). My contention is that the black essentialism of the one-drop rule is as integral to our understandings of both colonial and contemporary black/white social stratification in the former British empire and the future United Kingdom respectively. Furthermore, I would argue that across historical time and global spaces different structural principles based on popular folk conceptions of 'race' and hierarchy have been generated and justified, which illustrate the ways in which ideologies of sexualities and 'racial' differences are always intertwined.

The history of meanings of the word 'commerce' includes the exchange both of merchandise and of bodies in sexual intercourse. It was therefore wholly appropriate that sexual exchange, and its miscegenated product, which captures the violent, antagonistic power relations of sexual and cultural diffusion, should become the dominant paradigm through which the passionate and economic and political trafficking of colonialism was conceived. Perhaps this begins to explain why our own forms of racism remain so intimately bound up with sexuality and desire. (Young 1995: 182)

As I have already mentioned, popular folk concepts of 'race' and hierarchy began their ascendancy in Victorian anthropological discourses (Hannaford 1996; Goldberg 1993). If we take the publication of, to give its titles in full, *The Origin of Species by Means of Natural Selection, or The Preservation of Favoured Races in the Struggle for Life* by Charles Darwin in 1859 as our analytical starting point and the rediscovery of Mendelian genetics in 1900 as the pivotal end point, it becomes clear that there were historical events in both the United States and Europe which galvanised the production of so-called scientific knowledge for the purposes of legitimating white European and American racial supremacy as well as the subjugation of non-white people in the Americas, the Caribbean, and the newly formed imperial dominions in Africa and Asia (Malik 1996). In *Race, Culture and Evolution*, Stocking describes the specific focus of these supremacist scientific enquiries:

Darwinian evolution, evolutionary ethnology, and polygenist race thus inter-acted to support raciocultural hierarchy in terms of which civilized men, the highest products of social evolution, were large-brained white men, and only large-brained men, the highest products of organic evolution, were fully civilized. The assumption of white superiority was certainly not original with Victorian evolutionists; yet the interrelation of the theories of cultural and organic evolution, with their implicit hierarchy of race, gave it a new rationale. (Stocking 1982: 122)

In the early twentieth century, these dangerous ideas formed the basis of the Eugenics movements (Gosset 1965). It was Darwin's cousin Francis Galton who coined the word 'eugenics' and the phrase 'nature and nurture'. The scientific mission of the Eugenics movement was the eradication of 'inferior races' and the elevation of 'superior races' based on the idea that intelligence, criminality, and other social 'traits' were in and of themselves determined exclusively by heredity:

> I have never found an inter-mixed or inter-married white–negro couple where the stamp of social inferiority was not plainly traceable as the result … Intermarriages between whites and blacks, just as much as wrongful sexual relations without marriage, are essentially anti-social tendencies and therefore opposed to the teachings of sound eugenics in the light of the best knowledge available to both races at the present time … the conclusion would seem warranted that the crossing of the Negro race with the white has been detrimental to its progress. (Rogers 1944: 32)

In 1869, Galton looked at the distribution of intelligence within and between so-called different 'races'. Through quantitative measurements, he 'deduced' that the intelligence of 'Negroes' was, on average, two grades below that of Englishmen, while the intelligence of the 'Athenian race' of the fifth century was two grades above that of Englishmen (Galton 1870). It would follow from Galton's analysis that he would not advocate the mating of supposedly mentally inferior black Africans with supposedly mentally superior white Europeans. While diminished intelligence of the next generation was the excuse propagated by Galton for not condoning so-called mixing of the 'races', other scientists pointed to the 'weaker constitution' of 'racial hybrids'. Provine surmised that 'if these scientific proponents of racial supremacy argued that races of man differed in hereditary physical and mental characteristics then they would view crossing between distant races with suspicion or outright antagonism' (Provine 1973: 790).

This spurious campaign of selective breeding to ensure 'racial hygiene' and 'purity' culminated, of course, in the Nazi experiment and Hitler's Final Solution:

> Any crossings of two beings not at exactly the same level produces a medium between the level of the two parents. This means: the offspring will probably stand higher than the racially lower parent, but not as high as the higher

one. Consequently, it will later succumb in the struggle against the higher level. Such mating is contrary to the will of Nature for a higher breeding of all life. The precondition for this does not lie in associating superior and inferior, but in the total victory of the former. The stronger must dominate and not blend with the weaker, thus sacrificing his greatness. Only the born weakling can view this as cruel, but he after all is only a weak and limited man; for if this law did not prevail, any conceivable higher development of organic living beings would be unthinkable. (Hitler 1925: 258–9)

In *Showing Our Colors: Afro-German Women Speak Out*, Opitz (1986) describes forced sterilisations and abortions for German women who gave birth to 'non-Aryan' children, including Afro-Germans, who were themselves also involuntarily sterilised. In *Race and Empire in British Politics*, Paul Rich reveals the presumed 'moral problem' and the threat to 'racial hygiene' of 'half-caste' children in Britain in general and the port cities of Liverpool and Cardiff in particular (Rich 1986: 130–5).

In apartheid South Africa in the 1950s, the Immorality Act, which was 'to prohibit illicit carnal intercourse between Europeans and non-Europeans', the Group Areas Act and the Population Registration Act were all socially engineered to enforce particular beliefs about 'racial hygiene' (Banton 1967). The prevailing view was that white South Africans were 'pure' and black South Africans were 'polluted' (Comaroff and Comaroff 1991, Kuper 1974). The intention of such legislation was to protect the 'public health and safety' of the 'pure White Volk' who were not, as their black counterparts were, Biblical descendants of Ham.[5] Finally, in England, from Enoch Powell's 'Rivers of Blood' speech in 1968 to the 'political pornography' of the National Front in the 1990s, campaigns of racial hatred have, in part, encouraged acts of social exclusion and violence against anyone even mildy tinted with 'a touch of the tar brush'. British 'race' relations guru Michael Banton succinctly states: 'The metaphors of 'blood' and 'stock' have bitten deep into the English vocabulary and are unthinkingly but daily recapitulated by teachers, dramatists, journalists and politicians' (Banton 1967: 373).

Certain contemporary texts produced by black African American and white American/British academics seem to revert to a controversial 'race' science which reinforces the distorted principles of the earlier Eugenics movement (Kohn 1996). These texts include: *The Bell Curve* (Murray 1994) and *The g Factor* (Brand 1996). Murray and Brand, prospective heirs to the contentious throne held by Arthur Jensen since 1969, theorise about alleged links between 'race' and intelligence (Kohn 1996; Fraser 1995). African-centred counter-discourses are equally contentious. For example, *The Isis Papers* (Welsing 1991), advocates black supremacy based on the 'super-properties' of melanin (the pigment which lends colour to the skin and protects it from the harmful rays of the sun) which 'Blacks' are said to possess in greater abundance than 'Whites'. When will scholars learn that, in the words of Audre Lorde, 'The master's tools will never dismantle the master's house' (Lorde 1996: 158).

Un-Equal Under the Sun: Cultural Hybridities and Biology

> The events and situations that have produced racial blending reach far back into the misty and unrecorded annals of history. Whenever and wherever peoples move about, coming into contact with others different in race and culture, amalgamation and acculturation are possible. (Gist 1972: 1)

In other words, inter-group mating and marriages were and have always been commonplace. Hybridity named these acts of social transgresssion (Young 1995). Hybrid, meaning 'impure', 'racially contaminated', a genetic 'deviation', was the zoological term deployed to describe the offspring of 'mixed-race crossings'. In the twentieth century, 'hybrid' and 'hybridity' have been reappropriated to signal cultural synthesis. Indirectly, Malik speaks to the dialectical tension between biological and cultural notions of hybridities: 'The biological discourse of race and the cultural discourse of difference both arise from the inability to reconcile the two' (Malik 1996: 265). The major difficulty with the concept of cultural hybridity is the way in which it has been appropriated by mainstream academic discourse without recognition of its problematic origins in nineteenth century 'race' science fiction (Fisher 1995).

The presumption is that since the nineteenth century, discourses on hybridities have shifted their intellectual focus from the homogeneous, pseudo-scientific grafting of races to the fragmented heterogeneous multi-valent fusion of cultures. For example, Minh-ha points to the universality of the contemporary culturally hybrid condition: 'In the complex reality of postcoloniality it is therefore vital to assume one's radical 'impurity' and to recognize the necessity of speaking from a hybrid place, hence of saying at least two, three things at a time' (Minh-ha 1992: 140). In *Welcome to the Jungle: New Positions in Black Cultural Studies*, Mercer celebrates the advent of cultural hybridity as a (postmodernist) survival strategy: 'In a world in which everyone's identity has been thrown into question, the mixing and fusion of disparate elements to create new, hybridized identities point to ways of surviving, and thriving, in conditions of crisis and transition' (Mercer 1994: 5). In *Colonial Desire: Hybridity in Theory, Culture and Race*, Young substantiates:

Today the notion is often proposed of a new cultural hybridity in Britain, a transmutation of British culture into a compounded, composite mode. The condition of that transformation is held out to be the preservation of a degree of cultural and ethnic difference. While hybridity denotes a fusion, it also describes a dialectical articulation, as in Rushdie's 'mongrelization'. (Young 1995: 23)

Werbner and Modood have edited an anthology entirely dedicated to, and entitled, *Debating Cultural Hybridity*. In the introductory chapter, 'Dialectics of Cultural Hybridity', Werbner's closing remarks pinpoint the major problematic of discourses which celebrate cultural hybridities independent of their epistemological origins in scientific racism. She states: 'Hybridity as a loaded discourse of dangerous racial contaminations has been transformed into one of cultural creativity: 'insults' have been turned into 'strengths'' (Werbner and Modood 1997: 21). In essence, in England, there has not been a culturally hybrid rupture, which would transform the meanings of place and belonging for all her constituents. Rather, in an attempt to delude late twentieth-century rainbow members of the global village into believing that opportunities, resources, commodities, icons and even individuals are located on an imaginary gender-neutral level playing-field where everyone has equal access, cultural hybridities with their purported disconnection from 'race' science fiction have replaced biological hybridities.[6]

Place and 'Race': De/Territorialised Discourses of Gendered Identities

'Where'you from, La?' Susie suddenly asked one lunch break on the playing fields. 'Woolwich.' 'No, silly, where are you from, y'know originally?' 'If you really must know I was born in Eltham, actually.' 'My dad says you must be from Jamaica,' Susie insisted. 'I'm not Jamaican! I'm English!' 'Then why are you coloured?' Lara's heart shuddered, she felt so humiliated, so angry. 'Look, my father's Nigerian, my mother's English, alright!' (Evaristo 1997: 65)

So tell me ... what part of the world does your family come from?' 'Er, Ramsworth.' 'Yes, you live here, but where do you come from? Which country? Either Africa, South America or the West Indies, I figured. Or even an island in the Pacific.' I was definitely not a Maori. I'd gone off Maoris by then. I usually told people that I was from the Caribbean. That gave them a bit of a holiday. They went off for a couple of seconds under palm trees sun-bathing. I liked watching their faces when they did that. (Traynor 1997: 73)

These two extracts are from novels set in England, Bernardine Evaristo's *Lara* and Joanna Traynor's *Sister Josephine*. Each work also features a *métisse* woman as protagonist. However, in both instances, Lara and Josephine tangle with the twin torments of 'Englishness' being exclusively associated with 'whiteness' and the presumption that one's designated 'blackness' automatically afflicts one with a (mis)placed African diasporic condition. Never do 'white English' birth parentage or full-time English residence enable these characters to carve out territorialised spaces which reflect both the realities of cultural upbringing and the complexities of de-territorialised ancestries.

As I have defined it, the English African diaspora conventionally comprises African postcolonial constituents from the Caribbean, North and Latin America and continental Africa who find themselves in England for labour, schooling, political asylum or, frequently, by birth. However, scripted from a notion of 'home' as at once territorialised (English) and de-territorialised (African diasporic), *métis(se)* narratives demand a reconfiguration of the conventional (English) African diaspora. More pointedly, they map the specificities of the local, yet they also problematise the parameters and boundaries delimiting the local and the global:

> the local exists nowhere in a pure state ... the local is only a fragmented set of possibilities that can be articulated into a momentary politics of time and place ... this is to take the local not as the end point but as the start. This is not to idealise the local as the real, but to look at the ways in which injustices are naturalised in the name of the immediate. In conceiving of the local as a nodal point, we can begin to deconstruct its movements and its meanings. (Probyn 1990: 187)

Their critiques also confront racialised obstructions whereby 'whiteness' is deemed the normative and naturalised signifier by which deviations of 'blackness' are determined, as well as the presumption that 'Englishness' is synonymous with 'whiteness'.

In this de/territorialised place, the idea of 'home' has, by definition, multi-layered, multi-textual and contradictory meanings for *métis(se)* cartographers. In a travel essay chronicling his rediscovery of Britain, Nigerian and English writer Adewale Maja-Pearce wages existential war with the meaning of home experienced as competing and conflicting bi-racialised nationalisms:

> I had to learn as best I could to be at home, but even the word 'home' had complex connotations. Where was home? Was it Nigeria, my father's country? Or was it Britain, my mother's country? And how far did allegiance to the one involve a betrayal of the other? My inability to see was inseparable from the sense of betrayal.

If I didn't look, if I didn't admit the reality of the particular corner of the world in which I happened to be, in this case Britain – 'This blessed plot, this earth, this realm, this England' – then I couldn't properly live here. This in turn meant that I was released from the necessity of confronting the nature of my allegiance because to admit Britain, to say that I was British, was to deny Nigeria. I was like a man married to one woman but trying to remain faithful to another. If I wasn't careful I would lose both, and in the end I would be the one to suffer for it: to live like this is to condemn oneself to a half-life, which is the predicament of the outsider. (Maja-Pearce 1990: 12–13)

In lamenting the 'half-life' of the 'outsider', Maja-Pearce articulates for other transnational *métis(se)* subjects the complex nature of belonging. In addition, he conveys a broader collective African diasporic consciousness, forged from (post)colonial histories characterised by racism, sexism, class discrimination, ethnocentrism and other forms of oppression (Gilroy 1993). These transnational alliances are predicated on the profound paradoxes of citizenship (Gilroy 1996; Cohen 1994). Though daughters and sons of Africa's various diasporas are living in England, they must acknowledge the actual and significant impact of white English exclusionary practices on reconstructions of cultural and transnational local identities (Mercer 1994). Stuart Hall refers to this ongoing psycho-political project as 'Identity Politics One':

the first form of identity politics. It had to do with the constitution of some defensive collective identity against the practices of racist society. It had to do with the fact that people were being blocked out of and refused an identity and identification within the majority nation, having to find some other roots on which to stand. (Hall 1991: 41–68)

The outcome of the specification of Englishness as white is that sons and daughters of the English African diaspora, designated black, are denied full citizenship (Hall 1996). The one-drop rule means that *métis(se)* children with white English mothers or fathers are also denied access to an English identity which they can rightfully claim on the basis of parentage (Zack 1993).

As cultural critiques, the testimonies of the *métis(se)* individuals I worked with tackle these transnationalist concerns. Their stories also chart what Ang-Lygate refers to as 'the spaces of (un)location where the shifting and contextual meanings of diaspora reside – caught somewhere between, and inclusive of the more familiar experiences of (re)location and (dis)location' (Ang-Lygate 1997: 170). However, as cumulative text their individual evocations also illustrate the collective psychosocial problematics of the angst of a wider African diaspora in its specific geopolitical manifestations. In the conclusion to their edited collection *Place and the Politics of Identity*, Keith and Pile indirectly legitimate the (English) African diaspora as a shifting political space where senses of place are (re)negotiated and identities are (re)constructed:

> spatiality needs to be seen as the modality through which contradictions are normalised, naturalised and neutralised. Politics is necessarily territorial but these territories are simultaneously real, imaginary and symbolic ... spatiality should simultaneously express people's experiences of, for example, displacement (feeling out of place), dislocation (relating to alienation), and fragmentation (the jarring of multiple identities). Spatialities represent both the spaces between multiple identities and the contradictions within identities. (Keith and Pile 1993: 224–5)

Shifting the Margins to the Centre

Almost all of the sixteen *métisse* women and nine *métis* men who participated in this project in Bristol were born and came of age elsewhere (London, Birmingham, Liverpool, Manchester, Newcastle, Glasgow, Cardiff; the United States, Nigeria, Ghana, Jamaica).They had found their way to Bristol for education, work or personal reasons, and, for a two-year pregnant postmodern moment, this former slave port also functioned as a shifting political site for the individual redrawing of boundaries representing home, family and identity. Collectively, these crafted narratives of belonging drew marginalised social and political perspectives to the centre.

Although by no means definitive, photopoetic chronicles of childhood, the retelling of pivotal moments that shaped complex subjectivities, and frozen snapshots of experience reconstituted as structured anecdotes collectively recapture particular complex evolving everyday lived realities. The men and women who told me their stories all had black continental African or black African Caribbean fathers and white British or white continental European mothers. They were born between 1945 and 1975 in Britain, West Africa, and the Caribbean. A remarkable number have black Nigerian fathers and white English mothers.

I collected the original narratives in Bristol via open-ended tape-recorded interviews, between 1990 and 1992. Respondents' provided testimonies about their childhoods, gender politics, racial and ethnic identity, class background, nationalism, family, sexuality, creativity, parenting, and racism, among other topics. I acquired a separate notebook for each storyteller and recorded my responses to each of their storytelling sessions and kept track of the questions generated from each listening.

By the time the edited testimonies appeared as text, I had listened to them in full four times. The first time was immediately after each session. While their voices were still singing in my head, I formulated questions in direct response to their testimonies. These questions would serve as a guide, not as the basis, for the next storytelling session. I repeated this approach until the participants had finished testifying, at which point we had sucessfully reached the marrow – what is significant to each one of them in their everyday lives. I refer to this interview technique as the artichoke method. The ethnographer has to peel away many layers before the heart of the matter is revealed. Upon finishing the sessions, I listened to every single testimony again for insights and patterns. The third listening entailed laborious transcription, at times hindered by regional accents. The final listening was for clarification and verification of specific segments of testimonies.

When I began writing, I confirmed what I had suspected earlier – there was no way that I could adequately do justice to all twenty-five life stories. To include them all in the final 'polythesis', which ethnographic film-maker David MacDougall (1993) refers to as 'an interplay of voices' – and, I would add, ideas – would have been a lengthy process leading ultimately to my truncating their experiences. I tried working with fifteen, then nine, and finally six.

Selecting the final six was not easy. All twenty-five were eloquent, engaging storytellers. In order to produce a coherent final product which did not fragment or trivialise the experience of the individuals I had worked with, I needed to narrow the focus. I was particularly interested in the centrality of their white mothers in the retelling of their life stories.

In order to highlight the relationship between white mothers and one-drop-rule 'black' daughters, I decided to feature the narratives of six women – two sets of sisters and two women who had grown up in care with mother surrogates. Speaking with two sets of biological sisters enabled me to illustrate the similarities and differences in pathways to womanhood forged by two *métisse* daughters growing up with the same white mother. In the midst of the burgeoning Black Power movement, Akousa and Sarah were raised in Liverpool by a working-class white Irish mother, without their black Bajan (Barbadian) father. Yemi and Bisi were brought up in Nigeria during the turbulent postcolonial 1960s and neocolonial 1970s[7] by middle-class parents, a Northumbrian white English mother and a Yoruba black father. Ruby – Nigerian and English – and Similola – Tanzanian and German – spent their formative years in care in middle-class, all-white English and Welsh children's homes outside London and Cardiff, respectively. They were each socialised by mother surrogates prior to the explosive debates about welfare policy as it pertains to transracial fosterage, placement and adoption. To illustrate the ways in which *métisse* daughters narrate contested senses of place and identities which are both de-territorialised and bi-racialised, I have selected extracts from longer testimonies by Ruby, Akousa and Bisi.

Ruby[8] Marie Garson, an African Caribbean social worker, introduced me to Ruby. Ruby is a 43-year-old Nigerian and English social worker. She is the only one of the original twenty-five participants with whom I spoke exclusively in my home. This deprived me of a contextualised sense of who she was. Profound sadness laced with occasional happiness is the phrase that best captures my sense of her. Like many *métis(se)* individuals she is a survivor, a warrior on the front lines by virtue of her bloodlines.

What is black and what is white for me? In simplistic terms, it comes down to the colour of the skin as far as I'm concerned. I do distinguish between race and culture. So, I would call myself black and I would call myself British. Britishness is my culture, but because I'm black I will identify more from a racial point of view with other black people. Having said that, a lot of black people have different cultural backgrounds. Whether it's West Indian or Caribbean, African, American, there are those differences within that. I think that as black people, I would be very surprised to come across anybody who hasn't had some personal experience of racism somewhere in their life, in a way that a white person could not have. There's that shared understanding, that shared culture of racism that makes me feel closer to the black community in that respect. But, I am also British, so I guess that my values, my lifestyle and way of being are informed a lot by English culture. I used to feel uncomfortable about that at one time. But as I get older, I realise now that that is the way it is, Ruby, so why apologise for it. I can't turn myself into a black American or West Indian or something that's not who I am.

Once I came to the realisation that 'race' and culture are two different things, I found my own place in it more easy to define. Quite often people muddle the two together. If you're mixed-race, if you're not careful you can fall between two stools, where 'you're English, but you're not quite, 'cause you're black aren't you?' Or, 'you're not really black are you, because you're English? You're not one of us.' So, certainly if I'm talking to Caribbean friends or colleagues, or not even friends or colleagues, it comes up more with people I don't know. Where there's a taken for grantedness that I must be Caribbean in some way, and they're amazed when there are facets of the culture that everybody knows, and I say, 'I've never come across this before.' And it's like, 'Weehhh, where do you come from?' I say, 'London.' I've found myself in life having to explain to people that I might be black, but

I'm not Caribbean. I am English. These days I don't have a problem with that.

Akousa When I first met Akousa, I remember thinking how much she sparkled – her eyes, her smile, and her presence. My responding to her sparkling smile is humorous in that until recently, Akousa had always hated her smile. Her mother is Irish, her father Bajan. She is a Rastafarian, and yet is not seen as a typical Rasta woman. She sees herself as a black woman, and yet not everyone sees her as a black woman.

At the end of the day gettin' into me late teens, I didn't think much about meself because of all these conflicts that were startin' to come up from the past. Also new ones that were comin' in from other communities – black communities – that were really shockin' me. I mean there were times when I wouldn't show me legs. I'd go through the summer wearing tights and socks, 'Cause I thought they were too light and too white-lookin'. There was a lot of pressure. I remember one day I was leanin' up somewhere and this guy said to me, 'Boy, aren't your legs white?' I just looked in horror, and felt really sick and wanted to just run away. I was thinkin', God, why didn't you make me a bit darker? Why did you make so light? It took me years to reconcile that.

Because of what happened in the seventies in terms of the Black Power movement, especially in this country, if you weren't black like ebony then you just didn't have a chance basically. It was the most difficult time of my life – trying to sort out who I was now. Whereas before, I thought I knew who I was. My family comes from the Caribbean. I never brought me Mum into question. She seemed to take thing in her stride. I kept comin' home and I'd say to her, 'I hate all white people. Tonkers', or 'honkies', or whatever. There's me Mum sittin' there, and I just didn't think about it. It's hard work, but she's me mother. I don't think of her in terms of, 'me Mum, she's white, I shouldn't be sayin' these things.'[9] But on the other hand, me Mum never told me that I was 'half-caste' or 'half-breed' or anythin' like that. She saw me as a whole person. She told me, 'When you go out in the street, they're goin' to call you "nigger" they're not goin' to call you "light-skinned" or somethin' like that. They'll call you "black bastard".' No matter how light or how dark you are, that's the vibe.

I see myself as black. Other people see meself as bein' 'half-caste', as some like to call it. Like the Greek guy who said I should have an Irish map in one ear and an African one in the other. Therefore I should also have a Bajan one as well. and an English one, 'cause I was born in England. I could go on forever. When people bring those sorts of issues up, you sit down and you start questionin' yourself and askin' yourself, am I really who I think I

am? Who I've decided I am? All these people are tryin' to define who you
are, tellin' that 'You can't be black. Look how light you are,' 'Your mother's
white, so how can you be black?'

Bisi I met Bisi through an American woman in exile in Bristol, who, by
virtue of our similar backgrounds in the Arts, thought we would enjoy
meeting each other. However, Bristol being a very small city, Bisi had
already heard about me through mutual friends. Next to Sarah, I have
known Bisi the longest. Bisi and Yemi's father is Yoruba (Nigerian) and
their mother is English from Northumberland. Ycmi and Bisi have very
different temperaments, but just listening to them for a while and looking
at their faces, one knows that they arc sisters. They each have four children.
The father of Yemi's children is black Nigerian; the father of Bisi's children
is white English. Yemi grew up Nigerian-identified, while Bisi, who was
much closer to their white English mother, grew up with a more English
view of the world.

The question of what race are my children? What do they think? How do
they feel? It's difficult as well. I think Elizabeth said, 'I'm one-quarter
Nigerian, (very specific, very precise), but I'm three-quarters English,
Mummy.' Which is true. I ask my son sometimes, 'Do you think you are
white?' I don't know whether he says it to please me or not but he says,
'Well, no, not really.' And they use this dreadful term 'half-caste.' 'Af caste,'
they say, 'You are, aren't you Mum?' I say, 'What kind of a word is that ?
Half of what? How can one call oneself half of something?' I don't think
that's made any impression on them basically. Because it's the basic term
they use at school, and everyone knows what it means. 'I'm qua'a (quarter)
caste, aren't I Mum?' 'What do you mean, 'caste'? Do you know what it
means?'

Of course, Julia looks completely English. What are they to feel? Julia's
probably the child who'd have the least problems adjusting to a new
country.[10] She hasn't got this terrible sense of normal Elizabeth has. She's
outgoing. Actually they are all quite shy, funnily enough, apart from Emma.
Julia is more sociable than Elizabeth, that's why. She would have less
problems. You can't actually feed thoughts into your children. They are
aware that they are not completely British. Let's put it like that. I don't
know how far that goes. The words I put it in then are negative. They are
aware that they are not completely English. Is that being aware of something
positive or not? It's only through talking and discussing, that I know what
they think.

Being aware that one's system of ideas isn't absolute. It isn't the absolute,
the one above all others. There are many and they are all sort of parallel and

contradictory. If you are mixed-race, you belong in two (or more) cultural traditions, which may be mutually contradictory, you just have to find a middle space. As I said, this other woman who is Irish, her culture is something that will support her personality and at the same time oppress her. To come to terms with the ways in which it does that. The stuff about, you are never completely invisible or at home, you are always a bit of a stranger. Same status as strangers. My children are all English, and I still call myself a stranger.[11]

Parting Thoughts: 'Keeping England Clean'

Here then were the three Englands I had seen, the Old, the Nineteenth-Century and the New; and as I looked back on my journey I saw how these three were variously and most fascinatingly mingled in every part of the country I had visited. It would be possible, though not easy, to make a coloured map of them. There was one already in my mind, bewilderingly coloured and crowded with living people. (Priestley 1987: 380)

Priestley concludes his 1933 sojourn with the profound realisation that the meaning of Englishness is in the proverbial eye of the beholder. I now wish to end my intellectual journey with a critique of two examples from the media, which illustrate the ways in which deep-seated yet unspoken white English anxiety concerning racial infiltration by black 'alien settlers' still pervades popular discourse on nationalism and citizenship. It is 4 June 1998, one week before the start of the football World Cup in France. On 21 June 1998 occurs the fiftieth anniversary of the docking in Tilbury of the ship the *Empire Windrush*. Having travelled five thousand miles, 492 Anglicised Jamaicans, including Second World War veterans, began a new life in a different, less inviting 'Mother England' than they had imagined in the Caribbean. The neofascist slogan 'Keep Britain White' became an all too familiar refrain during this period of economic restructuring and social adjustment (Ware 1997).

Fifty year commemorative *Windrush* celebrations and radio and television documentaries abound alongside endless pre-World Cup programming and advertising, the former celebrating a multicultural Britain with a black population that is 'here to stay'; the latter, in subtle forms, holding on to a mythical notion of Englishness predicated on 'white purity'. Two of the most blatant suggestions of a spurious 'white Englishness' are adverts for two commodities which are synonymous with cleanliness and hygiene: soap and water. Both advertisements use representations of young children.

The first is a television advertisement for 'Ariel' soap-powder. A young white English male football enthusiast rushes home distraught, having 'dirtied' his football kit. His mother says: 'Don't worry, we will get your shirt white again'. She then demonstrates the special 'purifying' powers of Ariel, at which point the advertisement ends with the slogan: 'Ariel: keeping England clean'. The second is a billboard advertisement for Buxton water. In multicultural and multiracial Stratford, East London, just past the bus depot, looms larger than life a billboard depicting in the foreground three young white English boys with their faces painted with the Union flag. In the background, one can faintly discern a football crowd. To the left of the first young white English boy sits a visibly *métisse* young girl. The slogan is: 'Buxton: Found Purely in Britain'. There is another Buxton water billboard nearby, round the corner from Forest Gate railway station, on the side wall of an African Caribbean restaurant/café. On this version, the slogan is the same, as are the photographs of the three white English boys with the Union-Jack-emblazoned faces. This time, however, the *métisse* girl has disappeared.

As they say, the more things change, the more they stay the same.

Notes

Eternal gratitude to Ruby, Similola, Sarah, Akousa, Yemi and Bisi, without whose powerful testimonies my ideas would have existed as mere theoretical abstractions. My thanks also to the other ten women and nine men who participated in the original research project. Finally, thanks to Phil Cohen for his shrewd editorial assistance.

1. This chapter is an edited, updated version of the first chapter, 'Cracking the Coconut: Resisting Popular Folk Discourses on 'Race', 'Mixed Race' and Social Hierarchies', in Ifekwunigwe 1999.

2. For examples, see Root (1992); No Press Collective, *Voices of Identity, Rage and Deliverance: An Anthology of Writings by People of Mixed Descent*, Berkeley: No Press. 1992; Zack (1993); Lise Funderburg, *Black, White, Other: Biracial Americans Talk About Race and Identity*, New York: William and Morrow, 1994; Shirlee Taylor Haizlip, *The Sweeter the Juice: A Family Memoir in Black and White*, London: Simon and Schuster, 1994; Camper (1994); Root (1996); Zack (1995); Marsha Hunt, *Repossessing Ernestine*, London: Flamingo, 1996; *Absinthe, HypeNation: A Mixed Race Issue*, 9 (2), 1996. Also see *Inter-racial Voice*, the largest website edited by and about 'mixed race' people, founded by Charles Byrd: http://www.webcom.com/intvoice/

3. Although much has been written in the UK on 'hybridities', I am specifically referring to the paucity of recent social-science literature and fiction by 'mixed-race' writers about 'mixed-race' identity issues. However, two counter-examples are: Evaristo (1997) and Traynor (1997), by 'mixed-race' novelists with 'mixed-race' females as protagonists. Also see *New Mixed Culture*, a website founded and maintained by Sabu, the first artist in Britain to put his work on the web: http://www.1love.com

4. The term *métis(se)* is a 'French African', in particular Senegalese, re-appropriation of the continental French *métis(se)*. In continental French, *métis(se)* is synonymous with the derogatory English 'half-caste' and 'half-breed'; see Henri-Cousin (1994: 160). However, redeploying this term demonstrates the portability and mutability of language as well as its potential reinterpretation across national borders. My linguistic informants,

comparative literature Professor Samba Diop and cultural critic and ethnomusicologist Henri-Pierre Koubaka, are Senegalese and Senegalese–Congolese, respectively – that is, black continental African. They suggest that alternative translations of *métis(se)* both include and can extend beyond bi-racialised (black/white) discourses to encompass diasporic convergences across ethnicities, cultures, religions and nationalities.

In an English context, I offer *métis(se)* in part as a specific shorthand stand-in response to what I believe are the inadequacies of previous terms. In other publications (Ifekwunigwe 1997; Ifekwunigwe 1999), I have discussed the shortcomings of extant terms such as 'mixed race', 'mixed parentage', 'bi-racial', 'dual heritage', and so on. However, the primary reason for installing *métis(se)* as a lexical intervention is to free me momentarily from the tangle of terminology so that I may address more pressing and in fact derivative concerns such as racism and bi-racialisation. Perhaps from this we may imagine a future entirely free of the reinscribing badges of bi-racialised differences.

In short, for purposes of analysis, in the English African Diaspora, *métisse* (feminine) and *métis* (masculine) refer to individuals who, according to popular folk concepts of 'race' and by known birth parentage, embody two or more world views or, in genealogical terms, descent groups. These individuals may have physical characteristics which reflect some sort of intermediate status *vis-à-vis* their birth parents. More than likely, at some stage they will have to reconcile multiple cultural influences.

5. 'The sons of Noah were three in number: Shem, Ham and Japheth. ... That Shem was of the same complexion as Noah his father and mother – the Adamic complexion – there is no doubt in our mind. And that Ham the second son was swarthy in complexion, we have little doubt. Indeed, we believe it is generally conceded by scholars, though disputed by some, that the word Ham means "dark", "swarthy", "sable". And it has always been conceded, and never as we know of seriously disputed, that Japheth was white' (Delany 1879: 18).

6. In a footnote to the introduction to Lavie *et al.*, 1996: 24, Lavie reminds us that 'much of the work on "hybridities" is gender-neutral (for instance Paul Gilroy's)'. As a possible intervention, she advocates Donna Haraway's notion of a 'cyborg' wherein gender is necessarily marked: 'A cyborg is a cybernetic organism, a hybrid of machine and organism, a creature of social reality as well as a creature of fiction', Donna Haraway, 'A Cyborg Manifesto: Science, Technology and Socialist Feminism in the Late Twentieth Century', in *Simians, Cyborgs and Women in the Reinvention of Women*, London: Free Association Books, 1991 p. 149.

7. Since gaining independence from Britain on 1 October 1960, Nigeria has been plagued by tribal and economic conflict, including the Biafran civil war, a series of military coups, corruption at all levels of government and failed bids for democracy, which have resulted in severe abuses of human rights, most notably the assassination of Ken Saro Wiwa and nine other dissenters. In the words of the Igbo novelist and essayist Chinua Achebe: 'The Nigerian problem is the unwillingness or inability of its leaders to rise to the responsibility, to the challenge of personal example which are the hallmarks of true leadership'. See Chinua Achebe, *The Trouble with Nigeria*, Oxford: Heinemann, 1983, p. 1.

8. Unless otherwise specified, to protect anonymity, names and places have been changed.

9. This is a perfect example of the ways in which *métis(se)* people are forced to negotiate public and private spheres which negate and acknowledge, respectively, their white English parentage.

10. Bisi's observation that her one child who looks completely 'white' English is the one who would have the least difficulty adjusting to another cultural context is consistent

with Ruby's ruminations about her children. Obviously, in a world that still glorifies 'whiteness', those who are closer to 'it', or even embody 'it', are going to have an easier time in life.

11. Running like parallel lines throughout the testimonies are the twin themes of empowerment, which locates *métis(se)* people as cultural bridges and political agents, and of hopelessness, which highlights the intermingled psychosocial sensations of not belonging, being marginal, and being (in)visible. Without either putting words into their mouths or ignoring their cumulative and collective pain, my challenge was to create a socio-cultural context and a safe space for them to reframe the negativity that usually dominates most depictions of the lived experiences of *métis(se)* people in England.

Bibliography

Ahmad, Ajaiz (1995) 'The Politics of Literary Postcoloniality', in *Race and Class*, 36 (3): 1–20.

Ahmed, Sara (1997) 'It's a Sun Tan Isn't It?: Auto-biography as an Identificatory Practice', in Mirza 1997: 153–67.

Alibhai-Brown, Yasmin and Anne Montague (1992) *The Colour of Love*, London: Virago.

American Anthropological Association (1997) 'Draft Official Statement on "Race"', Washington: American Anthropological Association.

Ang-Lygate, Magdalene (1997) 'Charting the Spaces of (un)Location: On Theorizing Diaspora', in Mirza 1997: 153–68.

Anthias, Floya and Nira Yuval-Davis (1992) *Racialized Boundaries*, London: Routledge.

Anzaldua, Gloria (1987) *Borderlands, La Frontera: The New Mestiza*, San Francisco: Aunt Lute Press.

Bachman, John (1850) *The Doctrine of the Unity of the Human Race Examined on the Principles of Science*, Charleston, S.C.: Canning.

Back, Les (1996) *New Ethnicities and Urban Youth Cultures*, London: UCL Press.

Banton, Michael (1967) *Race Relations*, London: Tavistock.

Barth, Frederik (ed.) (1969) *Ethnic Groups and Boundaries*, London: Allen and Unwin.

Benedict, Ruth (1940) *Race, Science and Politics*, New York: Viking.

Benson, Sue (1981) *Ambiguous Ethnicity*, Cambridge: Cambridge University Press.

Bhabha, Homi (1994) *The Location of Culture*, London: Routledge.

Brah, Avtar (1996) *Cartographies of Diaspora*, London: Routledge.

Brand, Christopher (1996) *The g Factor*, New York: John Wiley and Sons.

Broca, Paul (1864) *Phenomena of Hybridity in the Genus Homo*, London: Anthropological Society.

Camper, Carol (ed.) (1994) *Miscegenation Blues: Voices of Mixed Race Women*, Toronto: Sister Vision Press.

Canclini, Néstor García (1989) *Culturas Híbridas*, Miguel Hidalgo, Mexico: Grijalbo.

Cohen, Robin (1994) *Frontiers of Identity*, London: Longman.

Colker, Ruth (1996) *Hybrid: Bisexuals, Multiracials, and other Misfits under American Law*, London: New York University.

Comaroff, Jean and John Comaroff (1991) *Of Revelation and Revolution: Christianity, Colonialism and Consciousness in South Africa*, Chicago: University of Chicago Press.

Davis, James F. (1991) *Who is Black?*, University Park, Penn.: Pennsylvania State University Press.

De-costa-Willis *et al.* (eds.) (1992) *Black Erotica*, New York: Anchor.

Degler, Carl (1971) *Neither Black nor White: Slavery and Relations in Brazil and the United States*, New York: Macmillan.

Delaney, Martin (1879) *The Origins of Races and Color*, New York: New American Library.

Diop, Cheik Anta (1991) *Civilization or Barbarism: An Authentic Anthropology*, New York: Lawrence Hill.

Diop, Samba (1993) Personal communication.

— (1998) Personal communication.

Dominguez, Virginia (1986) *White by Definition*, New Brunswick, N.J.: Rutgers.

Dyer, Richard (1997) *White: Essays on Race and Culture*, London: Routledge.

Evaristo, Bernadine (1997) *Lara*, Tunbridge Wells: Angela Royal Publishing.

Fanon, Frantz (1967) *Black Skin, White Masks*, New York: Grove Press.

Ferguson, Russell *et al.* (eds.) (1990) *Out There: Marginalization and Contemporary Cultures*, New York: New Museum of Contemporary Art/MIT.

Fine, Michelle *et al.* (eds.) (1997) *Off White: Readings on Race, Power and Society*, London: Routledge.

Fisher, Jean (1995) 'Some Thoughts on "Contaminations"', in *Third Text* 38, pp. 3–7.

Frankenberg, Ruth (ed.) (1997) *Displacing Whiteness: Essays in Social and Cultural Criticism*, London: Duke University Press.

Fraser, Steven (ed.) (1995) *The Bell Curve Wars: Race, Intelligence and the Future of America*, New York: Basic Books.

Friedman, Jonathan (1997) 'Global Crises, the Struggle for Cultural Identity and Intellectual Porkbarrelling: Cosmopolitans versus Locals, Ethnics and Nationals in an Era of De-hegemonisation', in Werbner and Modood 1997: 70–89.

Fryer, Peter (1984) *Staying Power: The History of Black People in Britain*, London: Pluto.

Galton, Francis (1870) *Hereditary Genius*, New York: Appleton.

Gerzina, Gretchen (1995) *Black England: Life Before Emancipation*, London: John Murray.

Gilroy, Paul (1987) *There Ain't No Black in the Union Jack*, London: Hutchinson.

— (1993a) *The Black Atlantic*, London: Verso.

— (1993b) *Small Acts: Thoughts on the Politics of Black Culture*, London: Serpent's Tail.

— (1996) 'Route Work: The Black Atlantic and the Politics of Exile', in I. Chambers *et al.* (eds.), *The Post-Colonial Question*, London: Routledge, pp. 17–29.

Gist, Noel *et al.* (eds.) (1972) *The Blending of the Races: Marginality and Identity in World Perspective*, New York: John Wiley and Sons.

Goldberg, David Theo (1993) *Racist Culture*, Oxford: Blackwell.

Goodwin, Brian (1994) *How the Leopard Changes its Spots*, London: Weidenfeld and Nicholson.

Gordon, L. R. (1995) 'Critical "Mixed Race"'? in *Social Identities* 1 (2): 38–395.

Gould, Stephen Jay (1994) 'The Geometer of Race', in *Discover*, vol. 15 (2): 64–9.

Gossett, Thomas (1965) *Race: The History of an Idea in America*, New York: Schocken.

Hall, Stuart (1991) 'Old and New Identities, Old and New Ethnicities', in A. King (ed.) *Culture, Globalization and the World System*, London: Macmillan, pp. 41–68.

— (1996) 'The Formation of a Diasporic Intellectual', in D. Morley *et al.* (eds.) *Stuart Hall: Critical Dialogues in Cultural Studies*, London: Routledge, pp. 484–503.

Hannaford, Ivan (1996) *Race: The History of an Idea in the West*, London: Johns Hopkins University Press.

Hashim, Iman (1996) 'Mixed Up or Just Plain Mixed? An Examination of the Construction of Identities in Individuals of Mixed Heritage as a Means of Exploring Debates Around Multiple Subjectivities', discussion paper in Sociology, Leicester University.

Henri-Cousin, Pierre (1994) *Diamond French Dictionary*, London: Collins.

Hernton, Calvin (1965) *Sex and Racism in America*, New York: Grove Press.

Hill Collins, Patricia (1990) *Black Feminist Thought*, Boston: Unwin and Hyman.

Hitler, Adolf (1992) *Mein Kampf*, trans. R. Mannheim, London: Pimlico.

Hoffman, Paul (1994) 'The Science of Race' in *Discover*, vol. 15 (2): 4.

hooks, bell (1992) *Black Looks*, Boston: South End Press.

Hyam, Ronald (1990) *Empire and Sexuality: The British Experience*, Manchester: Manchester University Press.

Ifekwunigwe, Jayne O. (1997) 'Diaspora's Daughters, Africa's Orphans?: On Lineage, Authenticity and "Mixed Race" Identity', in Mirza 1997: 127–52.

— (1999) *Scattered Belongings: Cultural Paradoxes of 'Race', Nation and Gender*, London: Routledge.

Jones, Joy (1994) *Between Black Women: Listening with the Third Ear*, Chicago: African American Images.

Jones, Lisa (1994) *Bulletproof Diva: Tales of Race, Sex and Hair*, New York: Doubleday.

Jordan, Winthrop (1974) *White Man's Burden*, Oxford: Oxford University Press.

Keith, Michael and Steve Pile (eds) (1993) *Place and the Politics of Identity*, London: Routledge.

Kiernan, V.G. (1972) *The Lords of Human Kind: European Attitudes to the Outside World in the Imperial Age*, Harmondsworth: Penguin.

Kohn, Marek (1996) *The Race Gallery: The Return of Race Science*, London: Vintage.

Koubaka, Henri-Pierre (1993) Personal communication.

Kuper, Leo (1974) *Race, Class and Power*, London: Duckworth.

LaForest, Marie Hélène (1996) 'Black Cultures in Difference', in I. Chambers *et al.* (eds.)*The Post-Colonial Question*, London: Routledge, pp. 115–22.

Lavie, Smadar *et al.* (eds) (1996) *Displacement, Diaspora and Geographies of Identity*, London: Duke University Press.

Lawrence, Cecile Ann (1995) 'Racelessness', in Zack 1995: 25–38.

Lorde, Audre (1996) *The Audre Lorde Compendium*, London: Pandora.

MacDougall, David (1993) 'The Subjective Voice in Ethnographic Film', paper presented at the University of California, Berkeley.

Mahtani, Minelle (1998) Personal communication.

Maja-Pearce, Adewale (1990) *How Many Miles to Babylon?*, London: Heinemann.

Malik, Kenan (1996) *The Meaning of Race*, London: Macmillan.

Mama, Amina (1995) *Beyond the Masks: Race, Gender and Subjectivity*, London: Routledge.

Marimba, Ani (1994) *Yurugu: An African-Centered Critique of European Cultural Thought and Behavior*, Trenton, N.J.: Africa World Press.

Mercer, Kobena (1994) *Welcome to the Jungle: New Positions in Black Cultural Studies*, London: Routledge.

Miles, Robert (1989) *Racism*, London: Routledge.

Mills, Charles W. (1997) *The Racial Contract*, London: Cornell University Press.

Minh-ha, Trinh T. (1991) *When the Moon Waxes Red: Reprsentations and Cultural Politics*, London: Routledge.

Mirza, Heidi (ed.) (1997) *Black British Feminism*, London: Routledge.

Moreno, April (1998) Personal communication.

Murray, Charles *et al.* (1994) *The Bell Curve*, New York: Free Press.

Nott, Josiah and George Gliddon (1854) *Types of Mankind*, Philadelphia: J. B. Lippincott.

Omi, Michael and Howard Winant (1986) *Racial Formation in the United States*, New York: Routledge.

Opitz, May (ed.) (1986) *Showing Our Colors: Afro-German Women Speak Out*, Amherst: University of Massachusetts Press.

Papastergiadis, Nikos (1995) 'Restless Hybrids' in *Third Text*, 32: 9–18.

Paredes, Anthony (1997) 'Race is not Something You Can See', in *Anthropology Newsletter*, vol. 38 (9): 1, 6.

Phoenix, Ann and Barbara Tizard (1993) *Black, White or Mixed Race?*, London: Routledge.

Phoenix, Ann and Charlie Owen (1996) 'From Miscegenation to Hybridity: Mixed Relationships and Mixed Parentage in Profile', in B. Bernstein and J. Brannen (eds.) *Children, Research and Policy*, London: Taylor and Francis.

Pieterse, Jan (1995) 'Globalization and Hybridization', in M. Featherstone *et al.* (eds.) *Global Modernities*, London: Sage, pp. 45–68.

Priestley, J. B. (1987) *English Journey*, Harmondsworth: Penguin.

Probyn, Elspeth (1990) 'Travels in the Postmodern: Making Sense of the Local', in L. Nicholson (ed.) *Feminism and Postmodernism*, London: Routledge, pp. 176–89.

Provine, William (1973) 'Geneticists and the Biology of Race Crossing', in *Science*, vol. 182 (4114): 790–96.

Ramdin, Ron (1987) *The Making of the Black Working Class in Britain*, Aldershot: Wildwood House.

Rashidi, Runoko (1985) 'Ancient and Modern Britons', in I. Van Sertima (ed.) *African Presence in Early Europe*, London: Transaction Press, pp. 251–60.

Rattansi, Ali *et al.* (eds.) *Racism, Modernity and Identity*, Cambridge: Polity.

Rich, Paul (1986) *Race and Empire in British Politics*, Cambridge: Cambridge University Press.

Rogers, J. A. (1944) *Sex and Race, Vol. III*, St. Petersburg, Fla.: Helga Rogers.

— (1952) *Nature Knows No Color Line*, St. Petersburg, Fla.: Helga Rogers.

Root, Maria P. (ed.) (1992) *Racially Mixed People in America*, London: Sage.

— (ed.) (1996) *The Multiracial Experience: Racial Borders as the New Frontier*, London: Sage.

Russell, Kathy *et al.* (1992) *The Color Complex*, New York: Anchor.

Sabu (1998) Personal communication.

Small, Stephen (1994) *Racialized Barriers*, London: Routledge.

Snowden, Frank (1983) *Before Color Prejudice: The Ancient View of Blacks*, Cambridge, Mass.: Harvard University Press.

Spencer, Jon Michael (1997) *The New Colored People: The Mixed Race Movement in America*, London: New York University Press.

Spickard, Paul (1989) *Mixed Blood: Intermarriage and Ethnic Identity in the Twentieth Century America*, London: University of Wisconsin Press.

Stanton, William (1960) *The Leopard's Spots: Scientific Attitudes Toward Race in America 1815–1859*, Chicago: University of Chicago Press.

Stocking, George (1982) *Race, Culture and Evolution*, Chicago: University of Chicago Press.

Stolcke, Verena (1993) 'Is Sex to Gender as Race is to Ethnicity?', in T. del Valle, *Gendered Anthropology*, London: Routledge, pp. 17–38.

Stonequist, Everett (1937) *Marginal Man*, New York: Russell and Russell.

Traynor, Joanna (1997) *Sister Josephine*, London: Bloomsbury.

Wah, Fred (1996) 'Half-Bred Poetics', in *Absinthe, Hyphenation: A Mixed Race Issue*, 9 (2): 60–65.

Walvin, James (1973) *Black and White: The Negro and English Society*, London: Allen Lane.

Ware, Vron (1997) 'Island Racism: Gender, Place and White Power', in R. Frankenberg (ed.) *Displacing Whiteness*, London: Duke University Press, pp. 283–310.

Weekes, Debbie (1997) 'Shades of Blackness: Young Female Constructions of Beauty', in Mirza 1997: 113–26.

Welsing, Frances Cress (1991) *The Isis Papers*, Chicago: Third World Press.

Werbner, Pnina and Tariq Modood (eds.) (1997) *Debating Cultural Hybridity*, London: Zed.

Williamson, Joel (1995) *New People: Miscegenation and Mulattoes in the United States*, London: Louisiana State University Press.

Wilson, Anne (1987) *Mixed Race Children*, London: Allen and Unwin.

Wolcott, Harry (1995) 'Making a Study "More Ethnographic"', in J. Van Maanen (ed.), *Representation in Ethnography*, London: Sage, pp. 79–111.

Young, Lola (1996) *Fear of the Dark: 'Race', Gender and Sexuality in the Cinema*, London: Routledge.

Young, Robert (1995) *Colonial Desire: Hybridity in Theory, Culture and Race*, London: Routledge.

Zack, Naomi (1993) *Race and Mixed Race*, Philadelphia: Temple University Press.

— (ed.) (1995) *American Mixed Race*, London: Rowman and Littlefield.

— (ed.) (1997) *Race/Sex: Their Sameness, Difference and Interplay*, London: Routledge.

11

It's Your World: Discrepant M/multiculturalisms

Barnor Hesse

Multiculturalism does not lead us very far if it remains a question of difference only between one culture and another. Differences should also be understood within the same culture, just as multiculturalism as an explicit condition of our times exists within every self. Intercultural, intersubjective, interdisciplinary. These are some of the key words that keep on circulating in artistic and educational as well as political milieux.

Trinh T. Minh-ha[1]

It's your world (and yours and yours and yours)

Gil Scott-Heron and Brian Jackson[2]

There is a brief but remarkable scene in Robert Wise's 1959 film noir, *Odds Against Tomorrow*, where a hustler character, played by Harry Belafonte, makes an impromptu visit to his former marital home and interrupts a social gathering there. Perplexed by his ex-wife's attempts to live a conventional upwardly mobile life with their young daughter in the atmosphere of 1950s white America, he both reminds and warns her: 'it's *their* world and we're just living in it!'. Whether or not she agreed, she did not reply. Instead she returned uneasily to a discussion with her white liberal friends that had begun to unravel, while he went back to planning a robbery in a difficult pragmatic alliance with a white southern racist whom he despised. Why begin a discussion of the politics of multiculturalism with an old black and white American film that I saw by chance late one Friday night on British television? The answer lies in the particular dramaturgical representation of national differences that the scene evokes. If we reflect on this it becomes possible to specify distinctive political characteristics of Western multiculturalism. First, it demonstrates that the same entanglement of 'race', gender and class can be lived, read and politicised in intensely different registers of the nation. Second, it illustrates how the proliferation of and interaction between cultural differences produce the recurrence of familiar and unfamiliar encounters, oscillating between temporary and permanent arrangements. Third, it reveals that there is little that socially fits together neatly, and that not everything is, despite overwhelming obstacles, irreconcilable. Fourth, it suggests political differences which convey histories of solidarity and opposition and their subsequent reversals, broken and repaired dialogues, and stark, solitary voices. Finally, the scene portrays a multicultural Western entanglement: it signifies an unyielding context of racialisation[3] in which the experience of related but differently empowered 'worlds', not only enhances and frustrates the desires for a representative or assimilable national formation, but also creates multiple possibilities of criss-crossing and cross-over identities which disrupt the centre of everyone's world.

Although this complex formation of multiculturalism underwrites Western national formations like the US and the UK, its Western political implications have been theoretically neglected in many contemporary debates. The concern here is to contribute to the development of a theory of the politics of multiculturalism, which can offer an account of its modern constitutiveness. The development of my argument is divided into four stages. It begins with a deconstruction[4] of Western multiculturalism. This reveals a racialised configuration of meaning that is conventionally repressed or disavowed in formal representations of the nation. Second, I comment on Charles Taylor's (1992) significant attempt to theorise the politics of multiculturalism as a 'politics of recognition'. I suggest that Taylor's intervention is problematic where it would expect to be at its most robust, and propose instead that the politics of multiculturalism be understood as a differential politics of interrogation. Third, I return to a conceptualisation of multiculturalism as a Western social formation in order to highlight that what is under interrogation is also resistant to being interrogated. Here I argue that multiculturalism is discrepant[5] because its contested, historic imperial formation is disavowed by hegemonic representations of the nation. I describe this as 'disavowed multiculturalism' because the dominant idealisation of the nation – nationalism – attempts to expunge its accountability to an imperial history. This formation of disavowal provides a surface of inscription[6] for political orientations or interrogations which valorise (or repudiate) multiculturalism as a national form without signalling the incompatible plurality of its discrete and blurred political discourses. I describe this diversity as 'representative multiculturalisms'. Finally I suggest that the multicultural is a constitutive form of Western national entanglement which has profound deconstructive implications for how we understand the politics of national identity. It produces the paradox of the multicultural impossibility of full national representation.

Deconstructing Western Multiculturalism

Since the 1980s, the concept of multiculturalism has undergone a profound transformation in cultural theory in the United States (see Giroux and McLaren 1994; Goldberg 1994; Shohat and Stam 1994). It no longer signifies simply the celebration or problem of cultural diversity, or the limited constitutional recognition of cultural difference; it can also refer to antagonisms between the sacred and the secular, educational pluralism and the distribution of democratic rights in relation to 'race', class, gender and sexuality. It has become a floating signifier[7] that blurs the distinction not only between different social sites of enunciation but between different Western national enunciations. This suggests that the thematics of multiculturalism in Western circulation define it as a constitutively undecidable formation, susceptible to radically different conceptualisations and social readings.

However, what is not covered by this framing is the Western status of this multiculturalism and its political implications. What currently circulates within the national discourses that traverse the Atlantic,[8] is a logic of multiculturalism that signifies cultural differences both contractively as 'race' and ethnicity and also expansively as including gender, sexuality, class, religion and so on. What these contracting and expanding poles of the multicultural suggest is not only the incidence of diverse cultural responses to the experience of national entanglement, but the political irreducibility of racialisation in any formation of Western multiculturalism. It is the articulation of racialisation in Western multiculturalism that is its configural dimension. Without this, neither the contractive nor expansive pole can be constituted. It is for this reason that multiculturalism in the West needs to be understood as discursively organised around the various discrepancies that circulate within the cultural afterlife of modern Europe's imperialisms.[9] Within this context, we need to address a racialised logic of modernity that projects through its Western circulation an ontological distinction between 'Europe–whiteness–masculinity' and 'Non-Europe–non-whiteness–femininity' (Cf. McKlintock 1995), where the former reflects singular normativity and the latter comparative pathology. It is this process of racialisation which inaugurates the discrepant formation of Western multiculturalism.

There is a highly significant dimension of temporal contestability here, which can be understood using James Clifford's (1992) idea of 'discrepant cosmopolitanisms'. This describes the outcome of modernity's unresolved historical dialogues between (and, I would add, within) national cultures in terms of 'continuity and disruption', 'essence and position' and 'homogeneity and difference' (Clifford 1992: 108). Mediated through imperial cultures of displacement and transplantation, discrepant cosmopolitanisms are 'inseparable from specific, often violent histories of economic, political and cultural interactions' (Clifford 1992: 108) which continually cross-cut 'us' and 'them'. It is useful to retain Clifford's idea of discrepancy to describe the West's imperial articulation of inconsistencies, antagonisms and inequalities. But this needs to be combined with the idea of discrepancy as referring to the conceptual avoidance and political marginalisation of these inconsistencies in the formal institution of national cultures. In this context, discrepancy in multicultural formations describes inconsistencies and antagonisms which are conceptually resistant to elimination and yet remain unthematised in various discourses of the nation. Theoretically it can be developed to suggest 'an inconsistency on the level of philosophical argumentation that cannot be mended but nevertheless makes it possible to obtain the desired authoritative results' (Gasché 1986: 126). In the analysis of the Western multicultural, this means that the exposure of evaded racialised contradictions and neglected imperial aporias (for example, slavery and liberalism, democracy and racism) in the formation of the nation actually constitutes the basis of the nation's idealisation. The discursive exposition of Western national formations identifies a significant range of conceptuality which 'instead of belying the philosophical enterprise, are rather constitutive of its successful completion' (Gasché 1986: 137). This suggests that in both the US and the UK, the hegemonic idea of the nation as a representative container of cultural differences relies on the conceptual repression of the historical impact and social incidence of the fusion between imperialism and liberalism. In other words Western multiculturalism is constituted not only through universal elaborations (rationality, liberty, tolerance, pluralism) but also through particular forms of disavowal which disregard the formative contamination of its universal ideals. It is this 'unthought dimension' (Gasché 1986) which has not been thematised and is generally displaced, outside the traditional problems of political theory. The discrepant describes the institutionalisation of antagonisms and inconsistencies and their conceptual disavowal or exclusion from the thematics of the nation.

What the politics of multiculturalism implies, at least provisionally, is the exposure of the discrepant in Western national formations, that is, the legacy and avoidance of their imperial implications in relation to contemporary cultural differences. These are entangled in the elaboration of normative inequalities, particularly implicated in the suturing of the liberal idealisation of universal values (liberty, equality, dignity) and the imperial particularist (white, masculine, heterosexual) application of its principles. It is the historical fusion of these inequalities in the formation of the West which produces the contractive and expansive poles of the multicultural.

Only here does it make sense to define the multicultural as the proliferation of and interaction between cultural differences. It still remains to be determined how the political contestation of cultural differences can be adequately theorised.

The Political Turn of Multiculturalism

So far I have suggested that much of the multicultural meaning of the Western nation emerges in relation to the racialisation of modernity (see Hesse 1993). The late modern forms of the UK and the US. retain in decisive terms the imprint of Imperial formulations.[10] The Western nation is a spatial and temporal construction of 'Europe' and its political encounter with the toleration, celebration and repudiation of 'non-European' cultural differences. In this sense there is nothing about the Western nation that naturally binds the people within its horizon. The imagination of the nation as a sovereign and limited community (Anderson 1983) is fractured by dispersed investments in that imagination. These look for a substantial return on their investment in the imagined community. What in this context might be a political theory of multiculturalism?

It has become almost obligatory now to consider the intervention of Charles Taylor's sophisticated formalisation of the theoretical structure of the politics of multiculturalism. This is becoming increasingly influential, particularly in the contemporary terms of political philosophy.[11] Taylor provides a compelling argument which situates what he describes as the politics of difference within the 'subjectivist turn of Western culture'. He derives from this the emergence of a theory of a politics of recognition within the tradition of Liberalism:

> A number of strands in contemporary politics turn on the need, sometimes the demand, for recognition. The need, it can be argued, is one of the driving forces behind nationalist movements in politics. And the demand comes to the fore in a number of ways in today's politics, on behalf of minority or 'subaltern' groups, in some forms of feminism and in what is today called the politics of multiculturalism. (Taylor 1992: 25)

What is most interesting yet generally overlooked in Taylor's essay is the strategic centrality of this opening paragraph. In contextualising multiculturalism as a variant of a 'demand for recognition', and in suggesting that it is substantively distinct from, although similar in the respect of 'recognition' to, nationalism, feminism and the politics of subaltern groups, Taylor defers any encounter with a political theory of multiculturalism as such. Instead he implies that it is reducible to a politics of recognition and is yet something specific. But this specificity is never actually illuminated, and not often even alluded to.

What does it mean to demand recognition? Taylor argues that there is a fundamental link between recognition and the integrity of personal identity: 'Non-recognition or misrecognition can inflict harm, can be a form of oppression, imprisoning someone in a false, distorted and reduced mode of being.' This arises in conditions where the attempt to be recognised in authentically chosen terms palpably fails. Hence the politics of recognition is a struggle for authentic identities in the culture; it demands that the democratic polity ensures equal recognition. This, suggests Taylor, has two significant political dimensions or orientations. The first, a politics of universalism, emphasises the 'equal dignity of all citizens' through the 'equalisation of rights and entitlements'. The second, in contrast, highlights a politics of difference; although this has a universalist basis, it should not be confused with the first. It emphasises a different sense of recognition, not so much equal dignity but equal distinction: 'The idea is that it is precisely this distinctness that has been ignored, glossed over, assimilated to a dominant or majority identity. And this assimilation is the cardinal sin against the ideal of authenticity' (Taylor 1992: 38). Whereas the politics of universalism is non-discriminatory and blind to the way in which citizens differ, argues Taylor, 'the politics of difference often redefines non-discrimination as requiring that we make these distinctions the basis of differential treatment' (Taylor 1992: 39).

A great deal of support for Taylor's position (see Gutman 1994) has turned on his sensitive rendition of a problematic status in the politics of difference. Before considering this, it may be useful to subject his ideas on the politics of universalism to a more incisive scrutiny. Taylor seems to think that historically the logic of universalism has gradually, almost inevitably, extended itself throughout the social, and as a consequence the principal of equal citizenship has become universally accepted. He cites the US civil rights movement in the 1960s as its 'greatest, most recent' example (Taylor 1992: 38). But there are two historical and theoretical weaknesses in this position which need to be addressed. First, the extension of the universal principle was hardly inevitable, nor did it historically remain the same principle that had initially been formulated. Taylor's historicity ignores how the US Constitution inaugurated by the 1776 Declaration of Independence did not apply the concept of equal citizenship (the Jeffersonian idea that 'all men are created equal') either to African Americans or to native Americans. In relation to African Americans, this non-extension of the principle was confirmed nearly a hundred years later by the famous Dred Scott decision of the US Supreme court in 1857, which upheld the claim that the provisions of the Constitution were not intended to apply to

African Americans (see Clarke 1994). In relation to this background, the civil rights movement represented neither a defence nor an extension of this principle, but its displacement and transformation in the articulation of a new principle which challenged rather than accommodated racism. In other words, the universal principle as it stood prior to the civil rights struggle was tied to the representative particularity of its enunciation: white America. The universal had not been articulated beyond this particularity. In this context what the civil rights struggle catalysed, and subsequently Black Power, the women's, native American and gay movements elaborated, was an interrogation of the nation's exclusiveness and an insistence on the transformation of this space to engage the heritage and affirm the rights of subjugated particularities. This suggests that it is the differential and representative political expansion of particularity which enables the articulation of a (new) universal principle, rather than the cultural discovery of European universals that are apparently self-generating and self-legislating.

The second weakness follows from the first. It concerns Taylor's tendency to emphasise the universal as a valorisation rather than a cultural and political articulation.[12] The problem of the principle of universalism and equal dignity in the US is that it was formed in articulation with European racism and white masculinity (see Carroll and Noble 1989). Taylor is holding on to the idea that there is a universalism without an influential particularism inscribed in the act of its enunciation or its application. What this fails to consider is that if a universal is articulated outside of particularity, then we need to ask what accounts for the particularity of its exclusions? Paradoxically, Taylor ignores (and also seems to reinforce) the basis upon which these exclusions are enacted. What Taylor identifies as outside the universalist politics of the 'public sphere' are precisely those issues or identities that have been conventionally excluded or suppressed by that sphere (black people, women, queers), which Taylor reproduces as the politics of difference, that is, the 'intimate sphere'. The problem for liberalism, as Taylor sees it, is that the politics of difference/multiculturalism cannot be 'assimilated' to universalism, because it either seeks recognition which is denied or it eschews the universal in the embrace of relativism. But this conceals a more decisive theoretical problem: how can the desire to preserve the sanctity of the universal, which gives rise to an unmarked politics of recognition (that is, affirming the legislative status of Western liberalism), be reconciled with the desire to defend the integrity of difference? It is the latter that effectively questions the particular historical, political and cultural articulation of the universal, and gives rise to what I call a marked politics of interrogation.

The Politics of Interrogation

If the politics of difference/multiculturalism were simply about the recognition of authentic identities and their cultural worth or value, we would still have to question whose recognition is sought and what is involved in the power to confer recognition and value. These are not questions that Taylor entertains. Although he refers to two politics of recognition – the universal and difference – located in the subjectivist, inward turn of Western culture, he is able to supply an intellectual genealogy only for the politics of universalism. It stretches from Rousseau through Kant and Herder to Hegel. Taylor's single textual reference for the politics of difference is Frantz Fanon. But Fanon is not situated in any intellectual context; he is not located in any corresponding turn in Western culture; he simply appears on the inassimilable edge of liberalism.

Taylor attributes to Fanon the view that violence, 'matching the original violence of the alien imposition', was the method to purge oneself of 'depreciating self-images' in the colonial situation, and this required a 'struggle for a changed self-image, which takes place both within the subjugated and against the dominator' (Taylor 1992: 65). This is an extremely tendentious yet conventional reading of Fanon, which underlines many liberal objections to his analysis. A more acute reading of Fanon's perspective might see that he is at pains to identify the complicity of Western values (for example, the politics of universalism and equal dignity) with their supposed antithesis. Fanon is not so much theorising the conditions of recognition as initiating a theory (and politics) of interrogation:

> The violence with which the supremacy of white values is affirmed and the aggressiveness which has permeated the victory of these values over the ways of life and of thought of the native mean that, in revenge, the native laughs in mockery when Western values are mentioned in front of him. In the colonial context the settler only ends his work of breaking in the native when the latter admits loudly and intelligibly the supremacy of the white man's values. In the period of decolonisation, the colonised masses mock at these very values and vomit them up. (Fanon 1967: 33–4)

There is cynical laughter and a hermeneutics of suspicion in this politics of interrogation.[13] In the black diaspora,[14] for example, it proceeds from a circumvention of Western culture. Circumvention emerges as an irruptive opening in a racially disciplinary political space; it incarnates the possibility of revising, challenging and changing the representational structure of impositional Western claims to universalism. With regard to its theoretical antecedents, black circumvention historically and metaphorically signifies the 'slave's representation and reversal of the master's attempt to transform a human being into a commodity' (Gates 1988: 128). Where it is sustained it initiates a political reversal; it turns subordination into insubordination and constitutes a series of tactical disruptions which expose an ethical precariousness in the racialised governance of Western culture. It creates the space of interrogation.

What I am calling the politics of interrogation places the European hegemony of Western culture in question; it announces itself as the place for questioning. Its theoretical orientation is derived from Merleau-Ponty. He suggests that interrogation resists engagement with the visible manifestation of the world as if it were a fixed or closed set of representations 'whose terminal product one supposes the world and things to be' (Merleau-Ponty 1968: 87). We can develop this to suggest two things in particular about the black diaspora's politics of interrogation in Western multiculturalism. First, it interrogates the relation of visible civilised grandeur to the invisibility of dehumanisation in constructions of Western culture; it 'interrogates so that something can be seen, something can be said, something can be known, something can be understood, something can be interrogated' (Silverman 1994: 35). Second, despite the apparent decisive quality of Euro-American significations (for example, the democratic accomplishments of the West), an interrogative practice questions whether these universal valorisations 'have a horizon of brute being and of brute mind, from which the constructed objects and significations emerge and *which they do not account for*' (Merleau-Ponty 1968: 97; emphasis added). In this double sense, the politics of interrogation is the articulation of an 'astonishment in the face of a perceived world'.

This is just one counter-lineage *within* Western culture that Taylor inexplicably neglects. It brings together the themes in the history of liberalism, Europe and the West which conventional political theory usually ignores: the complicity of the culture of universalism with imperialism (see Said 1993). The black diaspora is implicated in an interrogation of political modernity's articulation of the project of civilisation where the rights of Europe are promoted and imposed as 'good' for 'non-Europe'. This is a history from which perhaps only Herder, of the luminaries mentioned by Taylor, emerges honourably (see Pagden 1995). Within the terms of liberal Europe/America, equal respect for the individual was designed to admit no deviation; within the terms of colonial Europe/America, 'non-white' difference was tolerated and affirmed only within the diversity permissible within the racist regime of the 'good'. For iconic liberals of political modernity, such as John Locke and John Stuart Mill, both of whom were philosophically and administratively involved in the colonial enterprises of their time (see Parekh 1995), the articulation of British colonialism and English liberalism had two dimensions. First, in relation to the European *right*, individual liberty belonged to the 'civilised societies'. The 'right to non-intervention applied to the relations between civilised societies' (Parekh 1995: 94). Second, in relation to the non-European *good*, the improvement or development of the 'Other's good life could be introduced only from outside by Europe ('manifest destiny', 'civilising mission, 'white man's burden').

At this point we can state the principal strategic problem with Taylor's argument. It provides no logical space for these 'other' articulations in the conception of Western culture. Taylor's particular privileging of the universal, his unawareness of the tenability of a politics of interrogation, commits him almost to a dogmatic defense of a liberalism which does not recognise either past or prospective displacements or circumventions by the 'other'. Taylor forecloses the possibility of developing a credible theory of multicultural politics because he is dazzled by his own multicultural imaginary.[15] This is why his eventual recourse to a liberal fundamentalism[16] signals a strangely familiar illiberalism. The point is, as Bhikhu Parekh puts it:

> Liberals cannot consistently be dogmatic about their own beliefs and skept-ical about all others, or talk about an open-minded dialogue yet both exclude some and conduct the dialogue on their own terms. They need to take a sustained critical look at their basic assumptions that both generate and prevent them from noticing and restraining, their illiberal and inegalitarian impulses. (Parekh 1995: 97–8)

A political theory of multiculturalism needs to start in a place much different to that chosen by Taylor. In relation to Western multiculturalism it begins with an interrogation of the imperial construction of universal ideas like the West, Europe, 'non-Europe' and particularly the nation.

Disavowed Multiculturalism

We need to consider seriously what Homi Bhabha's (1994) invitation to reconceptualise the Western nation as one of the 'dark corners of the earth' can honestly mean in an account of modernity. Interrogation of its multicultural constitutiveness might begin with the fact that most accounts of modernity are 'structured around a gaze which goes from Europe towards the periphery' (Sayyid 1994: 277). They narrate legitimations which underwrite the Western nation's global domination and naturalise the contrast between what constitutes 'the West (Civilisation, Democracy, Rationality, Freedom) and its Other (Barbarism, Irrationality, Despotism, Slavery)' (Sayyid 1994: 277). Although the Western nation is an analogy of this symbolic order it cannot be encapsulated within any one cultural field. Western discourses of 'race' and ethnicity are themselves multi-culturally articulated through gender, sexuality, class, religion and so on (see Rattansi 1994). An articulation of multiculturalism as a social condition does not signify a single or unique origin but rather an imperial 'point of entanglement' (Glissant 1989). It is this point of entanglement which is also the symptom of the Western nation's repression of its accountability to that history.

In Lacanian psychoanalysis, a symptom is 'a particular, "pathological", signifying formation, a binding of enjoyment, an inert stain resisting communication and interpretation' (Zizek 1989: 75). This means that the multicultural provokes remembrance of a continuing imperial sense of the nation which can no longer be included within the universal liberal terms of its self-reference, yet must be referred to as an exterior, a resolved historical deviation from the inevitable ideals of Western freedoms. There-fore the multicultural becomes 'a stain which cannot be included in the circuit of discourse, of social bond network, but is at the same time a condition of it' (Zizek 1989). As a symptom, it is the trace of something which requires to be interrogated and understood but is assiduously covered over.

If the Western nation is a derivative of an imperial, symbolically dis-crepant order, it is because its 'past is present in the form of historical tradition' (Zizek 1989: 56), which has been sanitised rather than reclaimed in the popular consumption of the nation's ritualised heritage. Against this sense of the nation, to engage the multicultural is to work through the drama of the symptom which produces the 'symbolic reality of the past, long-forgotten traumatic events' (Zizek 1989: 56) that can no longer evade interrogation. Multiculturalism is the return of the national repressed. It takes refuge in the resilience of 'stains' that 'can never be fully expatiated' (Césaire 1955: 20). What is disavowed in the official versions of the Western nation is its implication both in the hegemonic construction of 'Europe' as the universal/ideal and its acculturation through and antagonism with the subaltern construction of 'non-Europe' as the differential/pathological (see Rattansi and Westwood 1994). If the Western nation is formed by this point of entanglement, then to enter this entanglement is to enter the West.

Western nationalism as disavowal During the late twentieth century, a white desire to escape democratic representations of that entanglement has recuperated the disavowals of Western nationalisms in a strategy to define the parameters of the national space so as to conjure up a racialised singularity out of a racialised heterogeneity (see Hesse 1997). Once the nation is articulated in terms of nationalism, it has to negotiate, if not 'subordinate the complex and multiple ways in which human beings define and redefine themselves as members of groups' (Hobsbawm 1990: 8–9). In order to construct a relation between these multiple definitions, nationalism conceives the nation 'prospectively' (Hobsbawm 1990). Yet what creates the culture of the prospect is a retrospective turn. The manifest national destinies of both the US and the UK were cultivated during the nineteenth century through appeals to the imperial essence of a mythical heroic, combative, masculinist Anglo-Saxonism. This illustrates one reason why, in a Western nationalist discourse, the nation is never where it is supposed to be; the metaphysics of national presence[17] are always inscribed in a temporal displacement; the past or the future beckons as it glistens. In either direction temporality can become a golden age, once it is organised for nationalist enjoyment. As Žižek puts it: 'All we can do is enumerate disconnected fragments of the way our community organises its feasts, its rituals of mating, its initiation ceremonies – in short, all the details by which is made visible the unique way a community organises its enjoyment' (Žižek 1990). In this way nationalism becomes the chosen people's spectacle.

But at the same time as 'we' consume our sameness, 'we' expel otherness. Nationalism is engulfed in fantasy, principally the fantasy of the other. In other words, the nation is 'what "always returns" as the traumatic element around which fantasies weave' (Salecl 1994: 211–12). The other threatens national identity because its habits, rituals and discourses have insinuated into 'our society', it interferes with the narcissism of our enjoyment of 'ourselves'. Where the politics of multiculturalism exhibits imperial symptoms of 'race', gender and sexuality, these insinuate multiple possibilities of dreaded encounters with otherness. What is often celebrated or derided as the politics of difference (see Young 1990) dislocates the nationalist enjoyment of identity. Where the racial–gender–sexual other persists in an affirmation of difference, he or she appears intolerant, inassimilable, a destabilising influence, a threat to our British or American way of life; 'if they adopt our customs, we then assume that they want to steal from us "our thing": the nation' (Salecl 1994). Not only is the representation of the nation subject to a differential politics of inter-rogation, it is disclosed through the contestation of different multicultural imaginaries.

Representative Multiculturalisms

The political question is: how do particular imaginaries articulate a conception of the nation through the multicultural and in relation to the national institution of disavowal? Imaginaries are important as political discourses because they express desires to overcome incompleteness or insufficiency in the construction of identities; they invoke perceptual objectives. The Lacanian concept of the imaginary covers the images of fantasy and the initiatives of lived bodily experiences, 'it is everything in the human mind and its reflexive life which is in a state of flux before the fixation is effected by the symbol, a fixation which at the very least tempers the incessant sliding of the mutations of being and desire' (Lemaire 1977: 60–61). It has been used in political theory to understand the logic and limits of discourses (Laclau 1990). There are three significant features relevant to my discussion of multicultural imaginaries. First, a multicultural imaginary incorporates the desire to define the absolute limits within which the nation is conceived. Second, it incorporates an interrogation of social incompleteness and discrepancy in the formation of the nation. Third, it incorporates an investment or disinvestment in any 'other' social vision of the nation. Multicultural imaginaries are visionary forms of 'situated knowledges' which draw on 'partial perspectives' (see Haraway 1991: 183–201) in a configuration of the nation. A multicultural imaginary is not a disembodied visualisation of all possible national representations; it is always positioned as a 'key practice grounding knowledge organized around the imagery of vision' (Haraway 1991). Although the nation is envisaged through differential interrogations, it is affirmed through particular imaginaries which give meaning to the proliferation of and interaction between its cultural differences.

Now if we take seriously the idea of different representations of multiculturalism, this suggests several multicultural interventions are entangled in expanding or contracting the political space of the nation. For this reason it is worthwhile referring to Peter McClaren's interesting approach to distinguishing different codifications of multiculturalism in the US (McClaren 1994a, 1994b). McClaren's point of departure takes the material relations of oppression as the terrain of a contested multiculturalism which signifies a 'forensic search for equality' (McClaren 1994a: 195). He describes his own theoretical objective as an 'initial attempt at transcoding and mapping the cultural field of race and ethnicity (in order to) discern the multiple ways in which difference is constructed and engaged' (McClaren 1994b: 47). While McClaren is alert to the need to delineate the multiplicity of articulations in the multicultural, and identifies conservative, liberal, left/liberal and critical variants, he is too easily seduced by categories that trace an untenable right–left continuum which confines the status of the political to a frontier between reform and revolution. In effect only the conservative and critical approaches are portrayed convincingly in his analysis; the former is indelibly marked by the politics of assimilation while only the latter has a 'transformative political agenda'. It is hardly surprising then that McClaren argues that only critical multiculturalism 'stresses the central task of transforming the social, cultural and institutional relations in which meanings are generated' (McClaren 1994b: 47). But this neglects to consider that this is precisely the orientation that all forms of political imaginary are motivated by. The idea that even the apparent stabilisation or conservation of meaning can occur without interventions to cohere contingencies or counteract disruptions needs to be rejected.

It would diminish the complexity of the politics of muticulturalisms to conceptualise it in McClaren's exclusivist terms. What concerns me more is how these various differences and similarities in social values are linked and displaced in political imaginaries, and how they project a codification of the nation. In order to illustrate this I want briefly to set out some of the political elements in four different multicultural imaginaries, which, although not exhaustive or shorn of different over-lapping tendencies, are sufficiently distinct in the Western nation. I describe these as: imperial, liberal, communitarian, feminist.

Imperial multiculturalism This is ambivalently hegemonic in Western nations, often in the form of a naturalised or rampant nationalism. It is stalked particularly by the legacy of white supremacy and the colonial inheritance. It conceives the nation as divided in terms of European and 'non-European' cultures or white and 'non-white' identities. It articulates multiculturalism in terms of a libertarian and anti-egalitarian assimilationism. It posits a 'common' national culture as a natural consensual obligation, where the value of universal liberty is compromised by conceptions of social justice that would restrict liberty. The multicultural imaginary constructs itself in the overarching shadow of a redeemable nationalism. It invests in a standard of culture or civilisation which racialised 'others' are expected to absorb, and disinvests in the idea that Western values are disturbingly contradictory. It espouses masculine individualism and cultural hierarchy. This is a hegemonic operation which requires differences in region, dialect and outlook to be absorbed within a prescribed national cultural standard. It inscribes a political frontier between itself imagined as the nation (the British/American way of life) and anything which is perceived as a threat to this (so-called 'multiculturalists').

Liberal multiculturalism This recognises the importance of social justice. It conceives the nation in terms of cultural majorities and cultural minorities, the socially advantaged and socially disadvantaged. It identifies cultural differences not in terms of cultural deprivation but of social inequalities, which are correlated with the absence of social and educational opportunities. It is underwritten by the Rawlsian retention of the primacy of liberty and the 'difference principle' (Kymlicka 1989), which affirms the equal distribution of social goods unless an unequal distribution would advantage the 'least favoured' (Rawls 1971). It prescribes a standard of individualism which people from any community or way of life should have the opportunity to achieve. This imaginary has a limited view of communities; its promotion of the individual citizen pursuing his/her rights provides an impoverished view of cultural antagonisms. Its investment in the universal ideas of liberty and equality and the mutual toleration of communities generates a multicultural imaginary that favours the proliferation of autonomous individuals bounded by a predetermined and consensually agreed conception of justice. It disinvests in the idea that universal ideas favour particular cultures or particular individuals.

Communitarian multiculturalism It envisages the nation as composed of discrete, regenerated and recoverable communities and social groups in which citizenship as a common public good is particularly important. This is seen as prior to and independent of individual desires and interests (see Mouffe 1993). It prescribes a standard of participation and recognition for various communities in the development of the nation, its laws and policies and hence civic virtue as a way of life. The participationist dimension, however, does not see the loss of community or a common good in terms of a lack of belonging. It emphasises the importance of differential political agency and efficacy in relation to conflicts between the possibilities available in different spheres of justice (for example, citizenship rights, income). This imaginary advocates the development of translational national principles of social distribution (see Waltzer 1983). The objective is to extend the 'unlimited and universally accessible participation of all in the consensual generation of the principles to govern life' (Benhabib 1992). It invests in the idea of discrete and accountable forms of representation and communal rights of self-determination, and disinvests in the idea of cultural assimilation.

Feminist multiculturalism What is often referred to as the politics of difference (Young 1990) finds its classical formative expression in the concerted interventions of black feminism to expand the conception of differential citizenship rights (see Hull *et al.* 1982). Black feminism has long occupied the foreground of engaging with the multiple articulations of different identities and 'developing a feminism rooted in class, culture, gender and race in interaction as its organizing principle' (Brewer 1993: 13–16). This basis of feminist multiculturalism informs an imaginary of the nation as divided into differential solidarities across communities and across nations. Its conception of the nation beyond the confines of parochial insularity and against the imperial hegemony of nationalism emphasises a transnational interdependence. For example, 'Within the interdependence of mutual (non-dominant) differences lies that security which enables us to descend into the chaos of knowledge and return with true visions of our future, along with concomitant power to effect those changes which can bring that future into being' (Lorde 1993: 486). This imaginary prescribes a democratic standard of polyvocality and multiple dialogues in the formation of social legislation and political conventions. It recognises not so much different conceptions of the good life, but different interdependent conceptions of its attainment. It multiplies the right to liberty, emphasising how its meaning is transformed in the simultaneity of individual, communal and gender interactions. Because these relations raise political questions defined by multiple articulations of power, it defines social justice in the form of redressing power which pervades the social, and cuts across the public, private and subaltern distinctions. Its identification of the differential terms of oppression and domination (Young 1990; Frazer and Lacey 1993) commits this imaginary to an investment in different social movements (for example, anti-racist, anti-sexist) engaged within distinct communities, and a disinvestment in the naturalisation of an amalgamated governmental regime of whiteness (Hesse 1997), masculinity and heterosexuality.

Conclusion

It is important to recognise that the representations of different multi-cultural imaginaries do not exhaust the discursive ramifications of multicul-tural constitutiveness. In one sense this suggests that the Western nation cannot be accounted for definitively in any particular representation of a multicultural imaginary. Although in Western multiculturalism it is the nation that attempts to fix and establish the order of cultural differences, the nation remains subject to the political play of different representative multiculturalisms.

What I have described as the politics of interrogation questions par-ticular concepts of national totalities or systems, but it does not preclude systematicity as such, because it is a politics that does not as yet question the idea of the nation. What is paradoxical about the politics of multi-culturalism conceived in this way is its parasitical deconstructive structure, the way it 'faithfully repeats that totality while simultaneously making it tremble, making it insecure in its most assured evidence' (Gasché 1986: 180). Primary amongst the most assured of Western evidences is account-ability to an origin of national identity. But Western multiculturalism as a discrepant form is indistinguishable from the critique of national origins conceived as a 'point of presence and simplicity to which reflection tries to return as an ultimate ground from which everything else can be deduced' (Gasché 1986: 180). It is only on the basis of this metaphysical conception of origin that the 'imagined community' (Anderson 1983) can be imagined systematically as a nation. Yet this is unmistakably the subversive locus of a disavowed multiculturalism. As Gasché argues, the first step in the deconstruction of the value of 'origin' is the pluralisation of origin, a recognition of its multiple inscription. It is precisely this which the discrepant constitutiveness of Western multiculturalism places on the national political agenda. It is the condition for the possibility of a differential politics of interrogation and its undecidable translation into multicultural imaginaries.

This is the point at which we encounter the multicultural paradox: the impossibility of national representation. We can see this, for example, in the difficulties that nationalisms predicated on a nation–state provoke but do not resolve. In this sense nationalism is a system which needs to express itself teleologically or eschatologically in order to secure an unquestionable foundation in an autochthonous people. But the chosen people are not reducible to nationalism; they may be gendered, sexualised, politicised in ways incompatible with its system. The paradox lies in the fact that any national system clearly 'implies a beyond to it precisely by virtue of what it excludes' (Cornell 1992: 2); the excluded is what remains. This encounter signifies the impossibility for nationalism or any configuration of cultural differences fully to absorb the possibilities of the national space; the limits of the system of configuration do not confront an opposition that can be overcome. In addition, the imperial history of modernity constitutes an excess that is disavowed in hegemonic representations of the nation as democratic. It is the excess of the remainder and the excess of the disavowal that institutes the politics of multiculturalism. In other words, Western multiculturalism is stretched between its disavowed imperial configuration as the social condition of any cultural enunciation of difference–identity/ otherness and its contingency in the diverse multicultural imaginaries of the nation. One way of writing this might be: Discrepant M/multi-culturalisms.

Notes

I would like particularly to thank Denise Noble and Ernesto Laclau for detailed comments on earlier versions of this substantially revised chapter; also Bobby Sayyid, Claire Alexander, Albert Weale and Hayley Bent for remarks and observations which helped me to think. (This chapter was previously published in *Social Identities*, vol. 3, no. 3, October 1997, pp. 373–94).

1. T.T. Minh-Ha, *When The Moon Waxes Red*, New York: Routledge, 1991, p. 107.

2. This is the opening chorus-line from the title track of Gil Scott-Heron and Brian Jackson's double album, *It's Your World*, New York: Arista Records, 1976.

3. Racialisation refers to modernity's reduction of human diversity and cultural representation to the limited iconography of 'races'. In the history of modernity, 'race' is initiated as a visual category of symbolic marking based on the European white gaze upon the bodies of the 'other(s)'. Racialisation is a concept of colonisation which divides the world conceptually into European and 'non-European', or white and 'non-white' bodies, as if this defined a natural, hierarchic division. In this binary process, white/European is assumed to be primary and 'non-white'/'non-European' is designated as secondary.

4. 'Deconstruction' here describes the discursive logic which reveals and resources the persistence of irreducible entanglements in attempts to clarify or distinguish the meaning of cultural and political articulations. This can be described as a structure of 'undecidability'. Undecidability describes that which resists semantic mastery, it covers all the meanings of ambivalence, ambiguity, equivocation and indiscernibility. It represents a limit, in so far as wherever it circulates meaning is unclear. In addition, undecidability is inexhaustible. As I suggest below, Western multiculturalism is undecidable in relation to different imaginaries of multiculturalism because they work to constitute a decision about the identity of the nation without securing an eventual, stable meaning for the nation, (see Gasché 1986; Laclau 1996).

5. There are a number of levels on which the concept of discrepancy works in this chapter. First, it describes those political inconsistencies and material inequalities which produce the cultural differences that define the frame of reference in Western multiculturalism. Second, it refers to how in the dominant national ordering these cultural differences can be recognised while the formation and incidence of related inconsistencies and inequalities are disregarded. Third, it suggests that because there are diverse representations of the meaning of national cultural differences, the discrepant re-emerges where different multicultural imaginaries replicate rather than challenge dominant forms of disavowal.

6. A 'surface of inscription' describes a formation conducive to bearing the imprint of a particular set of meanings (see Laclau 1990).

7. By 'floating signifier' I am referring to words or phrases that cannot be fixed to a particular or definitive meaning and are sufficiently ambiguous to signify a range of discrete meanings within definite parameters.

8. Perhaps a more useful designation of the sense of Western multiculturalism deployed in this article would be 'Atlantic multiculturalism'. It is based on the circulation of the political, cultural and economic inconsistencies and inequalities that arose with Western Europe's expansion into the western hemisphere since the 16th century. Paul Gilroy (1993: 15) has provided a lead in this thinking by suggesting that there are different claims that can be made for the modern history of the Atlantic other than as a sequence in European history, hence his account of the Black Atlantic describes the ocean's role as a conduit and surface of inscription in the circulation of black diasporic political and cultural forms. This approach can be combined with Edouard Glissant's (1989) 'creolisation' or Mary Louise Pratt's (1991) 'contact zone' or Avtar Brah's (1996) 'diaspora-space', which foreground the entanglement, antagonisms and cross-transformations of transcultural relations. The circumnavigation of the issues that flow from these formations shape Atlantic multiculturalism.

9. It is all too easy to obscure how the colonial empires of Europe have shaped modernity and the human geography and formation of nations. According to Anthony Pagden (1995), this imperial legacy has 'two distinct but interdependent histories'. The first begins in 1492 with the voyages of Columbus, which herald the 'European discovery and colonisation' of the Americas. Pagden suggests this period ends in the 1830s. The

second history begins in the 1730s, consolidates in the 1780s and is characterised by the 'European occupation of Asia, of Africa and of the Pacific'. As Pagden also notes, 'these second European Empires have only recently been dissolved, a process which for most of their inhabitants has been a slow and murderous one' (Pagden 1995).

10. This refers to the emergence of the Western nation and the counter-modern 'other cultures' through the Atlantic economy of slavery and global economy of colonialism.

11. See Gutman 1992, 1994; Foster and Herzog 1994; Kymlicka 1995.

12. In the process of articulation different elements of meaning are brought together and transformed in the logic of their inter-relatedness to produce a structure of meaning which is irreducible to the individual elements considered as a simple taxonomy.

13. I am suggesting here that there are different forms of affiliative expression in the politics of interrogation. Generally, the politics of interrogation announces itself as the place to question cultural hierarchies of domination and devaluation and their disavowal in discourses of democratic representation. Although I suggest that it emerges in relation to the imperial formation of the West, during the late twentieth century it has become expansive and increasingly differential in questioning the West's gender and sexual formations. I maintain, however, that the dimension of racialisation is integral to the politics of interrogation's agenda of questions. It should also be noted here, in order to understand the discussion that follows, there is an undecidable relation between the politics of interrogation and a particular multicultural imaginary or a combination of elements from different multicultural imaginaries.

14. 'Black diaspora' is used descriptively here to define the affiliative dispersal and Western circulation of various political and cultural discourses and dialogues that enunciate the histories, popular sentiments and debates among people of African descent.

15. In my discussion below of different multicultural imaginaries, I suggest there are distinct discourses which validate different national visions of the multicultural. I am suggesting that Taylor's analysis is implicated in one or more of these imaginaries (liberal and communitarian multiculturalisms), as indeed is my own analysis (communitarian and feminist multiculturalisms).

16. See Taylor (1992: 63) 'without compromising our basic political principles'; 'Liberalism is also a fighting creed'.

17. Jacques Derrida (1973) uses 'the metaphysics of presence' as a portmanteau of terms to describe the privileging in Western philosophical discourses of what appears to be conceptually fixed in place, available, retrievable, demonstrable: unquestionably there. This neglects the conceptual significance of the margin, the emergent, the opaque, the residual, the indistinct, the ambivalent (see also Gasché 1986).

Bibliography

Anderson, B. (1983) *Imagined Communities*, London: Verso.

Benhabib, S. (1992) *Situating the Self*, Cambridge: Polity Press.

Bhabha, H. (1994) *Locations of Culture*, London: Routledge.

Brah, A. (1996) *Cartographies of Diaspora*, London: Routledge.

Brewer, R.M. (1993) 'Theorizing Race, Class And Gender: The new scholarship of Black feminist intellectuals and Black women's labor', in S.M. James and A.P.A. Busia (eds), *Theorizing Black Feminisms – the visionary pragmatism of Black women*, London: Routledge.

Carroll, P.N. and D.W. Noble (1977/1988) *The Free and the Unfree*, New York: Penguin.

Césaire, A. (1972) *Discourse on Colonialism*, New York: Monthly Review Press.

Clarke, P.B. (1994) *Citizenship*, London: Pluto Press.

Clifford, J. (1992) 'Traveling Cultures', in Grossberg *et al.*

Connolly, W. (1991) *Identity/Difference*, London: Cornell University Press.

Cornell, D. (1992) *The philosophy of the limit*, London: Routledge.

Derrida, J. (1978) *Writing and difference*, London: Routledge.

Derrida, J. (1973) *Speech and Phenomena*, US: Northwestern University Press.

Fanon, F. (1967) *The Wretched of the Earth*, Harmondsworth: Penguin.

Foster, L. and P. Herzog (eds) (1994) *Contemporary Philosophical Perspectives on Pluralism and Multiculturalism*, Amherst: University of Massachusetts Press.

Frazer, E. and N. Lacey (1993) *The Politics of Community – A Feminist critique of the Liberal–Communitarian debate*, Hemel Hempstead: Harvester Wheatsheaf.

Gasché, R. (1986) *The tain of the mirror*, London: Harvard University Press.

Gates, H.L. (1988) *Signifying Monkey*, London: Oxford University Press.

Giroux, H.A. and P. McLaren (eds) (1994) *Between Borders*, London: Routledge.

Gilroy, P. (1993) *The Black Atlantic*, London: Verso.

Goldberg, D.T. (ed.) (1994) *Multiculturalism*, London: Routledge.

Glissant, E. (1989) *Caribbean Discourse*, US: University of Virginia.

Grossberg, L., C. Nelson and P. Treichler (eds) (1992) *Cultural Studies*, London: Routledge.

Gutman, A. (ed.) (1992) *Multiculturalism and the politics of recognition*, Princeton, N.J.: Princeton University Press.

— (ed.) (1994) *Multiculturalism*, Princeton, N.J.: Princeton University Press.

Haraway, D.J. (1991) *Simians, Cyborgs and Women*, London: Routledge.

Hesse, B. (1993) 'Black to front and Black again – racialization through contested times and spaces', in M. Keith and S. Pile (eds), *Place and the politics of identity*, London: Routledge.

— (1997) 'White governmentality: urbanism, nationalism, racism', in S. Westwood and J. Williams (eds), *Imagining cities: signs, scripts, memory*, London: Routledge.

Hobsbawm, E.J. (1990) *Nations and Nationalism since 1780*, London: Chatto and Windus.

Hull, G., P. Bell-Scott, and B. Smith (1982) *All the Women are White, all the Blacks are Men, but some of us are Brave*, US: Feminist Press.

Kymlicka, W. (1989) *Liberalism, Community and Culture*, Oxford: Oxford University Press.

— (1995) *Multicultural Citizenship*, Oxford: Oxford University Press.

Laclau, E. (1990) *New reflections on the revolution of our time*, London: Verso.

— (ed.) (1994) *The making of political identities*, London: Verso.

— (1996) *Emancipation(s)*, London: Verso.

Lemaire, A. (1977) *Jacques Lacan*, London: Routledge and Kegan Paul.

Lorde, A. (1993) 'The Master's Tools will never dismantle the Master's house', in Charles Lemert (ed.), *Social theory: the multicultural and classic readings*, Oxford: Westview Press.

Merleau-Ponty, M. (1968) *The Visible and the Invisible*, US: Northwestern University Press.

McClaren, P. (1994a) 'Multiculturalism and the post-modern critique', in Giroux and McClaren.

— (1994b) 'White terror and Oppositional agency: towards a critical multiculturalism', in Goldberg.

McKlintock, A. (1995) *Imperial Leather: race, gender and sexuality in the colonial context*, London: Routledge.

Mouffe, C. (1993) *The return of the political*, London: Verso.

Pagden, A. (1995) *Lords of all the World: Ideologies of Empire in Spain, Britain and France c. 1500–c. 1800*, London: Yale University Press.

Parekh, B. (1995) 'Liberalism and colonialism: a critique of Locke and Mill', in J.N. Pieterse and B. Parekh (eds), *The Decolonization of Imagination*, London: Zed Books.

Pratt, M.L. (1991) *Imperial Eyes*, London: Routledge.

Rawls, J. (1971) *A theory of justice*, Oxford: Oxford University Press.

Rattansi, A. (1994) 'Western racisms, ethnicities and identities in a post-modern frame', in Rattansi and Westwood.

— and S. Westwood (eds) (1994) *Race, modernity and identity*, Cambridge: Polity Press.

Salecl, R. (1994) 'The crisis of identity and the struggle for hegemony in the former Yugoslavia', in Laclau 1994.

Said, E. (1993) *Culture and Imperialism*, London: Vintage.

Sayyid, B. (1994) 'Sign 'O' Times: Kaffirs and Infidels fighting the Ninth Crusade', in Laclau 1994.

Shohat, E. and R. Stam (1994) *Unthinking Eurocentrism*, London: Routledge.

Silverman, H.J. (1994) *Textualities – Between Hermeneutics and Deconstruction*, London: Routledge.

Taylor, C. (1992) 'Multiculturalism and the politics of recognition', in Gutman 1992.

Waltzer, M. (1983) *Spheres of Justice*, Oxford: Blackwell.

Young, I.M. (1990) Justice and the politics of difference, Princeton, N.J.: Princeton University Press.

Zizek, S. (1989) *The Sublime Object of Ideology*, London: Verso.

— (1990) 'Eastern Europe's Republics of the Gilead', in *New Left Review* no. 183, September/October.

12

The Sacred and the Profane

Desirée Ntolo

Jewish and Black

Well now, where does my story begin?

I believe that to answer that question, I should take you as far back as two thousand years ago, to the time of the destruction of the Temple in Jerusalem by the Romans. My ancestor was an Essene who, like many of them, had openly become a follower of Rabbi Yeshua Bar Joseph of Nazareth while remaining a fully practising Essene. He was 30 years old at the time of the destruction of the Temple, and he and his fellow Essenes regularly gave shelter to some of Rabbi Yeshua's chosen apostles and disciples. Two years before the destruction of the Temple, all the Essenes, who had been quite numerous but lived in three separate groups, gathered together, their prophets having foreseen future events. With them was John, son of Zebedee and apostle of Yeshua, who was now an old man. Their meeting was to decide about their future and a way to ensure the survival of their faith. They decided that they should separate and go, if possible, to foreign countries.

Many Essenes decided to go to Tibet; some chose Persia and India, some Egypt and elsewhere in North Africa; some headed toward the European countries. A lot more chose to go to Ethiopia and the rest chose to remain in Palestine. My ancestor was among those who went to Ethiopia. For a while he lived with the Falashas on an island in an Ethiopian lake. Then he befriended a young Hebrew man who was an ambulant merchant, travelling south by boat to African coastal cities, selling fabrics to rich indigenous inhabitants, kings and dignitaries. His friend got him interested in his travelling salesman's business and they began to sail together regularly.

That is how they arrived one day at the coasts of the country now known as Cameroon. It used to be their last stop before they returned to Ethiopia, and they usually remained there up to a full month before they set sail again. My ancestor's friend already had a woman there, with whom he had two children. There my ancestor was introduced to a pretty girl with whom he fell in love.

The settlement where they lived was requisitioned by the authorities, on the advice of Christian religious leaders, and turned into a leper colony. Many leprous people were moved into it. All but one family, to which we are distantly related, left that settlement and went to live elsewhere, about forty kilometres away, in another county, but they have kept in touch with us up to this day. The rest became contaminated and died as lepers. That leaves my family proper and a 'cousin family', with whom we live in the same village, in two groups. We moved quite a few times in the early years of this century, before my great-grandfather and the son of one of his second cousins came back to settle where my family still lives, in a small village in the south of Cameroon, called Olamdoe. In it I was born in the late 1950s.

We are still called the 'Engolki'. We are still despised, we are still insulted, we are still provoked. All members of my family are black, like the rest of the villagers, but they call us foreigners all the same, and they still say that we do not belong in their midst. Still my family is very large, because it comprises not only those descended from my own grandfather, but those from his brothers, sisters and direct cousins. A very, very large family.

Before my great-grandfather David Metogo died, my grandfather, who was called Solomon Ondoua-Metogo, married my grandmother Marguerite, the daughter of a Presbyterian deacon. She gave birth to two daughters and a son. The first daughter was my mother, Rachel Ondoua-Elono. The second was my aunt Naomi Ondoua-Mbolle; and finally my uncle David Ondoua-Metogo. The Jewish element in our family is still very strong. We practice circumcision, we eat kosher food, we observe all purification rites. I observe the strict laws of shabbat, and my shabbat is observed on Saturday, as it should be. My grandfather and grandmother brought me and my sister up. My uncle having shown little interest in acquiring the tradition in matters of God after he went to college, and my sister preferring to go and stay with our mother at every opportunity, I was the only one left to sit and listen to my grandfather, asking him deep questions and willing to learn when he offered to teach and train me.

Talmudic tuition was available to girls and boys equally. Right from the start, there was no sign of the pharisaic chauvinism that survives in Orthodox Jewish communities. Normally in the patriarchal way, the teachings are passed on from father to son, but it was different in my family. Even though as Jews we were Orthodox, as Essenes there was not that chauvinism towards women. Both boys and girls got the Talmudic teachings if they were interested. Those who showed outstanding abilities in the teachings were the ones who were chosen to get the Kabbala, the secret teachings. As my grandfather was getting on in years, he had to choose someone to receive the teachings. So he chose me instead of my uncle. He gave it all to me; all the rules, the legacy of the ancient wisdom from Moses. Thus I inherited all the Essene rabbinical, talmudic and kabbalistic lore and treasures that should have gone to my uncle.

I am very lucky to be so rich in my inheritance. Because of this, I found myself in a kind of religious no man's land; not a Christian, even though believing in Jeshua of Nazareth, and not quite an Orthodox Jew. That is why I needed somewhere else in order to practice my religion in the way to which I am accustomed.

Space for Faith

The only way I could practice my faith was to have somewhere close at hand where I could go, mostly for prayers. We have to pray three times a day: morning, noon, and in the evening, sometimes at midnight. Every month I need purification. In the Essene training we also do Angelic Communions; communion with certain angels every day of the week, to build and celebrate the Holy Temple of God inside us.

Now, I cannot do all this inside the house in which I live. It has to be outside, or somewhere where I can touch the floor, which must be an earth floor, with no concrete on it. It is to be what we call an oratory, a sanctified place, dedicated only to prayer. There are also certain traditions unique to us which demand that we build such a place. For example, when someone dies we usually tie a piece of cloth, usually white cloth, around our wrists. We call it a mourning band. It allows one to be in touch with the spirit of the dead person for a whole year. If you had done something wrong to that person while they were alive and were not there at the time of their death, so that you never had time to say sorry, you may use the mourning band to communicate with them and say: 'I did this or that to you; please forgive me.' Also, if that person had done something to you and you never forgave them, you can use it to forgive them and make peace with them in the same way. After a whole year, on the anniversary of their death, there is a festival to celebrate the departure of the person, and also to free their spirit so that it can continue on with its life in whatever the Lord has decided for them. At that time all the mourning bands are burnt and the ashes are buried in the Tabernacle.

Since I came to Britain, many members of my family back in Cameroon have died, so I have accumulated a considerable number of mourning bands. But I have been unable to burn them, because I have nowhere to perform the ceremony. So, truly, these spirits, even though they have been freed by all my relatives in Africa, have not yet been freed by me. My grandmother wrote to me and said that there were three members of the family whose spirits had appeared to her complaining that they were in limbo and waiting to be freed. This might sound incredible, but it is because we are so down-to-earth and close to nature that we can communicate with spirits in this way!

When a child is born, there is the tiny bit of the umbilical cord which is left attached to the baby's navel after the cord is cut. When this falls, we do not just throw it away. We keep it in remembrance of the deep mystery of how the Lord makes a woman bear a child in the womb and keep it alive, fed, warm and growing until it is big enough to be born. We respect that miracle. And because of deep spiritual laws connected with the creation of a human being, we bury that tiny bit of umbilical cord in the consecrated place. The foreskin of the circumcised boy child is also given the same treatment and buried in the same way. My last two children's ceremonies have therefore not been properly carried out. My son is still awaiting circumcision because I did not have anywhere consecrated to bury his foreskin. He should have been circumcised when he was eight days old, now he is already 3 years old.

One of the most important parts of our religion concerns the rites of purification. In Cameroon we used to have purification pools, which we used regularly at certain times of the month, especially for women. For example, if I cannot purify myself at the time of the month when I have my period, so I can sleep with my husband, then deep inside that hurts me very much because I know that I am defiling him. I do not feel clean. In all the eleven years I have been in this country, I have never once been able to purify myself in this way, as I could not find any place for that. If you have grown up and lived in a certain way, if you cannot say your prayers in the way you are used to, if you cannot purify yourself in the way you are supposed to, if you cannot carry out the various observances and devotions that are laid down in your faith, then you live a life that is not your own. You can no longer practice the traditions in a proper way to pass on to your children. That is why I said that living in this, my house, was like living in an open prison, because I was not really free to practice my religion, to be me. This was something that was tearing me apart; to be like that for eleven years. So finally I came to feel that I was dying slowly. The only answer I had, the only thing I could do, was to build that oratory. Everything in my life was tied to that.

The Oratory

When I started building I used traditional methods. I used just mud and water. I constructed it in the same way we build houses in Africa.

Most houses in villages are built of mud, even if they have concrete floors
or wall rendering. And you do not see them falling down. They last and
last. Of course there are different methods of construction. They can be
either square, round, rectangular, or in the form of a pyramid. If the walls
are very thick, you do not need foundations. For my purpose, it had to be
made so that I could be in touch with the earth when I was carrying out
my devotions. All you need is a flat area like in my garden, where you can
build up the walls. The soil is mixed with water and the heap is built up
vertically in walls. The soil is a living thing. If you leave it there it will just
bond and establish itself. Plants will grow on it. It is exactly the same
principle that is involved in building a mud hut with thick walls. Of
course, the walls must be straight. Once you have put it up and you have
put the roof on, it will stay there for a hundred years. In fact, if I had
wanted to make it even stronger, and for it to last longer, I would have
added some straw, but that was not necessary for what I wanted.

In my village in Cameroon, building a house does not cost much in
labour, as all the members of the community are willing to give their help
free for building houses. In fact, all houses are built with the help of the
whole community. But, of course, in this country things are much more
complicated, people are selfish and there is absolutely no community spirit.
Things cost much more money and the buildings are ugly and do not last
long.

So I started building and for the first time I managed to do my purification and to burn the mourning bands. It was about half-finished when
I wrote to the Council, telling them what I was doing. I explained to them
all the reasons why I wanted to have a mud hut. It was a very long letter!
I told them that I did not know if I was breaking any laws or needed
permission. The people from the Planning Department sent someone to
have a look. This young man was very excited by it. He stood in front of
it and took photographs and said it was fantastic and that he had never
seen anything like it before. He told me that I should get in touch with the
local newspapers so that they may write about it but I was not interested.
Then I found out later that they got in touch with the press anyway. The
people from the Planning Department said that there had never been a law
in the history of the United Kingdom against the building of such structures like the one I had put up, and, at the size it was, as far as they were
concerned the building could stay. They also said that they would have to
consult the Housing Department, my landlords. If they said that it was
OK then I could keep it.

But when the people from the Housing Department came, everything
changed. They started bringing political issues into the matter. The man
told me: 'If we start allowing a black lady to build a mud hut, we are going

to see mud huts sprouting up everywhere. Why should we allow someone coming from Africa to build a mud hut in our conservative British area. It will offend local people.' They said that some neighbours had complained, but that was a lie. The people in the houses around me all signed a petition saying that the hut should stay. Then the Council people later said that some people round the back complained, but these people are so far away that I do not even regard them as neighbours. There is a piece of waste ground between us. So somehow they imposed their own priorities and brought up all these issues which had never even entered my mind when I was building the hut. They completely swept aside everything I had said about my reasons for building it. They said they had a duty to conserve their country so that it was part of the Essex tradition, not part of Africa.

On another visit one man from the Council said to me: 'Well, if you were white it might be a different story, but we can't let "you" get away with it, it would set a bad example to the other Blacks and we have enough trouble with them as it is.' Afterwards he denied having said any such thing when I told him that I would reveal what he had said. He said: 'If you quote any of that, I'll just say you made it up and it will put you in a bad light.' That was very upsetting. To hear them go on, you would think that I wanted to turn my garden into an African jungle or to build a special greenhouse to grow palm trees in. Actually, I have heard that people can get grants for building such things! But I was not making such demands. All I wanted was an oratory, somewhere to practice my religion in the best way I know how, for me to actually live like a human being. I explained to them over and over again why the building had to be made of earth and not of any other material, but they just did not seem to listen. Some of the letters they wrote were written in such a way that they gave me to understand that the house was theirs and that they could do what they liked to me. But they never made clear what had actually been decided or by whom so it was very confusing.

Enter the Media

After that first visit of the Housing Department Officials, they must have made a report because the Council people started to play dirty. When the newspaper reporters went to them, they said: 'The lady is homesick, she is tired of living in England, she hates it here and she wants to go back to Africa.' And the media just followed the Council's line. When they came to interview me I told them what I have just told you. But no matter what I said they decided that the Council's declaration was the most newsworthy. It just came out as this homesick African lady who wanted to build a mud hut in her back garden to remind her of home. They'd sit round and say: 'Tell us about yourself.' Then they'd ignore or twist what I had said. They made a lot of the fact that I had so many children and that they were noisy and loved pop music. So what? I have six children and they are normal healthy children, so of course sometimes they are a bit noisy. But the media turned it into a story about how I wanted this place to go to, to escape from my noisy children so I could have a bit of peace and quiet! Or else they made me out to be an eccentric, someone who just took it into their head to build a mud hut one day, just for the hell of it.

The worst example of media attack was the article written by Barbara Amiel in the *Sunday Times*. She argued that I should abandon central aspects of my faith in order to 'fit in' and be accepted as 'English'. I regard that as an insult. When I first came here I only spoke my mother tongue, Ewondo, and French. I taught myself English. Who can say that I have not adapted? I cook English food better than some English people. I do not only eat African food! So in all these ways the media completely misrepresented the issue, which I felt was a horrible injustice.

Demolition Squad

As for the Council, they were afraid that if I was allowed to keep the structure it would be used as a precedent by other tenants to gain more control over their environment. So the next thing they did was to send in some people to knock it down. These three men came with all their equipment but they could not knock the hardened walls down. They took the roof off and did not stop at that; they used saws to damage the roof timbers so that they could not be used again. If they had known how I had built the roof, the timbers could have very simply been lifted off and re-used; there was no need to cut them. They even cut off the doors that were lying aside on the floor, waiting to be fitted. They damaged these by cutting the wood into pieces so I could not re-use the doors. A really criminal act of vandalism.

The policeman who came with the demolition team stood close to me and had this amazing whispered conversation with me. The way he spoke to me, it seemed to be a very personal matter. He also seemed to know a lot about me personally. 'Are you surprised that we are knocking your hut down? Well, we have to do it. The whole matter has gone on long enough!' As I asked why they were destroying my timber: 'You started it, you started it,' he retorted. 'You bastard Jews want to take over the world. We have to put an end to this, it has to finish now. Gone on long enough.' I could not believe it. If anything, I have hidden the fact that I was a Jew to the media even though I had mentioned that I was an Essene. How did he know about me having any connection with the Jews? I did not ask for a penny. I used all my own savings to build the hut, and they were trying to destroy it while accusing me of pushing them around!

When I complained at the Council people's constant visits to my oratory and their intrusion on my devotions, they told me: 'If you want us to leave you alone, you've got to let us get our way.' I explained that they were desecrating a holy place, but they just did not care. According to their attitude the house belonged to them and I could not have a holy place in it. It was quite an amazing scene on the day when the Council officials visited. I expected a few of them to come, but I was absolutely amazed to see at least fourteen gentlemen standing outside my house. As they stood a while waiting for the leader of their group, my protective neighbours thought that they had come again to cause me more upset and they began to heckle them and shout at them. 'Heh! What else do you want with Desirée? Go away and leave her alone!' Finally their chief arrived, and I forced them to take their shoes off. Some of them were quite excited and complied with my unusual demand. They did not mind. It came with the job. But it had been raining and many of them were angry and very reluctant to take their shoes off to go into my garden, but I had already written to their offices over this and they knew ... It was quite hilarious to see these suited gents filing through my humble house with their shoes in their hands and I mercilessly standing there with a determined expression on my face. There was one particular old man who was very angry over this, and when they came out again at least nine of them arrogantly walked through my house wearing their shoes, refusing to take them off again, some commenting on the poverty of my home and the uselessness to take their shoes off. I saw the old man who was angry at taking his shoes off gesticulate that allowing me to build the oratory was absolutely out of the question. Then they told the media people that the structure was dangerous, that lumps of earth might fall off it. In fact it was rock solid. It was so strong that they could not actually knock it down, as they did not understand how it was built.

All the time the structure was being attacked, my neighbours were shouting at them to leave the hut alone. After that, because of what they had done to it, I did not want to keep it. They had taken the roof off, so I could not burn incense, and it was no longer a holy place to me. It had been totally desecrated. So I began to take the walls down myself. But even for me this was very difficult. The Council officials must have been frightened that the hut would stay there for a long time, since it was raining every day and the walls were still standing, contrary to their previous preposterous statement that the 'structure was dangerous' and about to collapse so they went to court to force me to totally demolish it. They took me to court to force me to do something that I was doing anyway. They even came to me to threaten that I would have to pay the costs of their legal action. They said that they would also seek to repossess the house, to evict me, if I did not comply. Later, when they were asked by the journalists, they denied having said any of this or having asked me to pay for their legal action, but I have this in writing.

The case came to court in January 1993, and I defended myself. The judge listened to the whole story and then he admonished the Council for the way they had handled the case and rejected their request that I pay the costs of the case. What a waste of taxpayers' money. He said that I could not be stopped or impeded from practicing my religion. He told me to demolish the rest of the walls and told the Council to seriously consider my application for a new structure, but that I should also go along with their requirements as to the outside look of the new structure. I could then build a mud wall on the inside. Now for my part, I have agreed to build the outside structure to Council specifications, and I hope that my landlords will understand my need for an oratory and remember the promise made to me in Court.

Repercussions

As a result of all this business I have become quite famous around here, but not always to my advantage. People notice and stare at me where they did not before. I have become more conscious of how people regard me. Some are quite hostile. As a result of the publicity and the bad way the media reported on the issue, I started to receive a lot of hate mail and death threats from all sorts of people, especially from groups like the British National Party, but I also got a lot of support from the Jewish and black communities.

Being Jewish and black can have its advantages as well as its problems! The congregation of the synagogue next door, and even Jews who did not worship there, were very helpful. They came to visit me. When they saw the building they used to say: 'Oh, that's beautiful, not at all what we have been led to believe from the newspapers.' We have had a lot of cases of anti-semitism in our area, so I would have really understood if they had not wanted to get involved and put themselves in a position of suffering even more discrimination, but they stood by me. I also got a lot of support from the black community and from the Commission for Racial Equality, and a human rights organization called SAFF, who advised me on my rights, and wrote letters to the police, the Council and to Jewish organizations. My main problem is that, in a sense, even though I have been granted planning permission for the new structure, I am still back to where I started. I still have nowhere to practice my religion, and I have no money left to pay for more materials to rebuild the Tabernacle.

Assimilation Games

We talk about living in a multicultural society. It is supposed to welcome, or at least tolerate, differences. Look, here we have people from many different cultures and religions: Jews, Hindus, Buddhists, Muslims, Christians, Mormons, pagans and/or atheists, witches, and more. We all live together, we cohabit without stepping on each other's toes. It is wrong for English people to tell everyone else to adapt to their ways, to be like them. The expression that the man from the Council and Barbara Amiel used was 'assimilate'. They both said: 'You've got to learn to assimilate to the British way of life.' That means 'Stop practicing your religion and become a Christian. You should start to celebrate Christmas and Easter.' It is like someone telling you to get rid of your own soul. You cannot. I would have to die inside to become what they wanted me to be. If English people went to Cameroon, even if they took out Cameroonian nationality, no-one there would say to them that they had to stop celebrating Christmas and start worshipping their Cameroonian ancestors! The Englishman can go on celebrating Christmas till the cows come home and still be an accomplished Cameroonian in other respects.

Appendix: Publications currently available from the Centre for New Ethnicities Research

Ranjit Arora, Reena Bhavnani, Phil Cohen, John Twitchin *For a Multicultural University* ISBN 1 874210 60 8 54pp A4 £8.00

Les Back *Young People, Community Safety and Racial Danger* Finding the Way Home Working Paper 5 Rights and Wrongs: Youth Community and Narratives of Racial Violence A4 £5.00

Les Back, Phil Cohen, Michael Keith *Issues of Theory and Method* Finding the Way Home Working Paper 1 ISBN 1 874210 21 7 £5.00

Les Back, Phil Cohen, Michael Keith *First Takes – Critical Ethnographies of Race, Place and Identity* Finding the Way Home Working Paper 2

Phil Cohen *Home Rules: Some Reflections on Racism and Nationalism in Everyday Life* ISBN 1 874210 03 9 52pp A5 £5.00

Phil Cohen *Forbidden Games: Class Race and Gender in Playground Cultures* ISBN 1 874210 67 5 42pp A4 Illustrated £5.00

Phil Cohen *The Last Island: Essays on England and Dreaming of 'Race'* ISBN 1 874210 31 4 64pp A4 Illustrated £9.95

Phil Cohen *Strange Encounters: Adolescent Geographies of Risk and The Urban Uncanny* Finding the Way Home Working Paper 3 A4 £5.00

Jeremy Cooper, Tarek Qureshi *Through Patterns Not Our Own* ISBN 1 874210 15 2 80pp A4 £5.00

Derek Kirton *Race, Identity and the Politics of Adoption* ISBN 1 874210 16 0 34pp A4 £5.00

Michael Keith *Making Safe – Young People, Community Safety and Racial Danger* Finding the Way Home Working Paper 4 A4 £5.00

Tim Lucas, Tahmina Maula, Landé Olumide Pratt and Sarah Newlands *Dialogues in Research Practice* Finding the Way Home Working Paper 7 A4 £5.00

Phil Marfleet *The Refugee in the 'Global' Era: Europe Confronts the Third World* ISBN 1 874210 26 8 42pp A4 Illustrated £6.00

Ian McDonald and Sharda Ugra *Anyone for Cricket? Changing Cricket Cultures in Essex and East London* ISBN 1 874210 95 0 72pp A4 Illustrated £9.95

Nora Räthzel and Andreas Hieronymus *Young People, Community Safety and Racial Danger* Finding the Way Home Working Paper 6

Derek Robbins *Citizenship and Nationhood in Britain* ISBN 1 874210 50 0 30pp A4 £3.00

Linda Rozmovits *Shylock – the Infamous Secret Jew* ISBN 1 874210 45 4 34pp A4 £3.00

Sara Selwood with Bill Schwarz and Nick Merriman *The Peopling of London: an Evaluation of the Exhibition* ISBN 0 904818 73 X 126pp A4 Illustrated £9.99 Jointly published by the Museum of London and CNER

Couze Venn *Occidentalism and its discontents* ISBN 1 874210 02 0 60pp A5 £5.00

Index